THE WILL TO CLIMB

ALSO BY THE AUTHOR

No Shortcuts to the Top:
Climbing the World's 14 Highest Peaks

K2:
Life and Death on the World's Most Dangerous Mountain

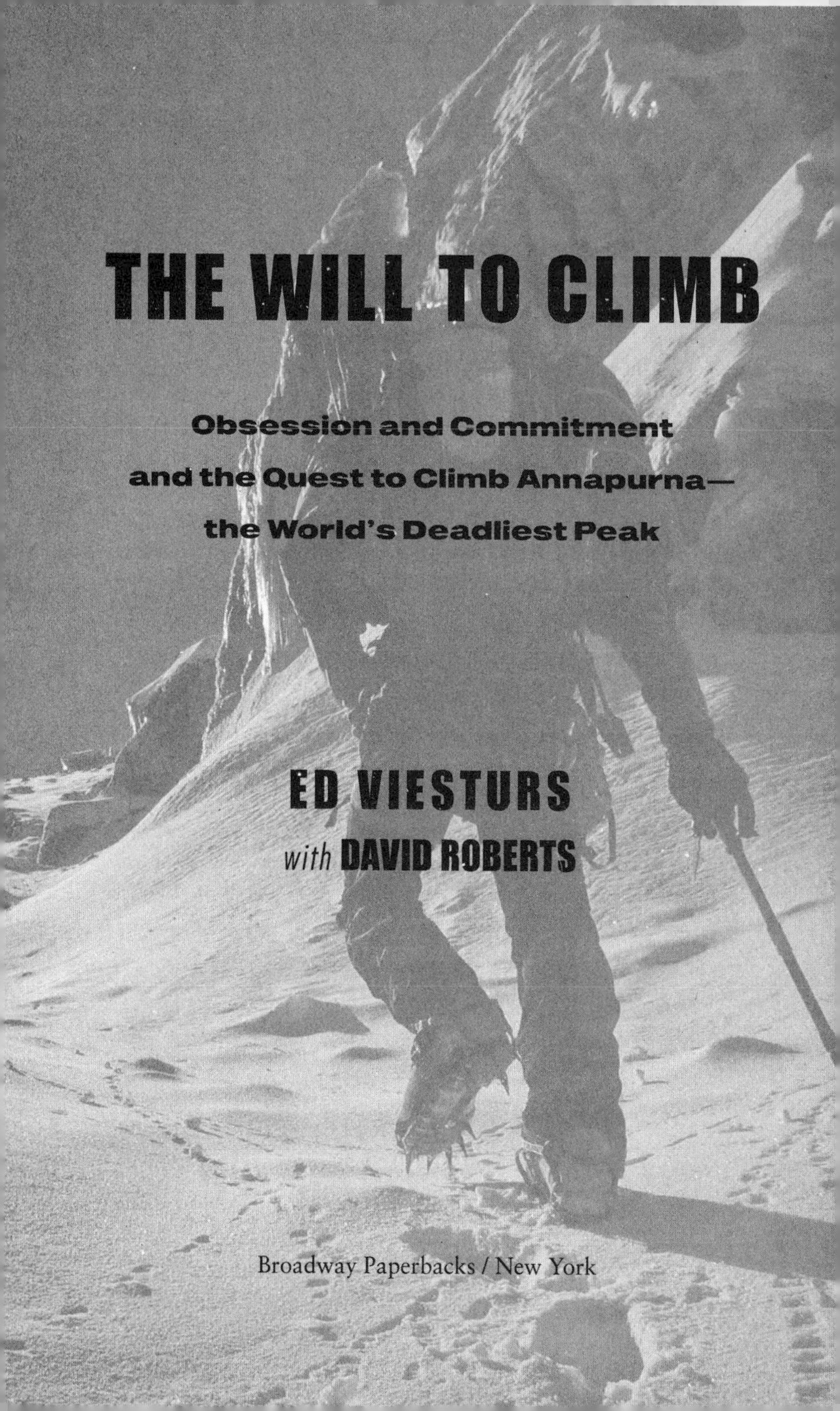

THE WILL TO CLIMB

Obsession and Commitment and the Quest to Climb Annapurna—the World's Deadliest Peak

ED VIESTURS

with DAVID ROBERTS

Broadway Paperbacks / New York

Published in the United States by Broadway Paperbacks, an imprint of the Crown Publishing Group, a division of Random House, Inc., New York.

www.crownpublishing.com

BROADWAY PAPERBACKS and its logo, a letter B bisected on the diagonal, are trademarks of Random House, Inc.

Originally published in hardcover in the United States by Crown Publishers, and imprint of the Crown Publishing Group, a division of Random House, Inc., New York, in 2011.

Library of Congress Cataloging-in-Publication Data

Viesturs, Ed.

The will to climb : obsession and commitment and the quest to climb Annapurna—the world's deadliest peak / Ed Viesturs, with David Roberts.

p. cm.

1. Mountaineering—Nepal—Annapurna. 2. Mountains—Nepal—Annapurna—Difficulty of ascent. 3. Mountaineers—Nepal—Annapurna. 4. Annapurna (Nepal)—Description and travel. I. Roberts, David, 1943– II. Title.

GV199.44.N46V54 2011

796.52'2095496—dc22

2011011680

ISBN 978-0-307-72043-6

eISBN 978-0-307-72044-3

Printed in the United States of America

Book design by Leonard W. Henderson

Cover design by Nupoor Gordon

Cover photograph by Jimmy Chin

10 9 8 7 6 5 4 3 2 1

First Paperback Edition

To my loving wife, Paula, who was with me in my thoughts and in my heart, step by step, moment by moment, as I lived my dream of reaching the summit of Annapurna, my fourteenth 8,000-meter peak.

And to our children, Gilbert, Ella, Anabel, and Nina—our constant source of love, warmth, and entertainment.

"Mountains are not stadiums where I satisfy my ambition to achieve. They are the cathedrals where I practice my religion."
—Anatoli Boukreev

"There are other Annapurnas in the lives of men."
—Maurice Herzog

CONTENTS

FOREWORD

In July 2009, I found myself climbing Mount Rainier, the huge, snow-covered, 14,411-foot-tall volcano in Washington State, with Ed Viesturs. I wasn't exactly sure what I was doing there, but before our two-day ascent was over, I'd realize that getting to the top of that mountain would be the hardest physical, emotional, and mental challenge I'd ever faced.

In a sense, I'd been sandbagged by Tod Leiweke, the CEO of the Seattle Seahawks at the time. Ed, who lives on Bainbridge Island, just outside of Seattle, is a passionate football fan. Before the 2005 season, Tod and his staff had been brainstorming to find a local celebrity to help connect fans to the Seahawks. Tod had been to one of Ed's charitable talks, so he suggested, "How about Ed Viesturs?"

The upshot was that Ed gave a motivational speech to the Seahawks just before their first game. Later that season, for another game, he was designated the team's Twelfth Man, whose duty is to raise the Seahawks' 35-foot-long flag up a pole overlooking one of the end zones at Qwest Field. That was the year the Seahawks made it all the way to the Super Bowl. Ed had arranged for all the players to receive miniature carabiners—devices symbolizing the teamwork of climbers roped together—after each victory. After the contest that clinched the NFC West division title, the team gave Ed the game ball. After the Super Bowl, the Seahawks also gave Ed an NFL Championship team ring.

The relationship between mountaineer and football team resulted in Ed's guiding Tod up Mount Rainier in the summer of 2008. And though he found the climb a stern challenge, Tod decided to repeat it the following summer with a new cast of characters as a fund-raising event for a local charity, the United Way of King County. Tod had talked Jim Mora, the Seahawks' head coach at the time, into joining the team. Then, one day as I was about to start a league meeting in Dallas, Tod said, "Roger, one quick question. Will you climb Rainier with us to help our local United Way?"

"Sure, no problem," I answered, then turned my attention to the meeting.

It was only sometime later that I took stock and thought, *What did I just do?* I'd never climbed so much as a big hill before, but I'd certainly seen Rainier rearing its massive bulk nearly three vertical miles above Seattle in the southeast. Nevertheless, I was determined to go through with it.

In early July, we all met at Paradise, the trailhead for Rainier. Besides Mora, Leiweke, and me, there were several local community leaders and four professional guides led by Ed and Peter Whittaker, co-owner of Rainier Mountaineering, Inc. It was as a guide for RMI that Ed got his start as a climber in his early twenties. By July 2009, he'd climbed the mountain a remarkable 203 times! Rainier was obviously a piece of cake for Ed. In 2005, he'd become the first American to climb the fourteen highest mountains in the world—all without bottled oxygen. He's still the only American who's pulled off that feat. And just two months before our rendezvous at Paradise, he'd climbed Mount Everest for the seventh time.

I trained for the climb by running in my neighborhood with a loaded backpack and jogging up stairwells in New York City, carrying weights in each hand, but nothing prepares you for altitude. Ed and Peter put us through our paces, training us on how to carry our ice axes, how to self-arrest with them if we slipped and fell, even how to walk on snow in a way that minimized our exertion. I survived this initial challenge, although one of my fellow climbers dislocated his elbow.

The first day we went from Paradise, at 5,400 feet, to Camp Muir, at 10,000. It's a grueling ascent, but essentially just a hike. The real climbing starts above Muir. That night we slept in prefab huts and planned to get up shortly after midnight to set out for the summit well before dawn. Ed and Peter had stressed over and over again the importance of keeping hydrated; I think I drank almost two gallons of water that evening. That meant I had to get up frequently during the night, clamber down from my third-tier bunk, put on all my clothes, and go outside to relieve myself. Even in the dark, the view was stunning. I could see other giant mountains in the distance, including Baker, Adams, and Saint Helens. After a while I gave up trying to sleep; Coach Mora and I just stayed up and stared at the magnificent vistas before us.

A cameraman who'd joined our team to shoot the climb for NFL Films caught my exchange with Peter Whittaker at twelve thirty A.M. on summit day. Peter asks me, "Roger, how do you feel?" I answer, "I feel good. Zero sleep." What I remember saying, however (and what must have been cut out of the film), was, "I feel like crap; why do you care?"

We took off by two thirty, roped close together in groups of four with our guides in the lead. For the first time in my life, I was wearing the metal spikes attached to my boots that climbers call crampons. I was feeling a combination of anxiety and confidence. I would have been happy to start even earlier—I wanted to get going.

As we started up, I thought, *This is like playing golf with Tiger Woods your first time on a course. I'm definitely out of my league.*

Yet I was moving along pretty well until we suddenly bumped into a crevasse that ran smack across our path. One thing I've got to chide Ed and Peter for is that during our training they told us all about the dangers of avalanches, falling rocks, and altitude sickness. Peter almost morbidly described the 1981 accident when a collapsing ice cliff snuffed out the lives of eleven climbers at a place right on our ascent route. (I'm not sure I needed to hear that little story.) But they never said a word about crevasses.

It was still dark. I couldn't see the bottom of the crevasse. I just froze. Ed said, "You can do it." I answered, "Yeah, but what comes after this?" "It gets harder," Ed admitted.

When I lifted my head to look upward, I saw the headlamp cones of climbers far above us. It seemed as though they were climbing into heaven. I thought, *I didn't come up here to die.* Ed and Peter were just standing there staring at me. They were eager to keep us moving, but I knew they were worried about whether they could get me to the top after all. It was only later that I learned that this was the exact place on Rainier where the 1981 catastrophe had struck.

The crevasse looked twenty feet wide. It was actually probably about thirty inches. I guess that my type-A personality kicked in then. Besides, I couldn't bear the thought of passing Jim Mora on his way down boasting about having summited while I had turned back.

Peter and Ed had just stepped over the crevasse. I definitely jumped it.

A little later the sun came up, and we could see everything. I'd never beheld a view quite so impressive. We clumped onward, and suddenly we were on the summit. We all cheered and embraced one another. Ed and Peter heartily congratulated me. It was one of the greatest experiences of my life.

Like Ed, I firmly believe that the lessons you learn from climbing a mountain translate into your "regular" life. On Rainier, I had to prepare meticulously, overcome fear and self-doubt, dig deep, and push myself. And I learned the incalculable value of good teamwork. If I'm roped to someone else and I fall, there's a good chance he's coming with me.

All those lessons apply almost daily to my work as commissioner of the NFL. I have to prepare for many challenges and face a regular diet of adversity. I need discipline. I have to push myself hard. And I've always made sure I was surrounded by the right teammates or colleagues—people I can count on in a pinch.

One of the stories that Ed told me early on was about how he turned back only 300 feet short of the summit of Everest in 1987 on his first Himalayan expedition. He knew he could make it to the top, but he wasn't sure he could get down alive. That turnaround is an incredible statement about Ed's discipline. That's what makes him a safe mountaineer. If I'd been in the same situation, I'm afraid I'd have told myself, *I'm this close, I'm going for it.*

In this book about Annapurna, Ed writes a lot about his fear of that deadly and treacherous mountain. It's hard for me to imagine Ed Viesturs being afraid of anything, but at the same time I can comprehend the difference between Rainier and a mountain almost twice as high and infinitely more dangerous. And I can imagine the gulf between a two-day ascent on a peak like Rainier and a sixty-day expedition to an 8,000-meter giant. What's impressive is how on Annapurna Ed turned his fear of the mountain that he called his personal nemesis into fuel to meet its challenge, which he finally did on his third attempt in 2005.

Ed and I have stayed good friends since Rainier. Last fall I was in Seattle for meetings. I had a two-hour window of free time, so I called Ed up and asked if he could meet me for lunch. "Gosh, I'd love to," he said, "but my son Gil is playing in his peewee football league game, and I've volunteered to move the chains." I said, "I'll help you." Throughout the first half, Ed and I were the chain crew and Ed kept the fact that I was actually the commissioner of the NFL under his hat. Somebody finally tipped off the parents about the guy measuring first downs. One of the coaches, I'm told, said to his son at halftime, "Why didn't you tell me that was Roger Goodell!" I'm glad they didn't notice. It was fun watching the kids play.

Someone recently pointed out that Ed and I are almost exactly the same age, both born in 1959 (I'm four months older). We were both fifty years old when we climbed Rainier together. I'll tell you this, though—and my wife will vouch for it—Ed's a lot younger-looking than I am. He could still pass for late thirties.

I'm not sure I'd ever climb Rainier again—or any other mountain—but if I do, it's going to be with Ed Viesturs.

Roger Goodell, commissioner, National Football League

THE WILL TO CLIMB

ONE

THE BRICK WALL

In April 2000, I started hiking in to Annapurna, at 26,545 feet the tenth highest mountain in the world. My three teammates were all veteran climbers. Neal Beidleman, an aerospace engineer from Aspen, had been with me on K2 in 1992. An exceptionally strong climber, he probably would have made the summit that year, except that job pressures forced him to return to the States before we could get in position to go for the top.

Neal recommended Michael Kennedy, with whom he'd done a lot of routes around Aspen. I'd never climbed with Michael, but I'd met and liked him. He'd never been on an 8,000-meter peak, but I had the highest respect for his amazing climbs in Alaska and the Karakoram. I also knew him as the longtime editor of *Climbing*, a magazine he'd singlehandedly turned into perhaps the best mountaineering journal in the world.

My Finnish friend Veikka Gustafsson was fast becoming my favorite partner in the Himalaya. Annapurna in 2000 was our sixth expedition together; eventually we'd pair up on no fewer than eleven attempts on 8,000-meter peaks.

By the spring of 2000, I'd been going after those 8,000ers for thirteen years straight, since my first attempt on Everest in 1987. Annapurna was, in fact, my twenty-third such expedition, during which I'd reached the summits of ten of the fourteen highest mountains in the world without using supplemental oxygen. Since 1994, I'd decided to go for all fourteen, a goal I'd originally thought was far beyond my grasp or means. Now that I had the support of sponsors and a modicum of celebrity, I could seriously devote my life to what I called Endeavor 8000, my campaign to stand on top of all fourteen. That in doing so I might become the first American to accomplish the feat never had more than a secondary importance to me. It was first and foremost a personal quest—to test my skills and endurance against the highest and some of the hardest mountains on earth.

I was forty years old that spring. I've always been a conservative climber, but by 2000, I had added reasons why it made sense to be cautious in the big ranges. In my twenties, when I had set out on my first expeditions to 8,000ers, I was single, so I didn't have the responsibilities and commitments that I started to accumulate as I got older. I was completely focused on my climbing and on figuring out how to scratch out a living at the same time. By 2000, however, I was married to Paula, whom I'd met and fallen in love with six years before. Now we had a two-year-old son, Gil, and as I left for Annapurna, Paula was six months pregnant with our second child. Ella would be born on June 25.

Of course Paula worried about my going off on expeditions, and I could no longer nurse that clean-cut conviction that exposing myself to danger on a big mountain was entirely my own concern. Paula saw how diligently I trained and prepared for each expedition, and she always trusted that I would make prudent decisions, but we both understood that on an 8,000er, I could never completely eliminate the element of risk. For Annapurna, I took along a satellite phone, with which I promised to call her as often as I could.

My choice of teammates was hardly accidental. As my regular partner, Veikka was a shoo-in. Like me, Michael and Neal were married and had kids. All three of them were mature, seasoned mountaineers; Michael, who would turn forty-eight on the trip, was almost a decade older than I. Veikka and I had decided that to tackle Annapurna, we wanted a strong team of four, rather than our usual team of two. I figured I could count on Neal's and Michael's judgment and expertise to help keep all of us safe. As I wrote in my diary on March 30, our very first day in Nepal, "Excited to check out Annapurna—but will be very wary & cautious about the ascent. I know the 4 of us are all very conservative & will always shy away from anything that is not acceptable risk."

Supporting our four-man climbing team would be the invaluable Dorje, a Tamang from the Makalu region of Nepal, who'd already been with Veikka and me on other expeditions, helping out with logistics and cooking at base camp. With minimal gear and no oxygen supplies to cart up the mountain, however, we would rely on no other Sherpa support.

After buying supplies in Kathmandu and hiring forty-four porters, we took an arduous ten-hour bus ride to the hill town of Beni, situated only twenty-five miles as the crow flies from Annapurna, though much longer by the trails we would have to hike. Beni's a squalid, depressing outpost—as I wrote in my diary, "A real dump of a place—end-of-the-road truck stop. Muddy and unkempt. Terrible service, shitty food." From Beni we hit the trail north along the banks of the great Kali Gandaki. Once we got away from the truck stop, we passed through a series of pleasant, clean villages—Tatopani, Dana, Kabre, Ghasa, and eventually Lete. I was surprised at the caliber of the tourist lodges in these little towns, which have flourished in recent decades as the Annapurna circuit trek has gained a certain cachet as one of the best long-distance hikes anywhere in the world. In Tatopani, for instance, our breakfast consisted of cinnamon rolls, eggs, potatoes, and steak. You could even buy beer in these lodges.

At the village of Lete we left the main trail, crossed the Kali

Gandaki, and headed east across a series of passes and gorges until we entered the deep ravine of the Miristi Khola. The scenery is stunning as you pass through bamboo and evergreen forests and hillsides lush with rhododendron. But it's a grueling and even dangerous passage: you climb 4,000 feet to one pass, then immediately descend 3,000 feet on the other side, and so on. In places, the grassy slopes we traversed were so steep that a slip off the trail by a heavily loaded porter could have been fatal. You almost think you ought to have crampons and an ice ax on those slopes. To help finance his expedition, Veikka had brought along four trekkers from Finland, clients paying handsome fees for the privilege of going to base camp with an expedition of "real" climbers. By the time these four reached base camp, on our sixth day out of Beni, they were (as I noted in my diary) "completely spent, almost shattered."

The hike to Everest base camp on the Khumbu side is a straightforward trek, made by hundreds of tourists every spring season. On the north, or Tibetan, side of Everest, you can ride in a truck all the way to base camp at 18,000 feet. But the hike to Annapurna base camp on the north is a very serious proposition, not for the faint of heart, the out-of-shape, or anyone with a fear of heights. As I would later recognize, that trek in to the lower slopes of Annapurna amounts to by far the most difficult approach posed by any of the fourteen 8,000-meter peaks.

I felt good on the hike in, and relished its strenuous ups and downs as training and acclimatization for the mountain itself. And the four of us got along splendidly. But what added a huge bonus to the experience was my awareness of the history of the route. Almost exactly fifty years before our hike up the Kali Gandaki and into the Miristi Khola, a French expedition had stormed the same approach to Annapurna, after wasting a month reconnoitering the mountain's neighbor, Dhaulagiri, the sixth highest mountain in the world. The maps of the day were so inaccurate that by the time the French had sorted out the topography and established a base camp under Annapurna's northern flanks, they had less than three weeks left to attempt the climb before the summer monsoon shut down the whole Himalayan chain.

At the age of sixteen I read Maurice Herzog's classic account of the 1950 expedition, titled in English simply *Annapurna*. It's no accident that that book remains the bestselling mountaineering account of all time, for the story Herzog tells is at turns thrilling and excruciating, triumphant and heartrending. On June 3, Herzog and Louis Lachenal reached the summit. It was not only the first 8,000er ever climbed—Everest would not fall for another three years—but it remains forever the only one of the fourteen highest mountains on which the first party to attempt it succeeded in reaching the summit. The team's retreat, however, turned into a desperate ordeal. In the end, Herzog would lose all his toes and fingers to amputation on account of the frostbite he incurred on summit day, but he declared in *Annapurna* (and has steadfastly maintained ever since) that his life was magically fulfilled by the team's accomplishment. The ascent was, he wrote on the last page of the book, "a treasure on which we should live the rest of our days."

More than any other adventure book I've read (and as a teenager I avidly devoured both mountaineering and polar narratives), *Annapurna* inspired me. It was the single most important push in the determination I formed by the age of twenty to become a mountaineer myself. The six principal French climbers—Herzog, the leader; the ace Chamonix guides Lachenal, Lionel Terray, and Gaston Rébuffat; and the two superb "junior" members, Marcel Schatz and Jean Couzy—were heroes of mine. No, they were beyond heroes; they were legends in my imaginative universe.

In 2000, on the hike in, day after day I was acutely aware that we were following in the footsteps of those pioneers. And I was impressed with how blithely they had solved the puzzles of that treacherous approach, especially without reliable maps and with the monsoon threatening to arrive far too soon. Exhilarating though it was to retrace the path discovered by the French, I carried with me in 2000 a certain burden of anxiety, even a taste of dread in my throat. We knew by now that Annapurna was one of the most dangerous mountains in the world. For every three climbers who reached its summit, one died trying. In those stark statistical terms, Annapurna was the deadliest of all fourteen 8,000ers, even more perilous than K2.

It was not by accident that I had put off attempting Annapurna for more than a decade. Only after 1994, when I made the decision to go after all fourteen 8,000ers, did Annapurna cross my radar screen as a future objective. I knew I couldn't put the mountain off indefinitely, but I wanted to make sure I had a wealth of experience under my belt before I made an attempt. A big part of the challenge for me in 2000 was seeing how well I might stack up against those brilliant French climbers who, when I first read about their great ascent, had seemed almost mythical figures. We planned to try the same route the 1950 expedition had put up—which angles across a monstrously large snow-and-ice bowl constantly menaced by avalanches and teetering seracs, before breaking through the massive ice cliff the French called the Sickle, which forms the upper brow of the whole face. But just how dangerous was that route? What would the conditions on it be like in the spring of 2000?

Between 1951 and 1999 seven expeditions had succeeded in repeating the French route. But another thirteen had failed. And during that time, on the French route and its variant to the east, known as the Dutch Rib, no fewer than ten good climbers had died. During some years—1990 and 1997, for example—despite a number of high-powered expeditions converging on Annapurna's flanks, not a single climber reached its summit. In contrast, on Everest, you had to go all the way back to 1974 to find a year when no mountaineer stood on top.

On April 8, Neal, Michael, Veikka, and I reached base camp, a flat spot on a lateral moraine at 13,500 feet, with even a few tufts of grass sticking through the rocks. Another 13,000 feet of mountain thrust into the sky above us. During the next few days, as we watched the mountain and studied the upper part of the north face, we silently came to a unanimous conclusion. Annapurna was going to be a tough and scary climb.

My first book, *No Shortcuts to the Top,* is a memoir about climbing the fourteen highest mountains without bottled oxygen. Endeavor 8000 took me eighteen years to complete, stretching across thirty expeditions. The climax of the book deals with my five-year battle with Annapurna, which proved so daunting that I started thinking of it as my personal Nemesis. It took me three tries before I finally reached the summit of the peak that the French had so boldly climbed (albeit at such a grim price) in 1950. During my first two attempts, Annapurna thwarted my best efforts so insidiously that I began to think there was no way I could climb it within the limits of my own judgment of acceptable risk. I squarely faced the possibility—and said as much to my friends and sponsors—that, if necessary, I'd close the roster at thirteen, leaving Annapurna unscaled.

In my second book, *K2: Life and Death on the World's Most Dangerous Mountain,* I focused on the second highest mountain in the world, a peak so beautiful and formidable that I had begun referring to it as the holy grail of mountaineering. Climbing K2 in 1992 was a crucial turning point in my life, giving me the first inklings of an ambition to climb all fourteen 8,000ers. But it was also the closest call I had ever had (or have ever had since) in the mountains. I still regard pushing on to the summit with Charley Mace and Scott Fischer on August 16 in the face of a fiendish gathering storm as the one big mistake in my climbing career, the one time I didn't listen to the voices in my head warning me about what might happen, the one time I violated my own strict rules about acceptable risk.

The immediate spur for *K2* was the 2008 disaster, in which eleven climbers from several different countries died in a single thirty-six-hour period, one of the worst tragedies in big-range history. But I also devoted a chapter to my own 1992 ascent. I didn't want simply to repeat what I'd written about K2 in *Shortcuts,* and I found that several more years' perspective on that pivotal climb provoked a whole new series of insights into my adventure. I also went back to my K2 diary and found that quoting extensively from what I'd written at the time would give a rawer but perhaps more truthful take on the emotional roller coaster of that long summer in the Karakoram. In the rest of the book, I spend a chapter each recounting what I viewed as the six most interesting seasons in K2's history, including the 2008 disaster, and distilling the lessons I thought one could learn from each of those campaigns.

A good portion of *Shortcuts* is given over to my struggles on Annapurna. In this new book, *The Will to Climb,* once again I have no desire to recycle what I wrote five years ago, shortly after finally getting to the top of Annapurna. And once again the perspective of distance on those three expeditions gives them a new slant in my memory. I've reread the three diaries I wrote in 2000, 2002, and 2005, and I intend to quote from them at far greater length than I did in *Shortcuts.*

As I did with *K2,* in this book, besides retelling my own adventures, I will focus on some of the most memorable achievements that have taken place on Annapurna, starting with the French first ascent. The history of Annapurna, however, is in crucial ways quite different from that of K2. K2's past is marked above all by controversies and catastrophes. And on that mountain, there has been no clear relationship between success as defined by getting to the top and success in terms of interpersonal loyalty and courage. In 1953 the American expedition to K2 failed to climb higher than 25,700 feet after one member, Art Gilkey, was stricken with thrombophlebitis. Giving up all hopes of the summit, his teammates tried desperately to lower him, strapped immobile to a makeshift litter, down the mountain—an effort that came close to costing all of them their lives. In my mind, that effort was not a failure, but rather one of the inspiring triumphs in climbing history of what its leader, Charlie Houston, called "the brotherhood of the rope."

Conversely, the following year, 1954, a massive Italian expedition succeeded in placing two men on the summit, claiming the first ascent of K2. But the team was so riddled with dissension, rivalry, and accusations of criminal negligence that its bitter legacy has been more than half a century of lawsuits and irreparable breaches of friendship. It's hard to think of a poorer model for "success" on one of the great mountains of the world.

In *K2,* then, I tried to sort out the lessons learned from the six most interesting campaigns on the mountain by analyzing mistakes made by the various teams, as well as shining examples of self-sacrifice, teamwork, and heroism.

Curiously, despite how dangerous Annapurna is, its history is highlighted not so much by controversies and disasters as by truly bold and innovative ascents pulled off by visionary mountaineers. It's those deeds that I intend to focus on in this book.

I've always believed that what you learn in the mountains can be directly applied to the rest of your life. Meditating on what Annapurna has meant to me plunged me into a realm of reflection that I never contemplated in either *Shortcuts* or *K2.* It took a great deal of commitment for me to go back to Annapurna for a third time, especially after I'd become convinced that there was no reasonably safe route anywhere on the mountain (another aspect in which the peak is unique among the 8,000ers). I'm a firm believer in the value of commitment—without it, I could scarcely have climbed a single 8,000er, let alone all fourteen. But I'm leery of commitment's close cousin, obsession.

My partner in 2002, the dazzlingly gifted Frenchman Jean-Christophe Lafaille, did battle with Annapurna not for five years, but for ten. J.-C. unabashedly referred to his involvement with his own nemesis as an obsession. He even titled his climbing memoir *Prisonnier de l'Annapurna* (Prisoner of Annapurna). Getting to the summit at last was, in his words, "revenge" on the mountain that had killed his mentor, Pierre Béghin, on J.-C.'s first attempt in 1992.

This book, then, is structured around the dichotomy between commitment and obsession, as revealed in the deeds of Annapurna's bravest and most skillful antagonists. Is it a dichotomy, however, or two points on a continuous spectrum? I'm not willing to make a simplistic black-and-white distinction, to claim that commitment is good, necessary, and sustainable (in life as well as in the Himalaya), while obsession is bad, dangerous, and most likely unsustainable. The whole business is more complex and subtler than that.

The issue of obsession and commitment in mountaineering brings in a host of other questions, ones that, curiously, climbers are not very good at addressing. Fear is an inevitable and even a useful component of the mountaineering game. Fear, like pain, is built into our very genes, for it helps to keep us alive. No matter how skilled a climber becomes, he or she never completely banishes fear (if you do, you're asking for trouble). But irrational fear, or fear out of control, can turn a climber into a quivering mess on the mountain. How do you manage fear on a climb? How do you use it to inform that ineffable but lifesaving mental capacity that we call judgment? How do you decide if your fear is teaching you to make the right decision? All climbers are afraid of giving up too easily, of chickening out, of "crumping"—to use the jargon invented by climbers to describe that demoralized state where you just want to throw in the towel and go home. But the opposite of fear isn't simply courage, or "guts," or daring. It's that exhilarating state we enter so seldom in life, in which you perform close to the limits of your ability in a situation where any mistake could have dire or even fatal consequences.

Another realm allied to commitment and fear is the remarkably broad spectrum between fulfillment and . . . well, what's the opposite of fulfillment? Disappointment? Frustration? Emptiness?

A successful climb can be one of the most fulfilling deeds of a lifetime. But sometimes it brings in its wake a sense of profound letdown, even of the kind of anomie where you don't know what to do with yourself next. Maurice Herzog felt lastingly fulfilled by his triumph on Annapurna, even though it cost him his fingers and toes. But his summit partner, Louis Lachenal, who subsequently lost all his toes, felt no fulfillment from Annapurna. Instead, he felt cheated, robbed of his legendary skill and grace. What accounts for the radical difference in temperament between two such men? Is there, in life or in mountaineering, anything like a magic formula for fulfillment? Is there a cure-all for emptiness?

What, indeed, are the lasting rewards of mountaineering, or of any passionate enterprise? What is the balance between triumph and failure? These are questions I ask myself every day, five years after I finished Endeavor 8000. What has it meant in the grand scheme of my life? What comes after it?

In the cast of characters who fill the pages of this book, as I ponder their stunning deeds on Annapurna, there is a remarkable diversity of temperaments and personalities, which gives rise to a comparable diversity of answers to the questions I've just posed. It's tempting to pair up some of these characters as face-to-face opposites: the patriotic romantic Herzog against the down-to-earth pacifist Lachenal; the sanguine, devout believer Tom Frost versus the dark fatalist Don Whillans; the stoic Jerzy Kukuczka, understating all his climbs, against the mystical Reinhold Messner, who recounted his own ascents in heroic terms; Erhard Loretan, sly, witty, even self-deprecating, contrasted with the solemn, media-driven Benoît Chamoux. . . . Some of those pairings were among teammates (Herzog and Lachenal, Frost and Whillans), some among intense rivals (Kukuczka and Messner, Loretan and Chamoux). And there were other stellar mountaineers who took on Annapurna's harshest challenges, and who stand in its chronicle in curious isolation, such as the Russian Anatoli Boukreev, whose limited command of English tarred him with the caricature of a dim-witted, obsessive superclimber, obscuring the thoughtful poet that emerged in his posthumously translated diaries and essays.

For that matter, J.-C. Lafaille and I became really close friends, sharing three expeditions to 8,000-meter peaks, despite the fact that I spoke no French and his English was sketchy at best. Somehow, though, we shared many great conversations about climbing, family, and life, and I felt honored that he confided in me about his dreams and fears. Yet we had differences in how we approached the high mountains, especially when it came to levels of acceptable risk. Seven years after we last stood on a summit together, I still puzzle over those differences, which ultimately led us along separate paths in the Himalaya and in life.

On April 8, from base camp, I finally called Paula on our sat phone. I realized that I should have called sooner, for when I got her on the line, she seemed irritated. As I wrote in my diary, "Should've called a few days ago, but didn't. Thought I would wait until we got here—but Paula was upset, understandably. I apologized but not sure that did any good." Within a few minutes on the phone, however, we were back on friendly terms. "Great to hear her voice & talk & catch up with her," I added in my diary. "Gil was asleep so I'll call back tonight to get him in the morning."

That little impasse was symptomatic of the new complexity that continuing to climb hard after marrying and having kids had brought to my life. Now, each time I left for an expedition, it was with a bit of a guilty feeling. I'd think, "Man, the minute I step out the door, Paula's work load increases. She'll be home alone, having to take care of the kids all by herself."

It wasn't just a matter of domestic logistics. In 2000, I missed Paula and Gil while I was on Annapurna. But I'd made it a cardinal principle never to shortcut an expedition because of those sorts of feelings, never to abbreviate a trip just to get home sooner. I was always committed to what I had undertaken, and Paula was fully supportive; she'd say, "Go do what you need to do." Her endorsement of my climbing from start to finish was critical to my pursuing Endeavor 8000.

And yet not calling her as soon as I'd said I would was a mistake that hurt her feelings badly. I've been accused of always blaming myself when things go wrong, but in this case my silence from April 1 through 8 really was my fault. Staying in touch was as important to me as it was to Paula, and the recent advent of small, handheld satellite phones had made regular communication around the globe possible, even from remote parts of the wilderness. But using the sat phone wasn't always a simple matter: it required finding the right moment to take a break during a busy day of trekking or climbing, and being in a location where you could get a good signal. The whole process was complicated by the twelve time zones that separated Paula and me.

On April 10, Veikka's four trekkers started their hike out. I wrote in my diary, "Trekkers are gone—yahoo! We have our own space." That sounds a bit heartless, but let's put it in context. The four Finns who hiked in with us were nice enough people, but Veikka had to take care of them, so he was constantly distracted. As long as they were with us, we had to share breakfast and dinner with them, and in effect keep them entertained. On an expedition, I prefer to be alone with my teammates, not sharing camp with superfluous people, so that I can focus on the task at hand. That's the reason I've never solicited base camp trekkers myself, even in the early days, when I could barely scrape up enough cash to go on each trip to an 8,000er.

During our first few days at base camp, we studied the mountain carefully, working out the first stages of our route toward Camp I. This side of Annapurna is so glaciated and complex that you need to establish a first camp before you even get a full view of the north face. The going above base camp isn't technically difficult, but that stretch is crevassed and threatened by cliffs and minor avalanche slopes that aren't even properly a part of the mountain. To avoid the broken-up glacier, we opted to traverse the rock slabs on the left instead, by a route that would lead us to Camp I. "Some loose funky stuff," I wrote in my diary, "ledges, gullies. Awkward bits that we fixed [with ropes] on the way up. Lots of exposure in places but solid footing on the rock." Even carrying heavy loads, however, we could scramble up and across these slabs fairly easily, wearing only our trekking shoes.

We were in high spirits those first days, and I stayed optimistic. By April 10 we had already deposited a good deal of gear at Camp I. I'd heard so many bad things about Annapurna, about how dangerous even the French route was, but I kept thinking, maybe it won't turn out to be as rough as people say.

Yet, slowly, doubts crept over us. On April 11, only three days after getting to base camp, our mood shifted slightly. From my diary:

> Clouds & wind from the N/NE this morning—something felt funky, like a change in the weather. At breakfast we all seemed ambivalent about going up. Outside we looked around, no one made any moves. I suggested a rest day & everyone agreed immediately.

In and of itself, that ambivalence meant little. After the arduous hike in and nine days of nonstop activity, we needed a break. Nobody had any real motivation that day. We figured, let's just park it.

Later during the trip, on one carry between base camp and Camp I, an avalanche cut loose above Veikka and me. It wasn't even sloughing off Annapurna, just off a subsidiary ridge on a nameless buttress on the approach to the peak. We took off running at top speed, actually sprinting across the sloping rock slabs—I called it a "hundred-yard dash" in my diary. We hid behind a big boulder while the debris thundered past behind us. At such an altitude, "running" becomes an anaerobic exercise. It took us fifteen minutes just to catch our breaths. I wouldn't call it a true close call, but it was certainly unsettling. If this kind of objective hazard could give us the willies way down on the approach to the foot of the mountain, what were we in for on the north face itself?

At the time, the only other team on this side of the mountain was a Spanish outfit. They were there to commemorate the fiftieth anniversary of the first ascent, but they didn't seem either very ambitious or particularly expert. After several days I wrote in my diary, "Met with the Spanish & they seem indecisive but will probably follow our lead." After we'd reached base camp, a third team arrived, made up of French guides, also bent on commemorating the landmark first ascent by their countrymen half a century before. These were a first-rate bunch; they had their act together from the start. As I always had on other expeditions, now we took the time to visit with the teams camped near us, in part to coordinate our efforts on the mountain, but more just to socialize. Our exchanges of food tilted in our favor, as we walked away with scrumptious meats and cheeses in return for our Pringles and M&Ms.

By April 12 the four of us were well installed at Camp I, with tents, fixed ropes, hardware, and ten days' food. I was still feeling optimistic. The next day, we finally got onto the mountain, as we pushed a route to look for a safe site for Camp II. "Good night's sleep," I wrote in my diary, "but awakened twice by big avalanche noise—then 30 seconds later our camp would get blasted by wind & spindrift. Scary, but our camp is very safe."

Scary and *safe*. Those two adjectives epitomized our experience during the next week—a constant vacillation between the two. On the thirteenth, we found a site for Camp II, where, the next day, we got our tents pitched tight to the lee side of a small ice cliff, above which the slope was seamed with huge, gaping crevasses. Whatever debris came crashing down from above, we assumed, would get sucked into those crevasses instead of pouring over the cliff above camp. Still, we were only at 18,400 feet. Eight thousand feet still to gain to reach the summit, with all the real difficulties ahead of us.

During the day of April 15 we hung out at Camp II—to acclimatize and to sit out a morning snowstorm. Our camp was Spartan: Veikka and I in our tiny tent, Neal and Michael in theirs. During our last several expeditions together, to save weight, Veikka and I had decided not to use two separate sleeping bags; instead, we brought a single down quilt that I had designed. The space inside our tent was so cramped anyway that to sleep you were forced to "spoon," so why not simply share that body heat? If you also have all your clothes on, the quilt provides sufficient insulation to keep you warm. Our kitchen kit consisted of a small propane burner head, a few canisters of fuel, a single small cooking pot for melting snow and boiling water, and one cup and one spoon per person. Our entertainment was minimal. I'd carry up part of a paperback book, and after I'd read several pages, I'd tear them out and give these "installments" to Veikka.

Our meals were as Spartan as our sleeping arrangements. Veikka's and my experience together had taught us what we knew we'd want to eat, and how little food we needed to bring. In general, your appetite decreases the higher you go. We'd worked out our standard menus. Breakfast was typically a couple of cups of coffee and a handful of granola with powdered milk. We'd fill our water bottles with sweet tea for drinking during the day. While climbing, instead of stopping for a true lunch, we'd snack on energy bars or gels, just to keep things simple. Back in the tent late in the day, we'd snack on dried fruit, nuts, crackers, cheese, and a little jerky. Dinner consisted of a cup of soup, a shared freeze-dried meal, a few cookies, and more hot drinks. Our choice of freeze-dried meals tended toward the hot and spicy. Even at a subzero high camp, we'd be sweating and taking layers of clothes off while eating one of these meals. I figured it was a benefit to climb into your sleeping bag with your system fired up by jalapeños and chili peppers. In the cold dry air at altitude, staying hydrated is a constant battle, and it took hours of melting snow in the morning and again at night to produce enough water to quench our thirst. On some occasions we'd be so exhausted from that effort that we'd skip dinner altogether.

A few odds and ends filled out our supplies. Our repair kit consisted of some wire, duct tape, cord, and a sewing kit. We had two first aid kits. I'd bring a substantial one, while Veikka swore by his own version: one Band-Aid and two aspirin tablets. Our personal hygiene items amounted to toothbrush and toothpaste, toilet paper, and some baby wipes.

Although the weather stayed fine during the next week, our doubts steadily grew. Something just didn't feel right. It was only April, but it seemed really warm. It was as if the mountain were melting and crumbling above us. Every day we'd see big avalanches pouring off one part or another of the north face, and during some nights, we'd be jolted out of our sleep by the sound of big slides crashing to the base. We still weren't fully committed to the French route, and we looked long and hard at the Dutch Rib, an apparently safer line to the east, first climbed by a Netherlander and a Sherpa in 1977. The Dutch Rib followed a protruding buttress of ice, snow, and rock, and it avoided the Sickle, the huge ice wall that hangs constantly over the French route. But just to get to the foot of the Rib, we'd have to traverse the plateau that was the catchment basin for many of the big avalanches coming from the north face and the Sickle above. How many trips back and forth across that dangerous slope would we be willing to make? How fast could we run from an avalanche with loaded packs? Probably not fast enough.

Then one day, peering through binoculars, Neal spotted a huge detached ice pillar precariously balanced directly above the top of the Dutch Rib. The size of a tall building, it looked ready to collapse at any moment. That alone made the Dutch Rib seem out of the question this season.

On April 16, after the four of us had climbed higher and I studied the upper face from a vantage point above Camp II, I wrote in my diary, "There is no safe way to get to *any* of the 'normal' routes. All threatened by a series of ice cliffs. The risks are too high & there is no way to justify attempting any of the routes." We agreed to dismantle Camp II, descend to Camp I, where we'd deposit the gear, then push on down to base camp to reevaluate our options.

I felt both puzzled and frustrated by our qualms about the face. I knew that since 1950 eight expeditions had succeeded in climbing the French route all the way to the summit. Except for the 1950 pioneers, I knew almost no details about the climbers who had made those ascents, not because I wasn't willing to do my homework, but because their accounts—in Russian, Chinese, and Korean, among other languages—were almost impossible to find. I began to wonder if those climbers had simply accepted higher levels of risk than we were willing to. But I also wondered whether conditions had been substantially better during the years those other teams succeeded. When you first read Herzog's account of dashing up the face in *Annapurna,* you get almost no sense that in May 1950 stuff was crashing down on all sides of the climbers. By 2000, however, I'd gone through the book countless times, and by reading between the lines, I'd come to understand that the French had had several close calls on the face. Even so, I wondered whether the spring of 2000 just happened to be a really bad season on the mountain.

When I reread my 2000 diary, I can see that the strain we were under was constant. I'd try to savor the good moments, as on April 16: "Celebrated Michael's 48th [birthday] with some Scotch. Had a great pizza dinner." And there was my sporadic contact with home: "I'm waiting up to call Paula & Gil. Nice to be *here* safe & warm while it's snowing all around." The weather had turned fickle, and now we had to be patient.

Base camp gave us a chance to rest up and feel safe. We slept much better without the constant strain of the mountain's dangers. We each had a one-man tent to retreat to, inside which we could escape with our books and music piped through our headphones. We gathered in our dining tent for the meals that Dorje magically concocted. Our appetites were much heartier at this lower altitude. We ate breakfasts of real French-press coffee, eggs, potatoes, and toast; lunches of fresh salads, tuna fish, and pasta; dinners of local rice and lentils, more pasta dishes, or, on occasion, Dorje's "everything pizza," which was piled high with cauliflower, ham, peas, sliced potatoes, onions, and liberal mounds of pungent yak cheese.

We spent much of our time engaged in conversation or playing heated hands of hearts. Base camp was also a place where we could look through the personal treasures each of us had brought along. Before each of my expeditions, Paula would write me a beautiful card, which I'd read on the flight over and carry with me in my pocket during the ascent. I also had a selection of family photos and a small bag of lucky trinkets in my "ju-ju" bag, which I always kept with me. Neal's and Michael's wives had sneaked "care packages" into their duffels, which they discovered only at base camp. These packages contained a trove of special treats, such as family photos, magazines, and gourmet candies and snacks. Neal's wife had thrown in the current copy of *Sports Illustrated*'s swimsuit issue, complete with 3-D glasses! That kept us howling with laughter for some time.

After two days at base camp, we decided to climb back up to Camp I, then scope out alternatives to the French route. "We will be *way* conservative about what we do," I wrote on the nineteenth, as if to convince myself we weren't simply being wusses. "Spent some time looking at routes but didn't come to any conclusions. I suggested we spend the day just watching the mountain & not yet climbing higher. Everyone agreed. Saw several big ones [i.e., avalanches] throughout the day—monsters."

On April 20 we pushed out of Camp I again, angling toward a line to the left of the north face proper. If we could get up this possibly safer route, we would need to traverse the east and central summits of Annapurna, both above 25,000 feet, just to gain the main summit. After several hours of climbing, Michael was in the lead. Suddenly he stopped. "I don't like these conditions," he said. We looked at one another, then seconded Michael's assessment. So we simply turned around and retreated. The mood was low in camp that afternoon. "We've looked at all the options, it seems," I wrote. "Not sure what to do at this point. Nothing feels right."

By 5:00 P.M., we had decided to give up our attempt on Annapurna. "The risks are too great—even for one round trip [to Camp II]," I wrote in my diary. "So tomorrow we'll start hauling our stuff to base camp." I felt, though, that I had to rationalize giving up. "I know I'm making the right decision—it feels right *not* to go back into that stuff. We had no close calls & that's the way it should be. . . . This mountain has too many uncontrollable risks."

I'll have to admit, however, that the setback stung. On only one other expedition, to the treacherous Kangshung Face of Everest in 1988, had I been stopped cold so low on the mountain. It was as if Annapurna were a brick wall and we had run smack into it. Our egos were bruised, even if our bodies were healthy. I had learned by now, however, to accept such a defeat. The mountain always calls the shots.

Only Veikka remained undecided. He talked that evening about maybe staying on and joining up with some other climbers, perhaps the French guides, to make one good effort on the 1950 route. He even pondered trying the route solo. I'm not sure he was really thinking of that possibility—it was more like he was thinking of thinking about it.

Shortly after midnight, he changed his mind.

There was a full moon that night. I was having trouble sleeping, but beside me, Veikka was deep in slumberland. Suddenly a deep, powerful rumbling sound tore through the silence. I scrambled half out of my bag and zipped open the tent door. Above me I saw a huge cloud of snow and mist. A gigantic avalanche was plunging down the north face. "Veikka!" I shouted, waking up my partner. "Look at that!" Soon he had his head out the door as well. In the blue glow of moonlight, the monster avalanche was boiling toward us. It was so huge and the distance it traveled was so great that it seemed to roll forward in slow motion, engulfing everything in its path. The sight was both mesmerizing and terrifying.

We shouted over to Neal and Michael in the other tent. "Get ready!" I yelled.

We knew we were safe, since we'd pitched Camp I a good two miles away from the base of the mountain. But we also knew that a slide as big as this one would push a veritable hurricane of wind and fine powder snow ahead of it.

It seemed to take forever for the avalanche to clear the face. At the last minute, I zipped shut the door and grabbed the tent poles. Veikka did the same, as did Michael and Neal in their tent.

When the blast finally hit, it was all we could do to hang on to our tent and keep it from getting blown loose. In the midst of the assault, Veikka and I stared at each other, wide-eyed. At last the wind stopped, but the spindrift took many minutes to settle over camp.

That was the biggest avalanche any of us had ever seen. It

remains today the biggest I've ever witnessed. (Only the avalanches I saw in 1988 tumbling off Everest's Kangshung Face were in the same league.) In the morning, we saw to our horror that the farthest-flung blocks of ice had come to rest only a couple of hundred yards short of our tents. The face of the mountain had been swept clean—features that we'd memorized over the previous ten days were simply gone. Had we been camped anywhere on the French route, the avalanche would have taken us with it. I can't remember which one of us said it, but we all shared the verdict: "Man, did we ever make the right decision!"

That day we packed all of our gear and descended to base camp. Before we left, I took a last look at the face. Later that evening I wrote in my diary, "Not sure what happened at our Camp II site—but it looks like it took a beating."

On April 25 we started the long, difficult hike out. We moved so fast it took us only three days to reach the hill town of Jomsom, an outpost on the Annapurna circuit trail that has a small airport. From there, with the assistance of a local fixer retained by our agents in Kathmandu, we arranged a flight out. We were back in Nepal's capital on April 28.

As it was, in 2000 we spent only eighteen days on Annapurna, if you count base camp as the beginning of the climb. Others have since asked me why we didn't stay on into May, in the hope that we'd get a better chance. By the time we left the mountain, there was still more than a month to go before the monsoon arrived.

The answer is fairly simple. That spring, Annapurna just wasn't going to get into the kind of shape we needed to climb it safely. Icefalls don't change substantially in only a few weeks, and we knew the constant activity—avalanches, collapsing seracs, falling rocks—wasn't going to abate anytime soon. That our decision to head home was a sensible one was borne out by the fact that in the spring of 2000 nobody got up Annapurna, not even the crack French guides. The highest anyone reached was 23,100 feet, still almost 3,500 feet below the summit. And I shudder to think of the risks taken by those guys who stayed on into May to get even that high.

By itself, that first defeat hadn't yet turned Annapurna into my personal nemesis. After all, there had been other 8,000ers I'd failed at on my first attempts: most recently, Dhaulagiri in 1998; Broad Peak the year before; Shishapangma in 1993; and Everest twice, in 1987 and 1988. I knew I could come back and give it another shot. The mountain would always be there.

But the brick wall we'd run head-on into on the north face haunted me for months afterward. Again and again my thoughts returned to the French in 1950. How had those guys—with infinitely poorer equipment than ours, with no other 8,000er yet climbed, and with Annapurna completely unexplored before their last-ditch assault—solved all the dangers of the face and pushed two men to the top just before the monsoon hit? Did they know something we didn't?

My God, thanks to World War II, none of those guys had ever been on an expedition before! All their climbing had taken place in the Alps. Maybe their very ignorance of the Himalaya had been a blessing in disguise. Maybe it was what they didn't know about big mountains that was their strongest asset.

Or maybe they really were the mythic figures they had seemed to me when I first read *Annapurna* at the age of sixteen.

TWO

A NEW AND SPLENDID LIFE

The first attempt ever made on an 8,000-meter peak came back in 1895, when a small party led by A. F. Mummery tried to find a way up Nanga Parbat, the world's ninth highest mountain, at 26,660 feet. Because it stands in relative isolation south of the formidable main chain of the Karakoram, the mountain—today in Pakistan, but then lying in British India—was relatively easy of access. But Nanga Parbat is a difficult, even treacherous mountain, and its Rupal face on the south lays solid claim to being the single tallest precipice on earth, rising in a single sweep almost 15,000 feet from the glacier to the summit.

Mummery was the finest British climber of his day, and his lead of the Mummery Crack on the Petit Grépon near Chamonix set a new standard of excellence and daring in the Alps. But, like other Victorian and Edwardian travelers in the Himalaya and the Karakoram, he underestimated the scale and danger of the world's highest mountains. After a bold reconnaissance of Nanga Parbat's west face, Mummery took only two Gurkha porters with him to explore an approach from the north. The three men were never seen again, nor have their bodies been found. In all likelihood, they were swept to their deaths by an avalanche.

K2, the world's second highest peak, was attempted in 1902 and again in 1909, with neither party getting higher than 21,870 feet. In 1938 and 1939, American expeditions made gutsy attacks on the southeast flank of the mountain (named the Abruzzi Spur after the leader of the 1909 Italian effort). I wrote about these remarkable expeditions in detail in my K2 book. On the second attempt, in 1939, the German-American Fritz Wiessner and his loyal Sherpa companion Pasang Lama reached 27,500 feet, only 750 feet of moderately angled snow slopes short of the top. But Wiessner had to turn back when Pasang refused to climb on into the night.

Mount Everest was not even reconnoitered until 1921, because of political roadblocks thrown up by the governments of Nepal and Tibet. But once the British won the cooperation of Tibetan authorities, they launched no fewer than seven attempts between 1921 and 1938 to climb the highest mountain in the world from the north. The most famous of these—indeed, one of the enduring legends in the annals of adventure—came in 1924, when George Leigh Mallory (the finest British climber of the generation after Mummery) and his young teammate, Andrew Irvine, disappeared around 28,000 feet on the northeast ridge, only about a thousand feet short of the summit. Today, only the most diehard partisans of that brave pair believe they could have reached the top before perishing.

Meanwhile, German teams focused on Nanga Parbat and on Kangchenjunga, the third highest peak in the world. On the latter mountain, expeditions launched in 1929, 1930, and 1931 ran afoul of the sheer complexity of the sprawling mountain. (Of all the 8,000ers, Kangchenjunga requires the longest and most circuitous approaches to the vast summit plateau.) None of the three attempts reached an altitude higher than 24,500 feet, still more than 3,500 feet below the top.

Nanga Parbat became the scene of repeated tragedy. The Germans made four attempts on the peak between 1932 and 1938, but they cost twenty-six lives. In 1937 a massive avalanche engulfed the team's high camp while the men slept in their tents. Seven Germans and nine Sherpa died in a matter of seconds. That event remains the single greatest catastrophe in the history of climbing on the 8,000ers.

From the autumn of 1939 through the summer of 1945, World War II effectively shut down big-range mountaineering on all continents. And for five years after the war, the political tensions that spilled out of that global conflict prevented climbers from returning to the Himalaya or the Karakoram. By 1950 the highest summit that climbers had reached was that of Nanda Devi, in northern India, at 25,643 feet (or 7,816 meters). That landmark ascent, whose altitude record would stand for fourteen years, was the achievement of a joint British-American team in 1936.

Thus by 1950, despite more than half a century of assaults by some of the best mountaineers in Europe and the United States (and by their Sherpa teammates), no 8,000-meter peak had yet been climbed. During that half century, Everest had effectively become the "British mountain," since no other nation had won permission to attempt it. Americans had put their dibs on K2, though Italians also coveted the handsome and daunting crown of the Karakoram. And tragedy or no, Kangchenjunga and Nanga Parbat were quintessentially German fields of mountaineering endeavor.

What seems curious in retrospect is that up until 1950 the French, despite producing a steady stream of superb climbers who were the equals of the best German, Austrian, Italian, and Swiss combatants in their native Alps, made almost no dent in the Karakoram or the Himalaya. Before then, the only French expedition ever launched against an 8,000er was a 1936 attempt on Gasherbrum I, the world's eleventh highest mountain. That team got no higher than 22,630 feet.

In 1950 the French as a people still felt the sting of the humiliation of World War II, during which the whole country was occupied by the Germans, only to be liberated after D-day by the brilliant attack of the Allied Forces. It's no coincidence that the first postwar French expedition to the Himalaya was conceived as a nationalistic effort, an attempt to restore Gallic pride by performing an audacious triumph of terrestrial exploration and adventure. Lucien Devies, the intensely patriotic president of the Club Alpin Français, chose the equally patriotic Maurice Herzog as the leader, despite the fact that Herzog had a far less impressive record in the mountains than did the three Chamonix guides Louis Lachenal, Lionel Terray, and Gaston Rébuffat.

On the eve of their departure the team gathered in the offices of the CAF in Paris. Suddenly Devies rose and read an oath the club would require each member to recite: "I swear upon my honor to obey the leader in everything regarding the Expedition in which he may command me." Free spirits such as Lachenal and Rébuffat were taken aback by this unanticipated demand, but one by one all the members spoke the oath.

In this sense the 1950 expedition was organized not only along nationalistic lines, but with military hierarchy. This would turn out to be the normal pattern for Himalayan expeditions in the 1950s and the first half of the 1960s, a fifteen-year span that saw the first ascents of all fourteen 8,000ers. It was a nationalistic era, with the cold war at its height and the European countries struggling to get back on their feet. Each expedition to an 8,000er was concocted as an exercise in patriotism. The teams were chosen not by old allegiances among friends, but in concerted campaigns to identify the finest mountaineers to represent their countries. Expeditions to the Himalaya during those years were like annual Olympic games. And the international rivalries waxed hot: the Swiss and the British dueling for Everest, the Americans and Italians trying to claim K2.

Since climbing nowadays is so individualistic, with national pride all but irrelevant, I've been asked sometimes how I would have reacted to the style of the 1950s. Frankly, that earlier nationalism doesn't bother me. I would have loved to climb in the Himalaya in the 1950s. Everything then was a true adventure, with climbers going off the map, discovering places no one else had ever discovered. If some leader had told me I had to recite a loyalty oath, I wouldn't have hesitated. If I had been one of the lucky few to be invited on an expedition to an unclimbed 8,000er, I'd have signed on the dotted line. For that matter, I've accepted the leadership of others on some of my expeditions, including the International Peace Climb on Everest in 1990, led by Jim Whittaker, and the 1996 IMAX filming project on Everest, organized by David Breashears. My attitude on those expeditions was, *Okay, you tell me what to do. I'll work my ass off doing it.*

Only once in my career, early on, did I decide to turn down an invitation to an 8,000er because of the bad vibes I'd picked up from the team. But in that case it had nothing to do with nationalism or autocratic leadership. Sometime in January or February of that year I was invited to a meeting of prospective climbers in Seattle. I was shocked that they were already squabbling among themselves in a pretty bitter way. I decided then and there that this was a gang I didn't want to be part of. Later I called one of the guys and said, "You're not even on the mountain, and you're already arguing? Thanks, but I'm not going." I'll never know how those antagonisms ended up playing themselves out on the mountain, but to their credit, the team succeeded in getting seven climbers to the summit.

In yet another respect the 1950 expedition was boldly ambitious. Rather than attempt a mountain such as Kangchenjunga or Nanga Parbat, on which previous expeditions had solved some of the puzzles of the approach, the French focused on two 8,000ers that had never been reconnoitered, let alone attempted. Looming some 220 miles west of Everest, Annapurna and Dhaulagiri are twin giants facing each other across the deep gorge of the Kali Gandaki. The tenth and seventh highest mountains in the world respectively, both peaks had been surveyed from great distances in the early nineteenth century (in fact, from 1808 to 1838, Dhaulagiri was thought to be the highest mountain on earth), but no explorers had worked out the approaches to either peak before 1950. The French team's mandate was not only to discover the best approach routes, but to attempt one or the other of the great mountains. If both proved beyond the party's capabilities, then bagging a lower summit or two in the Annapurna-Dhaulagiri massif would be the consolation prize. (In 1909 the Duke of the Abruzzi, after giving up on K2, attempted nearby Chogolisa, a much easier and lower peak. His team failed 850 feet short of Chogolisa's summit, but in reaching 24,275 feet, the Italians set a world altitude record that would stand for thirteen years.)

The choice of Maurice Herzog as the team's leader provoked controversy within French circles. As Lionel Terray would later write in *Conquistadors of the Useless,* one of the best climbing autobiographies ever written, Herzog's selection "caused a great deal of argument both then and later. . . . The objections were mostly on the grounds that he had done none of the greatest ascents of his day and could therefore not be considered one of its leading climbers."

A principal reason for putting Herzog in charge was that he and Lucien Devies were close friends. Both were staunch supporters of General Charles de Gaulle, and Herzog had served heroically in World War II. But critics pointed out that several slightly senior French alpinists with stellar records who might have made ideal expedition leaders—notably Pierre Allain and Armand Charlet—were passed over in favor of Herzog.

Yet this sort of choice of leader was far from abnormal on Himalayan expeditions in the 1950s and earlier. In 1953 the Himalayan Committee of the Alpine Club in London reneged on its choice of Eric Shipton to lead the expedition that would end up making the mountain's first ascent. Instead, the committee appointed Colonel John Hunt, whose own climbing record was little better than mediocre. Shipton had more experience on Everest than any other living climber, but he was thought to be too casual as a leader, and too fond of lightweight, fast-moving assaults on high peaks, to handle the massive logistical campaign the Alpine Club planned for 1953. Hunt was a military man through and through, and in the end he managed the logistics of that heavyweight attack with great finesse.

For that matter, in 1924, Mallory—who was not only the best British climber of his era, but also the one with by far the most experience on Everest—was not chosen to lead Britain's third attempt on the world's highest mountain. Instead, fifty-eight-year-old general Charles Bruce, a military man with more service in the army in India than experience on mountains of any kind, was appointed the leader.

There was no question, however, that Lachenal, Terray, and Rébuffat were among the finest technical climbers of their day anywhere in the world. Terray and Lachenal had formed an already legendary partnership, putting up extreme new routes all over the Alps. In 1947 they had made the second ascent of the north face of the Eiger, first climbed by a pair of Austrians and a pair of Germans in 1938, after the face killed eight of the first ten alpinists to try it. Rébuffat would become one of the best adventure writers of his day, a lyric rhapsodist at odds with all notions of "conquest" and military assault in the mountains. His masterpiece, *Starlight and Storm,* chronicled his becoming the first man to ascend what were then deemed the "six great north faces of the Alps," an achievement he would complete with a desperate struggle on the Eiger in 1952.

Jean Couzy and Marcel Schatz, at twenty-seven and twenty-nine, were only a few years younger than their more famous teammates, but they accepted from the start Herzog's decision to relegate them to a largely supporting role. Close friends and partners, Schatz and Couzy would take divergent paths after Annapurna. Schatz retired from climbing at the age of thirty, as he became one of his country's leading atomic scientists. Couzy, however, came into his own as a mountaineer, and would be the driving force on the 1955 expedition to Makalu, led by Terray, that made the first ascent of the world's fifth highest mountain.

The team was rounded out by three nonclimbers: Marcel Ichac, cameraman and photographer; Jacques Oudot, the expedition doctor; and Francis de Noyelle, its liaison officer.

At dawn on April 17, from the lowland village of Baglung, the climbers caught their first sight of Dhaulagiri, rising an astounding 23,000 feet above them far to the north. In *Annapurna,* Herzog records his teammates' ecstatic response, as they jumped naked out of their sleeping bags and tents to stare at the gigantic mountain and screamed with joy.

During the next month, the nine Frenchmen would steadily and dishearteningly learn how nearly impossible the challenge they had set for themselves would prove to be.

There are experiences in the history of mountaineering that no one else is likely ever to have. Among them was the vexing problem the French faced in April 1950. Both Annapurna and Dhaulagiri can be seen from more than a hundred miles away, they so tower over the lower summits in the range. But for the team to find its way through the labyrinth of foothills, canyons, and glaciers to the base of either mountain would tax and nearly defeat their finest efforts. The errors built into the best available maps by cartographers who were essentially relying on guesswork hugely complicated the problem. Time and again the French sent out reconnoitering parties to penetrate Dhaulagiri's defenses, only to end up separated from the mountain by high ridges that were never indicated on the maps.

In *Annapurna,* Herzog published on facing pages a pair of sketch maps of Dhaulagiri and its surroundings. The one on the left is based on the Indian Survey map; the one on the right reflects the reality that the team painstakingly discovered. The discrepancies are shocking.

I can't think of any mountaineer of my generation who has had to solve a comparably thorny problem. Sure, guys still reconnoiter the approaches to remote peaks in places such as western China before they can attempt to climb them. But local knowledge and the good maps produced by airplane and satellite surveys prevent today's climbers from stumbling into the kinds of dead ends that so frustrated the French.

In 1967 my co-author, David Roberts, organized the first expedition to a remote, unnamed range of difficult mountains in southwestern Alaska. But even though the range had never been explored, the U.S. Geological Survey maps of the region were dead-on accurate. Roberts's team of six was able to land by ski-equipped plane on the central glacier, where they set up a base camp, just as they had planned. Over the next seven weeks they made a bunch of first ascents, and after the expedition they had the privilege of giving the range its official name: the Revelation Mountains.

The pages of *Annapurna* devoted to the wild goose chase for an approach to Dhaulagiri amount to a chronicle of heartbreak and frustration. A sample dialogue between Herzog and Ichac, as they top out on what they think will be a crucial pass:

"Well I'm damned! A valley starting here—"

"It's not marked on the map," said Ichac. "It's an unknown valley."

"It runs down in a northerly direction, and divides into two great branches."

"No sign of Dhaulagiri!"

All this time, as the team frittered away the last weeks of April and the first weeks of May, the French knew that their window of good weather before the onset of the monsoon in early June was inexorably narrowing. On May 14, still stuck in the lowland village of Tukucha, the team met for what Herzog called "a solemn council of war." After an extended and rancorous debate, the men agreed to switch their objective to Annapurna. In effect, they were starting over.

The maps were every bit as wrong about Annapurna as they were about Dhaulagiri. In *Annapurna,* Herzog published another facing pair of sketch maps—Indian Survey versus reality—that once again document the stunning discrepancies. Fortunately, earlier during the expedition, on April 27, Couzy and Schatz, the two most junior members of the six-man cadre of expert mountaineers, had discovered a difficult but feasible route into the Miristi Khola, an eastern tributary of the Kali Gandaki, whose headwaters, the two men learned, drained the glaciers spilling from the north face of Annapurna. The Miristi Khola would prove to be the key to the approach, but it was such a savage gorge that Herzog at first doubted whether he could persuade the porters to carry loads up its steeply angled hillsides. As I mention in the first chapter, no other 8,000er has so difficult or dangerous a route of approach to what is now considered its "normal" route.

The path the French took up the Miristi Khola was in several crucial passages different from (and more dangerous than) the "improved" access route the four of us followed in 2000. Precipitous ravines forced the team to ford the river a number of times. Like most glacial streams, the Miristi Khola is bone-chillingly cold and tumbles in rapids through boulder-choked chutes. Herzog's fears were realized: again and again the porters refused to carry loads across the treacherous current. So the French took on the job themselves, crafting rickety bridges with fallen logs, or passing packs from boulder to boulder, or even wading the river with their boots on and heavy loads on their backs.

It is a tribute to the sheer drive and courage of those climbers that in only four days they reached a provisional base camp at the foot of the Northwest Spur, the nearest part of Annapurna itself to the upper reaches of the Miristi Khola. Yet now they made a decision that came close to costing them any chance of getting up the mountain.

Fired by his zeal as an alpinist, Terray lobbied hard for attacking the Northwest Spur at once, even though it was self-evidently a severe technical challenge. His enthusiasm won over an initially skeptical Herzog. During the next five days, first Terray and Lachenal and then Terray and Herzog pushed pitch after pitch up the steep pillar. Climbing of this level of difficulty had never before been accomplished in the Himalaya. But the Northwest Spur was yet another wild goose chase. After those five days of dogged effort, the men had reached a point only about 19,000 feet above sea level, more than 7,000 feet below the mountain's summit. The terrain was far too difficult for the Sherpa to climb, let alone to establish the necessary chain of well-stocked camps leading toward the top.

Five days of brilliant but wasted effort, with so few days left before the monsoon!. As it would turn out, the Northwest Spur would not be climbed until 1996, after numerous failed attempts, when a Pole and a Ukrainian in the vanguard of a crack Polish team finally succeeded in solving this daunting line.

More than a decade later, in his autobiography, Terray would look back on the attempt to climb the Northwest Spur as pure folly. "What ignorance of Himalayan conditions!" he wrote. "What an accumulation of errors of judgment!" Yet he retained a fierce pride about the climbing he had done on the spur: "Nothing will ever surpass those desperate days when I gave myself up to the struggle with all the strength and courage at my command."

It was Rébuffat, skeptical from the start about the Northwest Spur, who discovered the clever route through seracs and crevasse fields that at last led to the basin directly beneath the north face. Yet it was not until May 23 that the French team established a base camp there (they called it Camp I). The altitude of the camp was a paltry 16,700 feet—nearly 10,000 feet below the summit.

Once again, it is worth noting what frantic impatience the lateness of the season forced upon the French team. Three years later, on the first ascent of Everest, by May 23 the British had established a camp on the South Col, at 26,000 feet, a mere 3,000 feet below the summit, and that camp was supported by a string of no fewer than seven well-stocked camps snaking up the Khumbu Glacier, across the Lhotse Face, and through the Yellow Band. When Hillary and Tenzing finally made the summit six days later, that triumph came as the pinnacle of a massive logistical pyramid smoothly orchestrated by the leader, Colonel John Hunt.

I've often wondered if, for the French in 1950, a certain ignorance operated as bliss. At the base of the north face, the men seemed to have little sense of just how hopeless a task might be facing them. With no Himalayan experience among them, they seemed to treat Annapurna as they might have a big climb in the Alps—something on the order of the south face of Mont Blanc, perhaps.

In Herzog's book, as the men study that dangerous face, Lachenal suddenly declares, "I've found the route!" Itching to get started, he and Terray can barely be restrained. "A hundred to nothing!" Herzog quotes Lachenal as shouting in his ear. "That's the odds on our success!"

After our own crushing setback on the same face in 2000, when we reached an altitude of only a little above 18,000 feet and all four of us emerged from the expedition stunned by the dangerousness of the French route, I went back over *Annapurna* with a fine-tooth comb. My memory of the text was pretty accurate. Yes, here and there Herzog emphasizes the hazards of the face, as, for instance, the climbers prepare to cross a snow chute above their Camp II: "Seracs crashed down with hideous din, and the rumbling of avalanches put us all on edge." But, time and again, the six lead climbers push blithely across unstable snow slopes, beneath teetering towers of ice, and they never seem to lose the giddy optimism that Lachenal demonstrated crowing out loud to his teammates at Camp I. To my mind, it's even more astonishing that the French were able to place four camps at various poorly protected sites in the middle of that face. They slept in those scary camps, and persuaded their gutsy Sherpa to haul loads up to them. Only on June 2 did Herzog and Lachenal find a route through the ice cliff the team had named the Sickle and establish a relatively safe Camp V above.

Throughout that blitzkrieg assault, Lachenal's spirits remained sky-high. In his diary on May 25 he wrote, "Victory now seems assured." And on May 31, in a telegram to be carried out by a porter and wired to Lucien Devies, the expedition's patron back in France, Herzog described the route, insisting, "OBJECTIVE DANGERS FROM AVALANCHES AND SERACS SLIGHT."

It was only in 2005, after I'd finally made it to the top of Annapurna by the French route, that I came across a passage in Lachenal's posthumous memoir, *Carnets du Vertige* (Vertigo notebooks), that flatly contradicted all the cocky bravado of Herzog's account of the climb. Looking back on the expedition a few years afterward, Lachenal made a shrewd reassessment:

> At the base of Annapurna . . . we had only a few days left before the arrival of the monsoon. . . . This led us right away to choose an extremely dangerous route. . . . Today I believe that we took unheard-of chances [there]. . . . For the second ascent . . . I expressly advise against the route that we followed.

That particular passage was not published until 1996, and since *Carnets* has never been translated into English, I was unaware of it until a friend pointed it out to me. In my view, however, Lachenal's retrospective judgment about the danger of the route remains the definitive last word.

When I first read *Annapurna,* what inspired me most was how, as they made their desperate push up the north face, the French climbers carried out the job with perfect teamwork and gallant self-sacrifice. No single deed during that assault was more heroic than the one performed on May 29 by Terray. "The strong sahib," as the Sherpa called him, had been so far the driving force, leading more and harder pitches than any of his teammates. By all rights he deserved a chance to be in the first pair to attempt the summit. Instead, he gave up that chance by choosing to make an exhausting solo gear haul, as he descended from Camp IV all the way to Camp II and back again, simply to supply the upper camp with the necessities for a summit bid. In *Conquistadors of the Useless,* Terray called that decision a "bitter paradox," but one that he felt morally duty bound to enact. In *Annapurna,* Herzog quotes Terray as saying, "If only one party gets [to the summit], it may be because of the load that I'm going to carry up." And Herzog adds, "Terray's unselfishness did not surprise me—I had appreciated it for years."

I also deeply admired Herzog's performance during these last days of May. Whether or not he was less experienced than the Chamonix guides, above 22,000 feet he performed every bit as well as they did, and sometimes even exceeded their efforts. He truly led from the front, not from the rear, as all the best expedition leaders do.

It was also inspiring to read about how Couzy and Schatz accepted from the start that they would be relegated to the supporting role, with no chance for the summit themselves. It could be argued that those two men did more sheer logistical grunt work than any of the other climbers. And in the end they would play a crucial role in their teammates' survival.

So it was that on the evening of June 2, Lachenal and Herzog spent a sleepless night at Camp V, ready to go for the top in the morning. On the third, Terray and Rébuffat would carry their own gear up to Camp V, pitch a tent, and if possible make their own summit bid on June 4.

So far the monsoon had held off, but it might arrive any day. There was not a moment to be wasted.

In 2000, my co-author, David Roberts, published a book called *True Summit: What Really Happened on the Legendary Ascent of Annapurna.* It amounted to a thorough debunking of Herzog's account of the 1950 expedition in *Annapurna.* David's book caused a minor sensation in France, where it made the bestseller list.

Curiously, just like me, David had read *Annapurna* as a teenager and been deeply inspired by the story. Just as it had for me, that book more than any other convinced him to become a serious climber. In a 1980 essay for the glossy annual Sierra Club journal *Ascent,* David even went so far as to declare *Annapurna* the best mountaineering expedition narrative ever written.

Then one day in 1996, in a small French ski town, David met Michel Guérin, who was about to publish a French translation of one of David's climbing books. Michel reminded him of his pronouncement about *Annapurna,* then proceeded to explain why he vehemently disagreed with David's encomium on Herzog's book. Michel was in the process of publishing the first unexpurgated edition of Lachenal's *Carnets du Vertige.* And the chapters in that book about Annapurna, many taken straight from Lachenal's 1950 diary, represented an altogether different version from Herzog's of what went on during the expedition.

Initially devastated, David went on to spend two years digging his teeth into this "cold case" in mountaineering history. Since he reads and speaks French, he was able to find all the surviving comments about the expedition (many of them unpublished) written by Herzog's teammates—particularly the reflections of Terray,

Rébuffat, and Lachenal. In France, he interviewed the closest living friends and relatives of the six great Annapurna climbers. He also interviewed Herzog, who by then was the only one of the six still alive. (Lachenal, Couzy, and Terray had been killed in climbing accidents between 1955 and 1965.)

The upshot of *True Summit* is the contention that far from a marvelously cooperative "band of brothers" collaborating on an extraordinary first ascent, the 1950 team was ridden with dissension, acrimony, and envy. In David's view, Herzog's *Annapurna* is little more than a gilded fairy tale. The expedition made Herzog famous, and he remains today one of France's most hallowed sport celebrities. By the late 1990s, however, Lachenal, Terray, and Rébuffat were virtually unknown to the French public. Yet it was those three men, David argues, who were the real heroes of the expedition.

As I set off for Annapurna in the spring of 2000, David sent me a bound galley of his book, which would be published a few months later. At base camp, all four of us read *True Summit*. To me, the book was deeply disturbing. But I also didn't really buy David's analysis. We've discussed the question several times since 2000, and by now we've agreed to disagree. For me, *Annapurna* is still an amazing book, essentially a true story, and all six of the leading climbers' ability to pull together to save one another's lives far outweighs the kinds of squabbles and disagreements David dug up. Within most expeditions, conflict erupts—it's inevitable among a group of strong-minded mountaineers struggling to complete a stressful and lengthy project. And I still believe that Herzog was an inspiring leader.

After hanging on to the tent poles through the night, while a fierce wind threatened to collapse their tent, Herzog and Lachenal started out from Camp V at 6:00 A.M. on June 3. A little less than 2,000 vertical feet stood between them and the summit. For hour after hour the two men trudged up a monotonous and unrelenting snow slope. The going was not technically difficult, but the snow's texture varied maddeningly between hard crust into which their crampons bit firmly and softer stuff through which their boots sank, forcing them to posthole laboriously upward.

As Veikka and I would discover in 2005, that last summit slope of Annapurna, which faces due north, is one of the coldest places in the Himalaya. On June 3, 1950, almost at once both men felt their toes go numb. "Whenever we halted," Herzog would later write, "we stamped our feet hard. Lachenal went as far as to take off one boot which was a bit tight; he was in terror of frostbite."

Frostbite was a real threat. The single leather boots that Lachenal and Herzog wore were so inferior to today's double boots—plastic outer shell over a foam insert—that the numbing of the men's toes was almost inevitable. Even in 2005, on the summit slopes of Annapurna, despite our state-of-the-art footgear, with each step I took I had to make a conscious effort to wiggle my toes to keep the circulation going. Not doing so would definitely have resulted in frostbite and the possible amputation of some toes. Our Italian friend Silvio Mondinelli turned back that same day because he had started to lose feeling in his toes.

On June 3, 1950, as the climbers plodded on, Herzog lapsed into a trancelike state. "Lachenal appeared to me as a sort of specter," he recalled; "he was alone in his world, I in mine." But Lachenal was far more conscious of the danger, stopping again to take off his boots and rub his toes, eventually pleading, "We're in danger of having frozen feet. Do you think it's worth it?" Herzog's answer was to keep moving. In the Alps he had often felt his toes go numb, and he believed that by constantly wriggling them inside his boots he could keep the vital circulation flowing.

Sometime in midmorning, Lachenal abruptly halted. "If I go back, what will you do?" he asked his partner.

As Herzog tells it in *Annapurna,* he answered, "I should go on by myself."

"Then I'll follow you," Lachenal pledged.

From the first time I read Herzog's book, I was transported not only by the leader's courage and drive in pushing on toward the summit, but also by his partner's willingness to stay with him. Had the two men failed to get to the top of Annapurna, there would have been no classic tale of adventure, only another expedition narrative of a noble failure. Yet in view of the terrible frostbite Lachenal and Herzog did suffer that day, and with the experience of my own thirty-one expeditions to 8,000ers under my belt, I have to reconsider my teenage enthusiasm. I've always said that no mountain is worth dying for, and no mountain is worth the price of a serious, permanent injury. In Lachenal's and Herzog's shoes (literally) that day, I would have turned around. In my opinion, Lachenal's instinct to give up the summit was wiser than Herzog's determination to forge on at all costs. On an 8,000er, I'm not willing to lose digits for the sake of success, but other climbers are. You have to make your own choice in terms of the price you're willing to pay for a summit.

Yet as Herzog tells it, his own passion for pushing on won over his partner. "We were braving an interdict," he wrote, "overstepping a boundary, and yet we had no fear as we continued upward."

Herzog does not state the time, but it must have been midafternoon or even later before the two men emerged from a final couloir splitting a rock band and trudged slowly toward the summit. The passage in *Annapurna* recording the triumph is justly famous:

> Yes!
>
> A fierce and savage wind tore at us.
>
> We were on top of Annapurna! 8,075 meters, 26,493 feet.
>
> Our hearts overflowed with unspeakable happiness.
>
> "If only the others could know . . ."
>
> If only everyone could know!

At this point, Herzog's trance took over. He lingered on and on, staring at the view, taking pictures, even changing film from black-and-white to color. In *Annapurna* he recaptures the transport that engulfed him on the summit: "How wonderful life would now become! What an inconceivable experience it is to attain one's ideal and, at the very same moment, to fulfill oneself. I was stirred to the depths of my being. Never had I felt happiness like this—so intense and yet so pure."

In a far more pragmatic state of mind, Lachenal urged his teammate to start the descent. But Herzog pleaded for a few more minutes on top. Eventually Lachenal lashed out: "Are you mad? We haven't a moment to lose; we must go down at once."

Once again, as much as I admire Herzog and empathize with his rapture, I have to concede that Lachenal was using better judgment. Staying too long on a summit, indulging in the kind of ecstasy that seized Herzog, has cost more than one good climber his life. In a similar incident in 1978 my friend Jim Wickwire decided to linger on the summit of K2, while his partner, Lou Reichardt, demanded an immediate descent. In his climbing memoir, *Addicted to Danger,* Wickwire writes, "Elated and clearheaded, I wanted to stay awhile to take more photographs. Starved for oxygen and terribly cold, Reichardt wanted to head down immediately. We parted with the understanding I would follow in a few minutes and join him at camp, twenty five hundred feet below." A "few minutes" became twenty, the sun set, and realizing that he couldn't descend to high camp without a headlamp, Wickwire decided to bivouac alone in the open at nearly 28,000 feet. He barely survived the night. Those extra minutes on the summit taking photos nearly cost him his life.

Lachenal could wait no longer. He took off downward on his own. At last Herzog followed, but even though he moved as fast as he could, the gap between him and his teammate grew, until he could no longer see Lachenal ahead of him.

Meanwhile, ensconced in a second tent at Camp V, Terray and Rébuffat grew more and more anxious. Dusk approached with no sign of the summit pair.

Somewhere during the descent, still in a fogged, befuddled state, Herzog took off his pack, put it down on the snow, and removed his gloves to open it. Later he could not recall what task he was trying to perform. Having thoughtlessly laid his gloves beside the pack, he watched in horror as they rolled away down the slope below. "My gloves!" he cried out loud. In *Annapurna,* he records his instantaneous awareness of the meaning of that loss: "The movement of those gloves was engraved in my sight as something irredeemable, against which I was powerless. The consequences might be most serious. What was I to do?"

By his own admission, Herzog forgot that he carried a spare pair of socks in his pack. They could easily have served as emergency gloves. There is no doubt that high altitude and fatigue played a role in his making this critical mistake.

It was almost dark by the time Herzog reached Camp V. Hearing his footsteps, Terray and Rébuffat opened the door of their tent and thrust their heads out. "We've made it. We're back from Annapurna!" Herzog declared.

> Terray, who was speechless with delight, wrung my hands. Then the smile vanished from his face: "Maurice—your hands!" There was an uneasy silence. I had forgotten that I had lost my gloves: my fingers were violet and white and hard as wood. The other two stared at them in dismay. . . .

And where was Lachenal? "He won't be long," Herzog vowed. "He was just in front of me!" Only moments later, the three men heard a faint cry for help. The voice came from *below* them. In his haste to regain camp, Lachenal had slipped and fallen a hundred yards past the tents. At once Terray performed a brilliant glissade (sliding like a skier on the edges of his boots), reached his best friend, and helped him scramble and crawl back up to camp.

For Terray and Rébuffat there would be no summit attempt on June 4. Instead, the two men stayed up all night brewing hot drinks for their teammates. They also used the ends of their climbing ropes to whip Herzog's fingers and toes and Lachenal's toes in the hope of restoring circulation. This was the wisdom of the day for treating frostbite, but we know now that because of the damage it causes to frozen tissue, such treatment actually does more harm than good.

During the night, a storm swept in, and by morning the worn-out men poked their heads out of the tents to see only a wind-lashed whiteout. Camp IVA, briefly occupied on the way to V, lay not far below and to the west. Confident of making their way to that refuge, the men carried only one of their four sleeping bags with them. But in the whiteout, they got completely lost. As dusk once more approached, they walked in circles looking for any kind of familiar landmark, but found none. It seemed inevitable that they would have to bivouac in the open at 24,000 feet, and in a storm of such violence it would be unlikely that any of them could survive.

Then, by accident, Lachenal broke through a snow bridge and fell into a hidden crevasse. In despair, Terray called out his friend's name, only to have Lachenal answer, "I'm here!" Then: "It'll do for the night! Come along." He had tumbled a mere thirty feet down what Herzog called "a regular toboggan-slide." One by one, the other three men followed.

This "heaven-sent" shelter, in Herzog's phrase, saved the men's lives by protecting them from the worst of the wind and pelting snow. Even so, the ordeal in the crevasse drove the men to the very edge of endurance. Terray, the only one who had brought his sleeping bag, crawled into it, only to be overcome by a sense of selfishness; so he shared the flimsy down cocoon first with Lachenal, then with Herzog. Both he and Rébuffat spent hour after hour rubbing the frozen toes and fingers of their teammates. Snow sifting through the hole at the top of the crevasse showered the men, then melted, soaking their clothes. The cold was relentless as the climbers huddled for warmth and shivered uncontrollably.

At dawn Rébuffat was the first to scramble up the "toboggan-slide" and stick his head out of the crevasse hole. "Can't see a thing," he reported. "It's blowing hard." The men's spirits plunged another notch. But when Lachenal reached the surface, he saw only clear blue sky. "It's fine, it's fine!" he screamed with joy. It turns out that the day before, Terray and Rébuffat had taken off their goggles as they searched for the route. Despite the storm, sunlight filtering through the clouds had rendered them snow-blind.

All four men now emerged from the crevasse. They had taken their boots off during the night, and now Herzog could not force his frozen feet into his pair. In the end, Terray cut the boots halfway open so that he could jam the leader's feet inside, with only about half the hooks laced.

Now the four men faced a cruel dilemma. The two healthier climbers, Terray and Rébuffat, could not lead because of their snow-blindness, and the other two were too weak and lame to be of much use in finding the way down. All four lurched pitifully downward, arguing among themselves about the correct line. Yet throughout, Lachenal kept yelling that he could see Camp II, far below. Suddenly he began shouting, "Help! Help!"

Wrote Herzog, "Obviously he didn't know what he was doing. . . . Or did he?" One by one the other climbers joined in the cry for help. Then, miraculously, they heard an answering cry. "Barely two hundred yards away Marcel Schatz, waist-deep in snow, was coming slowly toward us like a boat on the surface of the slope." The gap closed. Schatz took Herzog in his arms, murmuring, "It is wonderful—what you have done."

Couzy was not far behind. The two junior climbers led their teammates past Camp IVA and all the way down to Camp IV. By now Terray's and Rébuffat's feet had begun to freeze as well. But all six men now dared to believe they would get off Annapurna alive.

This is what has always seemed to me so perfect about the Annapurna story. Terray and Rébuffat gave up their hopes of the summit to save the lives of the crippled Lachenal and Herzog. Then, when it seemed that all four men might perish, Schatz and Couzy found them and saved their lives in turn. And in the next few days, the brave Sherpa Ang-Tharkey, Pansy, Sarki, and Aila performed heroic tasks of their own to get the "sahibs" down the mountain.

At Camp IV the team was far from out of the woods. In the warmth of early June the north face was collapsing with a vengeance. During the descent the closest call came when Herzog, Pansy, and Aila, roped together, set off an avalanche. They cascaded toward a 1,500-foot precipice, only to have the rope snag on a protruding crest of ice, leaving Herzog dangling on one side, the two Sherpa on the other.

Nor was the ordeal over by the time all the climbers got safely off the face. In fact it had only begun. In the first decade of the twenty-first century, in such a predicament, the team might have been able to use a sat phone to call in a helicopter to whisk the invalids off the mountain. Such an option was of course impossible in 1950. The team would have to hike and be carried along the treacherous gauntlet down the Miristi Khola and through the foothills to Tukucha.

At Camp II the expedition doctor, Jacques Oudot, decided to give Herzog and Lachenal injections of Novocain in the groin. Not only were these shots hideously painful, but the two frostbitten men had to undergo them daily through the next several weeks. Once again the wisdom of the day, distilled from battlefield treatments of frostbite during World War II, would later prove fallacious. The injections were worthless.

It took a full month for the wounded caravan to retreat through the lowlands. Herzog and Lachenal had to be carried every step of the way in rickety chairs made of canvas and webbing, on the backs of porters and Sherpa who weighed less than the Frenchmen did. For days at a time Rébuffat, too, had to be carried. Among the principal four, only Terray hobbled back to civilization under his own power.

Despite regular dosages of morphine, Herzog and Lachenal were in almost constant pain. Herzog contracted a fever, grew delirious, had wild hallucinations, and temporarily lost all will to survive.

In the lowland heat, the men's frozen digits grew septicemic with bacteria. On July 2, still short of the nearest village, Oudot performed the first of the amputations, cutting off four of Herzog's toes and one little finger and several of Lachenal's toes. A few days later, in a railway car speeding the men toward Delhi, in 113-degree heat, he completed the operations. In a macabre gesture, Oudot swept the bloody dressings and several amputated digits out the train door. In the end, Herzog lost all his fingers and toes, Lachenal all his toes.

Success on the first 8,000-meter peak ever climbed thus came at a terrible cost. One might well wonder why such a grim story should inspire not only youngsters like me to become climbers, but generation after generation of impressionable and adventurous youths of both genders and scores of nationalities.

The answer lies squarely in Herzog's book. Although it would take him months to recover from his injuries, Herzog began to dictate his account from a bed in the American Hospital at Neuilly, a suburb of Paris. To lose all one's fingers and toes to frostbite at the age of thirty-one, as Herzog well knew, was an almost intolerable blow. Not only would he never climb again, but for the rest of his long life the simplest of daily acts, such as tying his shoelaces or putting on a shirt or even writing with a pencil, would verge on the impossible. Could any mountain triumph be worth such a sacrifice?

Herzog had not the slightest doubt about the answer. Annapurna, he was sure from the first days in the hospital onward, had fulfilled him for the rest of his life. In his book, he proclaimed that affirmation in almost mystical terms. As he wrote in the foreword,

> In my worst moments of anguish, I seemed to discover the deep significance of which till then I had been unaware. I saw that it was better to be true than to be strong. The marks of my ordeal are apparent on my body. I was saved and I had won my freedom. This freedom, which I shall never lose, has given me the assurance and serenity of a man who has fulfilled himself. . . . A new and splendid life has opened out before me.

It was not only his own sense of fulfillment that transported Herzog: he believed that on Annapurna he and his teammates had forged an indelible brotherhood. As he wrote, "Together we knew toil, joy, and pain. My fervent wish is that the nine of us who were united in the face of death should remain fraternally united through life." This ideal, too, inspired me when I first read *Annapurna,* just as it would a few years later when I read Charlie Houston's celebration of "the brotherhood of the rope" in *K2: The Savage Mountain.*

Annapurna ends with the most famous closing line in mountaineering literature: "There are other Annapurnas in the lives of men." I wholeheartedly subscribe to Herzog's belief that lessons learned in the mountains can be translated into other realms of life. I often end my talks and slide shows with a paraphrase of that closing line—paraphrase to suit our politically correct era, although it would be too awkward to emend Herzog's formula to "other

Annapurnas in the lives of men and women." Instead, I usually close by saying, "Each of us has his or her own Annapurna."

The achievement of claiming the first 8,000er galvanized the pride of all of France. Upon their return the climbers were hailed as national heroes, almost as supernatural beings. The showing of the film Marcel Ichac made during the expedition packed 2,500 spectators into a Paris auditorium. Appearing from backstage, the climbers were greeted with wild cheers. During the following year, the film was shown thirty more times in Paris alone, and various members of the team delivered talks and showed slides in three hundred venues all over France.

This frenzy of celebration had everything to do with restoring a nation defeated and occupied during World War II to a state that seemed to recapture some of its former glory. It is safe to say that no other mountaineering accomplishment—not even the first ascent of Everest by the British in 1953, news of which reached England in the middle of the coronation of Queen Elizabeth II—has ever given its home country such a surge of joy and self-esteem.

Herzog would go on to build a distinguished career on his leadership of the Annapurna venture, as he became both mayor of Chamonix and minister of youth and sport under President Charles de Gaulle. Nor was the sense of fulfillment that he proclaimed in the pages of *Annapurna* a fleeting thing: over the years since, he has reaffirmed it again and again. If anything, Herzog's sense of having gained "a new and splendid life" has become even more mystical over the course of his long life. In 2007, at the age of eighty-eight, he published a memoir of his life after Annapurna, titling it *Renâitre*—literally, "Rebirth."

What is vexing, and puzzling, and ultimately very sad is that Annapurna gave Louis Lachenal no sense of fulfillment to match Herzog's. In fact, the loss of his toes plunged the man into anguish and despair. France gave the Legion of Honor to both Herzog and

Lachenal (though not to the other members of the team), but the highest accolade his country could grant a civilian seemed to mean nothing to Lachenal. All that mattered was that he could no longer climb with the grace and skill that had made him a legend in the Alps. As Terray movingly writes about his best friend in *Conquistadors of the Useless,* "Once he had seemed magically immune from the ordinary clumsiness and weight of humankind, and the contrast was like wearing a ball and chain."

In compensation, Lachenal became a wild and reckless automobile driver. It was as if speed on the roadway took the place of the speed on cliff and couloir for which he had become famous. He decided to try to break the unofficial record for the fastest trip from Chamonix to Paris, ultimately whittling his time down to six hours and forty minutes. (This in an era before any of the high-speed *autoroutes* had been constructed. On those superhighways, today's best times are still only in the vicinity of five and a half hours.) Lachenal's driving terrified his wife and friends, and he survived several spectacular one-car accidents.

By 1953 he had begun to climb again and, according to Terray, within a year had almost regained the level at which he performed before Annapurna. Climbing had always been Lachenal's obsession, but now he grew even more driven in the mountains than he had been in the prime of youth. On a cold day with high wind in November 1955, Lachenal prowled the streets of Chamonix to find a companion with whom to make a ski descent of the Vallée Blanche above his hometown, finally recruiting a friend. The two men rode the *téléphérique* up to the Aiguille du Midi, then set off unroped down the glacier. For a skier of Lachenal's ability, this was a trivial descent. But without warning, he broke through a snow bridge and fell 150 feet into an icy crevasse. As he fell, he hit the back of his head on a bulge in the uphill wall of the crevasse. The blow broke his neck and killed him instantly. He was only thirty-four.

Ironically, Lachenal's death came not as a result of a reckless act, but thanks to sheer bad luck. Now, as then, every week scores of skiers routinely run the Vallée Blanche unroped or solo, and very few of them suffer serious accidents.

If disappointment or emptiness is the opposite of fulfillment, one wonders why Herzog and Lachenal had such diametrically opposite reactions to their astounding and costly triumph on Annapurna. Was it simply a matter of the difference in their temperaments?

A few clues to the despair that Lachenal felt after Annapurna came home to me only in 2005, when David Roberts translated for me several key passages from Lachenal's memoir, *Carnets du Vertige*. "For me," Lachenal writes about Annapurna, in a passage not published in France until 1996, "this climb was only a climb like others, higher than in the Alps but no more important." Another passage casts a new light on his decision to go on to the summit with Herzog, even though he knew that his feet were freezing. Of that pivotal moment, Lachenal writes, "Thus I wanted to go down. I posed the question to Maurice to find out what he would do in that case. He told me he would keep going. . . . I guessed that if he continued alone, he would not return. It was for him and him alone that I did not turn around."

If this is true—and why would anyone doubt it?—Lachenal's loyalty to his driven teammate emerges from the Annapurna expedition as perhaps its single most heroic (and at the same time, most tragic) deed. As a Chamonix guide, for Lachenal the duty to take care of his partner, whether he was a mere client or an equal on the rope, came almost as a gut-level reflex.

In this respect, my own makeup is closer to Herzog's than to Lachenal's. Climbing has given me, along with marriage and family, the greatest sense of fulfillment I've attained in my life. For me the fulfillment has come not from any single mountain or expedition, but from completing the eighteen-year quest I called Endeavor 8000. It's just my nature: when I set myself a challenge, I'm bound and determined to complete it. This applies even to relatively simple projects. If I'm building a new deck for our house and I leave a single nail unpounded, it will drive me crazy until I pick up my hammer and slam that nail home.

Climbing has also brought me some of the closest friendships of my life. When you rope up with a partner, you're literally entrusting him with your life, as he is his with you. On 8,000-meter peaks, Veikka Gustafsson became the person I trusted most to make all the right joint decisions, and it's with partners such as him that I forged the deep brotherhood that I had read about in *Annapurna* and *K2: The Savage Mountain,* and that as an aspiring climber I so envied and longed to find in my own life. As a teenager, I actually put up posters on my bedroom walls of my climbing heroes, guys such as Tom Hornbein and Jim Wickwire and Jim Whittaker, whose deeds I had only read about. That those guys subsequently became my good friends and even teammates was deeply fulfilling for me.

I have to admit that when I came home from Annapurna in 2005, having finally climbed all fourteen 8,000ers, I suffered a few spells of . . . well, not exactly letdown or disappointment. It was more like, *So now what do I do?* It didn't help when friends and acquaintances started asking me if I had retired from mountaineering. I was dumbfounded, but at least I could see a certain humor in their concern. I even went along with the joke for *Outside* magazine, posing for a portrait in which I pretend to hawk all my climbing gear in a yard sale.

That vague sense of letdown quickly passed. I've found plenty of other adventures to fill my time since 2005, including a couple of grueling Arctic trips on Baffin Island, one by dogsled and one man-hauling our sledges. I've climbed Aconcagua again, and even Everest in 2009, reaching the summit for my seventh time. In January 2011, I made my first trip to Antarctica, where I climbed its highest peak, the Vinson Massif. Meanwhile, I've worked as hard as I can to be a good father and husband for a family that has allowed me to spend lots of time out of sight on the other side of the globe.

In this book, as I ponder the other outstanding exploits in Annapurna history, and relive my 2002 and 2005 expeditions, I intend to keep my eye on those fascinating and paradoxical tensions that mountaineering inevitably elicits: the tricky balance between risk and reward; fulfillment as an outcome versus its bleak opposite, whether it manifests itself as emptiness or disappointment; and the thin line we climbers inevitably tread between commitment and obsession.

THREE

SOUTH FACE

The first ascent of Annapurna in 1950 opened the floodgates on the 8,000-meter peaks. Within the next fourteen years, all thirteen of the remaining highest mountains in the world received their first ascents. In 1953 it was not only Everest that got climbed—that same spring, the great Austrian alpinist Hermann Buhl reached the summit of Nanga Parbat, in the only solo first ascent any of the 8,000ers would ever see. (Buhl was, of course, supported by team members at lower camps.) K2 was claimed by the Italians the following year, Makalu by the French and Kangchenjunga by the British in 1955, and Lhotse in 1956 by the Swiss. The last of the 8,000ers to succumb—not because of its difficulty so much as because of the politics of access—was Shishapangma in Tibet, first ascended by a Chinese team in 1964.

In what was originally called the Golden Age of Mountaineering, all the highest peaks in the Alps were first climbed by Europeans and Brits, most of them between 1855 and 1865. The age ended with the tragic first ascent of the Matterhorn, when four of the team of seven led by the Englishman Edward Whymper fell to their deaths.

Pessimists predicted that climbing would go out of fashion for good after the Matterhorn was tamed. They could not have been more wrong. Instead, the generation after Whymper's tackled the more difficult ridges and faces of the highest mountains, and set their sights on slightly lower but even more technical first ascents, such as those of the Petit Dru (1879), the Grépon (1881), and the Totenkirchl (1881). By the 1930s two fiendish north faces had each earned the ominous sobriquet of the Last Great Problem of the Alps. After repelling numerous aspirants, some of whom died in the attempt, both the Eiger Nordwand in Switzerland and the north face of the Grandes Jorasses in France were finally climbed in 1938.

A century after the Golden Age had run its course in the Alps, a closely parallel history unfolded among the world's highest mountains. The Golden Age of Himalayan Mountaineering has become the label for the years from 1950 to 1964, when nationalistic frenzy drove the countries that competed in the mountaineering race to snag the first ascents of the fourteen 8,000ers. Yet even during those years, a handful of bold first ascents of peaks lower than the magical 8,000 meters were pulled off. The two most shining achievements were probably the climb of Muztagh Tower (7,273 meters) in the Karakoram by a crack British team in 1956, only five days before an equally crack French team reached the summit by a different route; and the brilliant climb of Gasherbrum IV, also in the Karakoram, by the Italians Walter Bonatti and Carlo Mauri in 1958. At 7,925 meters, Gasherbrum IV fails by a piddling 247 feet to be the fifteenth 8,000er; yet it is a sterner challenge to climb than any of the fourteen highest peaks—even K2 and Annapurna.

One of the great ironies of mountaineering history is that after reaching the summit of Mount Everest on May 29, 1953, Sir Edmund Hillary firmly believed that the mountain would never again be climbed. Why would anyone bother, he thought, once it had been done? By now, of course, Everest is climbed by as many as five hundred men and women in a single spring season. Its second ascent came only three years after Hillary and Tenzing's triumph, when a Swiss team repeated the British route on Everest and also bagged the first ascent of neighboring Lhotse, the fourth highest mountain in the world.

During this so-called Golden Age, attempts on other routes on the 8,000ers were virtually nonexistent. The stellar exception was the gutsy and dangerous line forged up the west ridge of Everest by Americans Tom Hornbein and Willi Unsoeld in 1963. Nearing the summit, the two men recognized that they had passed a point of no return: judging that they probably could not down-climb their route, they made the bold decision to go up and over the top and try to descend by the South Col route the British had pioneered, over terrain they had never before seen. Along the way, Hornbein and Unsoeld survived a bivouac above 28,000 feet, the highest then endured anywhere on earth. The pair's stunning deed was thus also the first traverse of any 8,000er.

The second ascent of Everest may have taken place only three years after the first, but that sort of repeat rate was very much the exception on the 8,000ers. Annapurna waited for twenty years before receiving its second ascent. But the British assault on the south face of the mountain in 1970 remains today one of the landmarks of Himalayan achievement.

Part of the reason for the delay was that Nepal closed all its mountains to outsiders between 1966 and 1969. With the lifting of the ban, mountaineers turned their attention once again to Nepal's 8,000ers, and the most ambitious among them decided to try routes more difficult than any tackled on the first ascents.

Actually, there were two British Annapurna expeditions in the spring of 1970. One, organized by various branches of the army, was composed of relatively little-known climbers. The team attacked the French route, and after a logistical struggle stretching over a month and a half (compared with the scant ten days during which the French stormed up the face in 1950), two men, Henry Day and Gerry Owens, reached the summit on May 20. It was they who made the second ascent of Annapurna.

The other British expedition was led by Chris Bonington. Thirty-five years old in 1970, he had forged a record as one of the finest British climbers in the Alps. Two of his greatest accomplishments were the first British ascent of the Eiger Nordwand in 1962 and the first ascent of the Central Pillar of Freney on the south face of Mont Blanc the year before—a long, exposed route that had become notorious because so many good climbers had failed on it, including Walter Bonatti, who retreated in a storm that took the lives of four of the seven members of a mixed French-Italian team. Bonington also had two Himalayan expeditions under his belt, one of which had succeeded on a difficult new line on the south face of Nuptse, the satellite peak to Lhotse and Everest that looms over the Khumbu Glacier.

Bonington's background was military: he had graduated from the Royal Military Academy at Sandhurst and served in the British Army in various capacities for six years, before resigning in 1961. In this respect, he was atypical of the gang of the top British climbers of the day, who tended to be anarchistic rebels or apolitical blue-collar blokes. (A disproportionate number of them made their living as plumbers.) But the military training had turned Bonington into a man with the perfect temperament to lead expeditions. The 1970 Annapurna assault would be the first occasion on which he served as a true "official" leader, but after that, he would organize and head many expeditions to the great ranges. He remains today the most successful leader of far-flung mountaineering ventures ever to take the field. Thanks not only to that leadership but also to his prolific writing, filmmaking, and lecturing, he is far and away Britain's most famous climber today.

Bonington chose the south face of Annapurna on the basis of a single photograph lent him by Lieutenant-Colonel Jimmy Roberts, also a military officer, but one of his country's foremost explorers of the Asian ranges. Planning at first a lightweight four-man expedition, Bonington was nudged to expand the team because of the self-evident hugeness and difficulty of the south face. In the end the team set out for Nepal with eight principal climbers and three other men serving in various supporting roles. Bonington chose his teammates mainly from cronies he had climbed with before, but they also happened to comprise a good portion of the best British alpinists and rock climbers of the 1960s. In his expedition account, *Annapurna South Face,* Bonington justifiably boasted, "The party . . . was certainly the strongest that had ever been assembled in Britain to tackle a Himalayan peak."

Unlike the north face by which the French had attacked Annapurna, the south face rises in one unbroken, gargantuan sweep more than 10,000 feet from the glacier at its base to the summit. Studying the Jimmy Roberts photo, Bonington and his teammates picked out at once what looked like the only conceivable route. Bonington had been warned about the dangers of the face by some of his few compatriots who had actually seen it. David Cox told him, "South face? I don't remember much about it; looked huge; yes, there were a lot of avalanches coming down it, but I think they were going down the runnels."

To avoid the "runnels," or chutes that gather falling ice and snow, the team plotted a line toward the western or left-hand side of the face, where a slightly protruding buttress rose steadily toward a 2,000-foot-high rock cliff. The Rock Band, as the team named this obstacle, commenced at the ungodly altitude of 22,750 feet. It would clearly form the "crux" of the route. But the whole face was unmistakably steep. One of the members later calculated that the average angle through the 5,000-foot rise from the beginning of the buttress to the top of the Rock Band was 55 degrees. This was actually steeper than the south face of Mont Blanc, where Bonington had made his breakthrough climb on the Central Pillar of Freney, and almost as steep as the legendary Walker Spur on the Grandes Jorasses.

The combination of sheer size, self-evident technical difficulty, and absolute altitude above sea level made it clear that nothing on this order had yet been attempted anywhere in the Himalaya or the Karakoram. Staring at the image in a color slide sent to him by David Cox, which he had projected onto his living room wall, Bonington thought, "It was like four different alpine faces piled one on top of the other—but what a line! Hard, uncompromising, positive all the way up."

Six of the seven teammates Bonington chose for the expedition were friends he had climbed with and learned to trust on the small crags of Britain or on big routes in the Alps. In terms of how the assault unfolded through April and May 1970, the team can be loosely characterized as falling into three groups. Five of the men might be called the "good soldiers," willing to put in day after day of fixing ropes and hauling loads to support whichever team happened to be in the lead during any given period. Then there was Bonington himself, who led not with a dictatorial iron hand, but by thoughtfully consulting the judgment of his peers before deciding who should do what. He also contributed his own share of load-hauling, and led some of the crucial pitches on the route. Rounding out the team were two brilliant climbers with huge egos, blazing ambition, and sharp tempers.

The four British "good soldiers" were Nick Estcourt, Martin Boysen, Mick Burke, and Ian Clough. The fifth was an American, Tom Frost, who had never before climbed with any of the Brits. The Cambridge-educated Estcourt was a civil engineer; Boysen, a teacher in a secondary school; Burke, a working-class lad who had dropped out of school at fifteen and made do with odd jobs between climbing trips; and Clough, with whom Bonington had solved both the Eiger and the Freney Pillar, who made a living running a small climbing school in the Lake District. Clough was, in Bonington's words, "the kindest and least selfish person I had ever climbed with." These four Brits ranged in age from twenty-six to thirty. The fifth "good soldier," Tom Frost, had been added to the team relatively late, after a publicity agent Bonington had hired asked him, "Couldn't you get in an American? It would make my job a lot easier in the States."

Thirty-three years old, Frost made a living by manufacturing climbing gear with the soon-to-be legendary Yvon Chouinard out of a makeshift garage turned smithy in Southern California. Although the Great Pacific Iron Works, as the two friends called their firm, would revolutionize climbing by crafting pitons and ice axes and other gear that was better than anything else available, their business in the 1960s was a shoestring operation. (Chouinard would go on to become a millionaire after he founded the outdoor clothing line Patagonia.) Although Frost was known to the Brits only by his climbing résumé, it was a sterling one, filled with first ascents of big walls in Yosemite and expeditions to Alaska, the Andes, and the Himalaya. Bonington sent a letter of invitation to California, and Frost accepted on the spot.

No American climber, however, could have been temperamentally more at odds with the British crew. Bonington and company tended to be hard-living iconoclasts: profanities regularly enlivened their speech, several were champion drinkers, and most of them smoked. Frost, on the other hand, was a Mormon who eschewed not only obscenities but smoking and all kinds of drink, ranging from alcohol to coffee and tea. As luck would have it, on Annapurna he would share a tent most often with Mick Burke, an inveterate chain-smoker (according to Bonington, Burke brought seven thousand cigarettes on the expedition, most of which he smoked himself). Although Frost (as nice a guy as Ian Clough, and equally unselfish) bit his tongue throughout the expedition, the difference in lifestyles would cause considerable friction.

The two superstars on the Annapurna team were Dougal Haston and Don Whillans. Bonington had met Haston, a Scot, on the ill-starred Eiger Direct expedition in the winter of 1966, during which the team leader, the charismatic American John Harlin, was killed when a fixed rope he was ascending broke and he fell 4,000 feet to his death. The tragedy caused the rest of the British-American party to lose all heart for the project—except for Haston, who teamed up with a competing German team to complete the hardest route done to that date in the Alps.

Twenty-seven years old in 1970, Haston was a hard person to get to know. As Bonington would characterize him in *Annapurna South Face,* Haston "has a reserve that is difficult to break through and yet at the same time is a very easy companion, whether drinking at the foot of the mountain or sitting out a storm half-way up." Other climbing companions of the Scot took a darker view of the man, who had gained considerable celebrity in Britain after the Eiger Direct. In *The Boys of Everest,* a group portrait of Bonington and his many stellar protégés, Clint Willis sums up that view:

> Dougal at moments tried to convince himself that he was indeed a kind of hero. His journals were laced with cutting and sometimes callow remarks about climbers who struck him as over-the-hill or unserious. He still sometimes cultivated the notion of himself as superman or artist—someone who lived with a purpose and vitality that set him apart.

Bonington himself was fairly blunt about the man's short fuse. Of Haston's apprenticeship as an alpinist, he wrote, "The group of Edinburgh climbers he went around with were a hard-drinking, antisocial lot who specialized in punch-ups and breaking up huts."

By 1970, Haston had taken over the directorship of the American School in Leysin, Switzerland, from his mentor, John Harlin, after Harlin's death on the Eiger. The school was a bohemian enclave for young Brits and Americans, with a strong emphasis on outdoor sports and counterculture studies. Ironically, Haston would meet his own untimely end in 1977, not on any of his daring ascents, but on a casual ski run behind the Leysin School, when he was caught in an avalanche.

The other superstar on Annapurna was Whillans, thirty-seven years old in 1970 (thus the oldest member of the team) and a plumber by trade. By 1970, Whillans was already a legend in British climbing circles, chiefly as a result of a string of unprotectable and gutsy climbs on cliffs and towers in Scotland and northern England, many of them unrepeated for more than a decade after his first ascents. Whillans had also been Bonington's steadfast partner on the Freney Pillar, and on two attempts on the Eiger Nordwand before Bonington succeeded with Ian Clough.

Yet Bonington hesitated long and hard before inviting Whillans to Annapurna, calling his selection "in some ways the most obvious choice of all and yet the one I had the most doubts about." Mixing bluntness with ambivalence, Bonington wrote in *Annapurna South Face*,

> He is undoubtedly the finest all-around mountaineer that Britain has produced since the war, but in the last few years he had let himself slip into poor physical condition, developing a huge beer-drinker's pot belly through lack of exercise and a steady intake of beer. He had lost interest in British rock climbing, and even in the Alps, preferring to go on expeditions to the farther ranges of the world. On top of this our relationship had always been strained. But I had done some of my best climbing with Don, and he was certainly the best climbing partner I have ever had.

Whillans's slide into fatness between expeditions would grow to become an integral part of his legend. Somehow he would always round into shape on the hike in to some Himalayan challenge and end up performing as well as or better than all his teammates. He was like the Keith Richards of climbing, smoking, drinking—

his body was definitely not his temple, but he could perform. Yet Whillans would die of a heart attack in 1985 at the age of only fifty-two, and more than one friend would believe that his dissolute ways contributed to his early demise.

In 2005, British climbing historian Jim Perrin wrote the definitive biography of Whillans, titled *The Villain: The Life of Don Whillans* ("the Villain" being one of the man's nicknames, which he himself fancied). Perrin's is one of the darkest accounts of the life of a mountaineer ever written, full of ruined friendships, deep funks and depressions, and drinking binges that border on the unimaginable. Yet through it all shines Whillans's genius as a climber, both on the crags of the Scottish Highlands and on the tallest and most difficult mountains on earth.

I was twelve years old when *Annapurna South Face* was published in 1971. Maybe five or six years later, shortly after I devoured Herzog's *Annapurna,* I read Bonington's book. It, too, gave a powerful boost to my ambition to become a climber. The glossy photos of difficult leads were breathtaking, and even with my limited mountaineering experience, I could see at once that nothing like this had been done in the Himalaya before 1970.

Rereading the book years later, I realized how it had Bonington's stamp all over it. With his military background and his passion for the tiniest logistical detail, *Annapurna South Face* is not only a great adventure tale, but also an almost obsessive testament to meticulous organization. The book ends with eighty-seven pages of appendices covering everything from medical supplies and preparations to a precise itemization of every bit of food the climbers ate to an anthropological treatise titled "The People of Nepal." In the medical section, under the subhead "Recommended Drugs," no fewer than ninety-four different medicines are listed, each with the exact quantity brought along specified. Thus: "Merocets" [a kind of cough drop]—1,000 lozenges"; "Tetralysal [an antibiotic]—1,000 tablets"; "Valium—100 tablets"; and "Novocain eyedrops—10 vials."

Other readers might have been put off by such fussy detail, but this was the kind of stuff I just ate up. I've always loved Bonington's books, and I read those appendices with as rapt a focus as I did the narrative of the expedition itself. I admit to having been something of a "gear freak" myself—back in college I had the original Chouinard catalog, REI catalogs, and many issues of *Mountain* magazine, and I'd spend hours poring through them. I couldn't afford any of that fancy equipment, but I could look at it. So when I read Bonington, I wanted to know exactly what those guys ate, what kind of boots they wore. Tables, lists, flowcharts—on such-and-such day, these two guys carried that much stuff up to Camp II, where they stayed two days. You didn't get this from Herzog, with his mystical, romantic bent. With Bonington, it was as if you were living the expedition day by day.

Bonington has a reputation for being equally fussy and obsessive when he gives a talk or a slide show. Other climbers have groaned while telling me about sneaking out of some auditorium to grab a beer as Bonington went on for twice his allotted time. But in the early 1980s, when I was a student at the University of Washington and saw him speak at Kane Hall on campus, I loved every minute of it. The talk lasted a full three hours, with an intermission. The place was packed, with people jammed in the aisles. Sitting casually at the edge of the stage, Bonington covered his whole career. He not only showed slides, but he also played tapes of inter-camp radio dialogue. It was like going to a great movie.

In another important respect, however, Bonington's book was the opposite of Herzog's. In the 1960s, along with opposing the Vietnam War and dabbling in sex, drugs, and rock and roll, a generation of younger adventure writers insisted on adopting a tell-it-like-it-was approach to expedition literature. In Herzog's *Annapurna* there's plenty of dialogue, and even arguments and criticisms among the climbers, but it's all in the service of a united team effort. The same is true in spades of Sir John Hunt's *The Ascent of Everest*—reading that book, you'd never suspect the slightest antagonism marred the teamwork of the British climbers who made the mountain's first ascent in 1953.

But in *Annapurna South Face,* Bonington hangs out all the laundry—clean as well as dirty—to dry. Often he quotes dialogue from memory, as Herzog does, but he also transcribes whole pages of radio discussion from one camp to another, which he tape-recorded for posterity. And plenty of that talk is acrimonious. It's clear from the book that while the Brits supported each other superbly on the south face, at the same time there was intense competition and rivalry among the team's members. In a way, it's amazing that Bonington was able to keep the expedition focused on a common goal, and it is a testament to the men's loyalty to their leader that some of them lent him their private diaries and letters, apparently giving him carte blanche to quote from them in the book.

Tom Frost recalls the process by which Bonington put together his book: "I was keeping a journal throughout the expedition. Afterward, Chris asked me if he could copy it. I said yes. I never had any say about what passages he used."

Remarkably enough, Frost believes today that he has never read *Annapurna South Face* in its entirety, but has only skimmed it. "A book like that's not my style," he amplifies. "I'm interested in the mechanics of an expedition, how the teamwork comes together. I'm not interested in the bickering among the climbers. That doesn't appeal to me at all."

Of course I would have given anything to be part of a team like the one Bonington assembled for Annapurna. But I would have cringed to find my sharpest criticisms of teammates quoted verbatim in the pages of the official expedition account. Yet even as a teenager, I knew that disagreements and tensions such as the ones Bonington aired in *Annapurna South Face* were the norm on serious adventure trips, and I confess to a kind of guilty pleasure when I first read the book, which was like eavesdropping on the nastiest exchanges between those teammates in the heat of battle. For me, the day-to-day details, disputes and all, painted a complete and accurate picture of expedition life.

As the size of the team expanded, what Bonington had initially conceived of as a lightweight expedition among friends grew to become a major undertaking. And it was here that Bonington the leader came into his element: he calculated all the logistics, did all the fund-raising, and became a tireless publicist for the project. In subsequent decades, he would perfect his skills as an organizer. No team leader in mountaineering history has ever gathered to his side such an all-star roster of colleagues—not only the guys on Annapurna, but such now-legendary climbers as Doug Scott, Joe Tasker, Peter Boardman, Dick Renshaw, Mo Anthoine, and Al Rouse. Clint Willis's group biography, *The Boys of Everest,* was originally going to be titled *Bonington's Boys.* All those years, it was as if Bonington chose an objective, then told his "boys," *Okay, I'll organize the expedition, I'll raise the money, why don't you guys come along?* Who wouldn't want to go on an expedition like that?

On the mountain, too, Bonington was an ideal leader. He never directed operations through binoculars from base camp, like such martinets as Ardito Desio on K2 or Karl Herrligkoffer on numerous expeditions. But he also never thrust himself into the front so that he could grab the summit. He always did his share of the hard work: carrying loads, fixing ropes, even leading tough pitches. But his attitude about bagging the summit was admirably restrained: *If it works out, I'll go to the top. If not, somebody else will.*

The 1970 Annapurna expedition grew to such mammoth proportions that the personnel eventually included not only the eight principal climbers and three supporting Brits, but also six high-altitude Sherpa, a television team, and a "kitchen staff" of four. On top of this, back in England, were three high-profile "patrons" (one of them Sir John Hunt), a four-person "committee of management," the publicity agent, and two secretaries. The list of companies that contributed gear and food—all these details are spelled out in Bonington's appendices—swelled to eighty-five firms. These donors of essential supplies included "Stewart & Son of Dundee Ltd.—Whisky," "Gauloises—Cigarettes," "Crosse & Blackwell Ltd.—Tinned fish," and "Ever Ready (G.B.) Ltd.—Batteries."

The great advantage the 1970 British team had over the French in 1950 was the approach march. Only a few routes to the bases of other 8,000ers are as straightforward as the trek to the south-facing Sanctuary, the interlinked glaciers that flow from the high ridgeline of the Annapurna massif.

In late March the team flew from Kathmandu to the hill town of Pokhara, where they hired 140 Gurkha porters. The hike in took only eight days of relatively gentle walking, most of it along the banks of the Modi Khola. By March 28 the men had set up a base camp beside the glacier just three miles south of the daunting line they hoped to climb on the huge face.

Despite the intense scrutiny Bonington and his teammates had devoted to the few photographs they had of the south face, all the men were worried about the safety of the route they had picked out. In a pub in north Wales during the months before the expedition, Bonington showed one of the photos to Joe Brown. A plumber like Whillans, and Whillans's steady partner when he was in his twenties, when the two men put up the hardest routes yet climbed in the British Isles, Brown was also one of the two men who reached the summit on the first ascent of Kangchenjunga, the world's third highest mountain, in 1955. (Brown famously dismissed the effort as "a long slog.") Now, in the pub, the congenitally laconic hard man studied Bonington's photo, then uttered a one-line judgment: "You'll be swept away by powder snow avalanches in the middle section."

So, at base camp, Bonington anxiously awaited the verdict of Whillans, who had gone up beneath the face and spent a long time studying the line. In *Annapurna South Face*, Bonington re-creates the exchange upon Whillans's return:

> "Did you see the Face?"
> "Aye."
> "What does it look like?"
> "Steep. But after I had looked at it for a few hours it seemed to lie back a bit. It's going to be difficult but I think it will go all right."

As he watched, Whillans had seen a huge avalanche come down just left of the men's proposed route. But he was convinced the line itself was relatively secure.

Still anxious, Bonington asked about the 2,000-foot cliff high on the route to which the team had already given a name:

> "What about the Rock Band?"
> "Steep, but a lot more broken than I thought it would be. I'm pretty sure the big groove up the front of it will be too hard for us, but there seems to be a line up to the left."

The challenge of the south face was so enormous that it dictated to the 1970 team two decisions that were, in a sense, conservative ones. By that year, the best climbers in Alaska and the Andes had begun to abandon the old-fashioned "expedition-style" tactics in favor of an "alpine-style" approach that was first developed in the European Alps. On an expedition-style ascent, the team builds a series of solid, well-stocked tent camps up the mountain, covering the same terrain many times in order to supply those camps with ample gear and food. Hundreds or even thousands of feet of thin nylon ropes are fixed over the pitches, to make load-carrying easier and safer than leading the pitches was initially. From the highest camp, near the apex of this logistical pyramid, at least two climbers go for the summit. If there's time and the weather holds, second and third and even fourth pairs also go for the top. An expedition-style assault on a major peak usually lasts from one to three months.

Using alpine-style tactics, the climbers place few or no fixed ropes, and their camps are supplied only with the lightest of tents or with bivouac sacks. Instead of a buildup of supplies in preplaced camps, the team makes a probe or two lower on the mountain. Then, carrying all the gear and food they might need, they go all-out in a single push for the summit. It's usually a one-shot deal: if the climbers can't get to the top on their main thrust, they typically use up all their hardware setting up rappel anchors to get down the route. A second attempt is usually out of the question.

Alpine style is cleaner and more elegant, and involves much less drudgery than expedition style. But it puts the climbers in far more vulnerable positions. In well-stocked tent camps linked by fixed ropes, climbers can wait out four- or five-day storms; with only bivouac gear and a few days' worth of food, the same storms force a retreat-or-die ultimatum upon climbers pushing alpine style. On the other hand, a lightweight, single-thrust ascent takes only a fraction of the time expended on the old-fashioned ascent by logistical pyramid. In Alaska, for instance, new routes of the sort that had taken teams more than a month to complete in the early to mid-1960s were being knocked off by 1970 in as few as three to six days.

But the true adaptation of alpine style to the high Himalaya would not arrive until almost a decade after 1970. There was a single shining exception: the first ascent of Broad Peak in 1957 by four Austrians, including Hermann Buhl, who had made the solo first ascent of Nanga Parbat four years before. On Broad Peak—

the only 8,000er first climbed alpine-style—the four men had no Sherpa support, used no bottled oxygen, placed no fixed ropes, and made their push from Camp III to the summit in only thirteen hours.

Still, Broad Peak was technically trivial compared to the south face of Annapurna. Bonington and company never even considered trying the great wall alpine style. From the start the plan was to rotate pairs of climbers in the lead, fix every difficult pitch with ropes, and put the rest of the team (including the Sherpa) to work hauling gear and food to solid tent camps at various perches on the route. Eventually this chain stretched through six camps between 16,000 feet on the glacier just before the start of the route to Camp VI at 24,000 feet halfway up the Rock Band.

Bonington also made the decision to use bottled oxygen on the mountain, even though the French had done without it in 1950. The leader's feeling was that hard technical climbing on the upper reaches of the wall would simply be too taxing for men gasping their lungs out in the thin air as they tried to acclimatize.

I've been asked many times if I thought the use of bottled oxygen on 8,000ers was unsporting, or even in a sense cheating, making the peak easier. Because I climbed all my 8,000ers without supplemental oxygen, I think I've been misunderstood as criticizing others who chose not to climb in the same style. For me it was always simply a matter of a personal choice. I've never had any quarrel with those who've used bottled Os to get up a peak, even when some of them were my teammates. And I certainly see nothing wrong with Bonington's decision to have his lead climbers strap on masks and regulators and suck in the helpful gas when they were struggling with tough rock and ice pitches above 24,000 feet. In my eyes, that in no way diminishes the achievement of their ascent.

One of the first tasks Bonington faced was to find the right pairings among his eight climbers. The first matchup he concocted would turn out to be the most critical of all. He decided early on that he wanted Whillans to start out in the lead, because he had more big-mountain experience (and, Bonington thought, a better "feel" for mountains in general) than any of the other members. But who would make the best partner for this often irascible and headstrong climber? As Bonington would later write,

> I was still not entirely certain how well Don would go; he was obviously not yet a hundred per cent fit, and his pot belly, though on the wane, was still there. It was seven years since we had climbed together . . . and I did not know whether he still had that tremendous fire that I had once known.
>
> I therefore selected Dougal [Haston] as Don's partner, for of all the team he seemed to have the greatest drive. On the approach march he was like a compressed spring, held under tension, just waiting to get at the mountain.

It would turn out to be an inspired pairing, not only on Annapurna, but also a year later, on the southwest face of Everest. A close friend of Haston's at the Leysin School later summed up to Haston's biographer, Jeff Connor, Dougal's view of the relationship between himself at age twenty-seven and his thirty-seven-year-old partner:

> Dougal said to me, "Whillans is the man." . . . There was this compassion about Don, which a lot of the people don't often attribute to him. On Annapurna, and on Everest later, when they ran out of food, it was Don who would open up the last can or tin of pâté and say: "Here you go, Jimmy, you eat this." Don survived on tea and cigarettes, and as far as Dougal is concerned, he told me later that Don saved his skin. He looked after Dougal, [who] called him "Dad."

By April 7, only a week after starting the climb, Whillans and Haston had pushed the route to the future site of Camp III, at 20,100 feet, more than 4,000 feet above base camp. That camp, pitched on a small snow saddle, was the launching pad for the assault on the true south face, rising another 6,000 feet above. All the real technical difficulties lay ahead. Yet the fast progress lulled the team into overoptimism. "[D]own at base camp that night," wrote Bonington, "we happily swilled Scotch and talked of knocking off the Face in the next fortnight."

The second pairing joined Nick Estcourt and Martin Boysen, who were already good friends. They would preserve their twosome throughout the expedition, and perform backbreaking work, mainly in the service of others in the lead.

During the first week of April, Ian Clough was having trouble with the altitude, and Mick Burke suffered from a bad case of hemorrhoids, so both men were hors de combat at base camp. Bonington made a third pairing of himself with Tom Frost. On April 14 those two men began the "real" climbing, on a fiendishly sharp and corniced ice ridge that rose abruptly out of Camp III.

One reason for the team's early optimism was the superb performance of the six Sherpa, who carried many a vital load up to Camp III and even beyond. And since the 1950s a minor revolution in the way Europeans (and Americans) interacted with the native peoples who aided their efforts had taken place. No longer were the porters called "coolies," or screamed and lectured at when they staged sit-down strikes on the hike in. Neither they nor the Sherpa were expected to serve the "sahibs" morning tea, or pitch their tents for them. In his book, Bonington captures the spirit of this enlightened new partnership:

> We certainly always treated them as fellow climbers and never allowed a Sherpa-Sahib relationship to creep in. They were undoubtedly fitter than we were, and on the

> carries were nearly always out in front. We openly respected them for this; they, on the other hand, respected our greater climbing experience on difficult ground.

In the end, the Sherpa would haul gear and food as high as Camp IV, at 21,300 feet, across some highly technical ground secured by fixed ropes. But above that camp, Bonington was unwilling to push the men from Nepal.

One night in Camp III, Bonington and Frost crawled into their sleeping bags, "me to read *Decline of the West,* a novel of sex, lust, and violence," the leader wryly observed, "he to read his Mormon testament, the only reading matter I saw him look at during the entire trip." There ensued a philosophical discussion about religion. It is evident that Frost hoped to convert the agnostic Bonington to his faith. Indeed, in a passage from Frost's diary that Bonington reproduces, the Californian revealed that in a discussion with his LDS ward president back in his hometown of Ventura, the man told Frost that "the entire expense and effort of building up the Church was worthwhile if only one individual was converted. . . . I may have the opportunity to explain this [to my Annapurna teammates] and be a proper example of the word of wisdom."

There is no faith on earth more diligent at seeking converts than the Church of Jesus Christ of Latter-day Saints. But Frost would make no inroads among the hard-living bohemians of the British team. Instead, as Bonington observed, "I couldn't help respecting Tom for his religious faith and the way he refrained from ramming it down any of our throats."

From the start, Frost sensed a gulf between himself and his teammates. "We definitely had an all-star team," he recalls. "The Brits were good, they knew their stuff. But they were all professional climbers. They wanted to look good on television, to advance their careers. Bonington cared only about success. He wasn't on Annapurna to have fun. But I was on holiday. I was there just to enjoy the climb, and for weeks I really enjoyed it." Among the Brits, Frost remembers, it was Martin Boysen with whom he got along best.

The ice ridge above Camp III dealt the team its first major setback. Frost insisted on attacking the ridge directly on its crest, while Bonington had a hunch about a better route skirting the crest. Deferring to Frost's experience on hard ice and snow in the Andes, he gave in and followed the American's lead. But Frost climbed so slowly that Bonington was soon, in his own words, "seething with impatience." Yet "once I had swum up the soft snow to him and then ventured onto the slope beyond I saw why he had gone so slowly: I had never been on such appalling snow. . . . I had the feeling that the entire ridge was honeycombed and could come tumbling down about me."

As it would turn out, the whole Bonington-Frost effort on the ice ridge would prove to be a mistake. Bonington calls the chapter devoted to it "Blind Alley." Days of perfect weather were wasted climbing the terrifying crest, and there was no way to place anchors in the soft snow and hollow ice firm enough to entrust fixed ropes to them. Eventually it was Whillans and Haston, coming up in support, who found the "bypass" route left of the ridge that got the team back on track.

As always in Bonington's book, the interpersonal is right on the surface. Realizing their error, Bonington admits that "I couldn't resist hitting out at Tom, saying, 'I wish I hadn't listened to you about the ridge.' " At once, however, he recognized the injustice of his complaint. The choice of the crest had ultimately been a mutual one.

During the following weeks, the expedition slowly crawled its way up difficult and scary terrain. At last the rotation system started to work its benefits. On April 23, more than three weeks after starting on the route, Nick Estcourt and Martin Boysen established Camp IV at 21,300 feet, at the top of the ice ridge. It would take another sixteen days before Camp V could be pitched, a mere 1,450 feet higher. In the meantime, Mick Burke had recovered from his hemorrhoid attack. Bonington paired him with Frost, and that duo established Camp V on May 9.

Above Camp V, however, the huge Rock Band soared. By now the optimism of early April lay in tatters. The climb had turned into an all-out struggle. Burke led many of the hardest pitches on mixed terrain on the left side of the Rock Band. Boysen, Estcourt, and Bonington were tireless in support, as they hauled loads up the ropes fixed by the lead climbers. Only Ian Clough, who still was suffering from the altitude, lagged behind. But rather than sit out the expedition at base camp, Clough made two gutsy efforts to overcome his nausea and weakness, as he carried loads first to Camp V and then, in a whole separate effort, all the way up to Camp VI at 24,000 feet.

Bonington is unsparing in his account of just how "knackered" these pushes left his teammate. Reconstructing dialogue as he paired with Clough on a grueling load carry, he writes:

> He succeeded in getting across the Terrible Traverse, but on the vertical ropes leading up to the crest of the ridge he just hung there like a lifeless sack.
>
> "It's no good, Chris, I'm pilloxed. I'll have to go down," he shouted.
>
> "You've only got another hundred feet to climb and you'll be at our high point," I shouted back. "All you'll have to do then is hold the rope, so that I can at least get another pitch done."
>
> "I don't think I could even do that."

At this point Bonington declared that he would climb on solo. The selfless Clough responded, "I can't let you do that, I'll get up somehow."

There were terrifying moments in the Rock Band as the climber leading a new pitch came close to the limits of his skill and endurance. Once, with Frost belaying him, Burke front-pointed fifty feet above on extremely steep, brittle ice without placing a single piece of protection. Then he stopped, exhausted, hanging on to the pick of his ice hammer, with just the front points of his crampons sunk into the ice, as he fought a rising panic.

> "Watch the rope, Tom," he called. "I could come off here."
>
> "How about putting in an ice-peg?" came the cool reply.
>
> "Christ, I'd forgotten about them!"

Grasping his ice hammer with a single hand. Burke fumbled for an ice screw, then barely managed to stab and twist it home.

Throughout the Rock Band, falling stones threatened the climbers on every pitch. In his diary, Frost wrote, "The high whistlers were coming down, occasionally landing close by . . . and I gave thanks many times for the protection I am being given. Sooner or later someone will probably be hit by this falling rock or ice."

By the beginning of May, morale had reached its nadir. Clough said to Bonington, "At this rate I don't think we've got much hope of success; at least we've put up a good show." Without answering, Bonington privately agreed with his partner's bleak assessment.

As frightening and dangerous as leading on new ground was, that was the job all eight climbers preferred to the debilitating work of fixing pitches, carrying loads, and establishing camps. Jumaring up a fixed rope, as one slides mechanical ascenders attached to one's waist and foot loops, can be a routine business. But if one carries a fifty-pound pack on a vertical or overhanging pitch, the strain is enormous and fear can easily overcome even an experienced climber. Fixed ropes are not fail-safe—they sway in the wind, scraping across cliff edges, and fray under the weight of climbers jumaring them. It was a severed fixed rope on the Eiger Direct in 1966 that sent John Harlin plunging to his death. Ironically, the last man up the fatal rope just minutes before Harlin was the much lighter Dougal Haston, who noticed the worn section of rope but failed to alert his partner to it.

Under the constant tension of the last week of April and the first several weeks of May, tempers flared, and a subtle game of maneuvering began to infect the teamwork that had held the party together like glue. A single list in Appendix A of Bonington's book ("Diary and Statistics") tells the whole story. The names of the eight principal climbers head eight columns. The rows calculate things such as "Total days at or above Camp IV" and "Total non-rest days at or above 20,000 feet." The three rows that leap out at you are "Days in lead," "Days moving camp," and "Days carrying loads." In other words, these stats quantify the "glory" part of the ascent ("Days in the lead," everybody's favorite assignment) versus the grunt work ("Days moving camp" and "Days carrying loads").

Bonington, Boysen, Frost, Estcourt, Burke, and even Clough have similar stats. Their total days of grunt work in support range from thirty-two (Clough) to thirty-eight (Estcourt). Haston's and Whillans's totals, however, are both twenty-six. But on the expedition, Whillans spent nineteen days in the lead, Haston twenty-two. The next closest is Bonington, with thirteen. Boysen and Estcourt, the real workhorses, got only five days each in the lead. Clough had only four.

The reasons for this were complicated. But one inescapable conclusion is that one way or another, Whillans and Haston manipulated the situation so they got the majority of the time out front. It wasn't simply because they were the strongest climbers; it was a combination of the luck of the rotation draw and Bonington's decisions as a leader. In consequence, among the team members, Haston and Whillans did the least hard work ferrying gear and food and establishing camps. They saved their energy, whether or not deliberately, so that they'd be in a position to go to the top.

As Tom Frost remembers, "Dougal was definitely the strongest climber on the team. The Sherpas had great respect for him, because he was so strong. And that's the reason Don attached himself to Dougal. Don was the master of expedition politics. On the other hand, Don turned out to be the second-strongest climber on the mountain.

"What bothered me, though, was that Dougal and Don were strong, but they were also lazy. The other guys, especially Boysen and Estcourt, really pitched in, they were really team players. But Don and Dougal formed a team of their own."

This discrepancy caused the hardest feelings within the crew during the whole two and a half months on the mountain. By May 13 the team had established Camp V at 22,750 feet at the base of the Rock Band. After weeks of tireless work in support, Estcourt and Boysen were looking forward to their turn to go into the lead. But that day, over intercamp radio, Bonington made a surprising decision. He would send Haston and Whillans straight from low on the mountain through the intermediate camps to take over the lead. In his book, Bonington never clearly explains his thinking, but it is evident that he thought that Haston and Whillans had the best chance of reaching the summit. The team was so far behind schedule that, like the French in 1950, the men in 1970 were already leery of the approaching monsoon.

Estcourt and Boysen were deeply disappointed, but they accepted the verdict with stoic resignation. But the more volatile Mick Burke flew into a rage, and even Tom Frost, who rarely voiced criticisms of any kind, bluntly told Bonington, "I think you've destroyed the spirit of the expedition by pushing Don and Dougal in front out of turn; it was a real stab in the back for Nick and Martin." In his diary, Frost wrote, "For the first time for me politics and personality problems rear their ugly heads and it ceases to be an idyllic, but becomes a normal expedition. As in life these schemers will drink from their own cup of wrath—time will tell."

Ever since 1970 the chief "schemer" has been assumed to be Don Whillans. The implication that lingers forty years later is that he planned his surge to the fore from the beginning. Bonington had made him the official deputy leader of the expedition, and Whillans knew that his old friend from the Freney Pillar respected his mountain judgment above that of all the other climbers. But what cemented the image of Whillans as schemer was how he dealt with his teammates' displeasure at the time.

My co-author, David Roberts, attended the annual meeting of the American Alpine Club in New York City on December 5, 1970. The featured presentation that Saturday evening was a slide show about Annapurna south face given by Frost and Bonington. The pictures left the audience breathless, but what David vividly recalls is Bonington playing tapes of the intercamp radio dispute over the May 13 decision. No one in the AAC had ever witnessed a show that brought home such an unexpurgated sense of what serious conflict on an expedition could be like. The voices were crackly with static, as, in Cockney and Lancashire and Scottish accents, the men volleyed their conflicting views. Then suddenly the gruff, gravelly voice of Whillans burst in, blasting his teammates as slackers and cowards in an obscenity-filled tirade.

Bonington published some of these dialogues in *Annapurna South Face,* with the expletives deleted. Among Whillans's remarks is the following:

> "Camp V isn't even consolidated and the progress of all towards Camp VI is so poor that it's had me and Dougal depressed all the way up the mountain. I don't know what Mick thinks he's playing at but Camp V is short and we want to get the route pushed out and unless they get their

> finger out [of their ass], push it out and establish VI or at least find a site, they should make way for somebody else to try. He's had a week and progress seems very poor."

Eventually Bonington interceded to try to stem the furor. "Stop, all of you. Cut it out," he shouted into the radio. "Everyone's trying their bloody guts out to do this climb, and I think we can sort this out without any kind of argument."

But the damage was done. The personal attack on Burke, who had led the hardest pitches on the whole route as he surged up the dangerous cliffs of the Rock Band, triggered his fury. Burke would die only five years later, on another Bonington expedition, when he disappeared near the summit of Everest after helping his team climb the magnificent southwest face. But during those five years, he never forgave Whillans, nor did the two try to repair the breach.

As Tom Frost puts it today, "Whillans was not the kind of person you want to be like. He was not a hero—he was more like a rock star."

The radio dispute on Annapurna became infamous in mountaineering circles. On a more traditional expedition, this would have been precisely the kind of dirty laundry the team would have shielded from public scrutiny. But Bonington had no qualms either about playing the tapes at slide shows or transcribing them into his book. Despite his conservative, military background, he has always been a firm proponent of the tell-it-like-it-is school of adventure journalism.

The episode lastingly stuck to Whillans's image, adding to the portrait of him as "the Villain." In Jim Perrin's biography under that title, he writes of this turning point on Annapurna:

> The team rapidly regrouped around the new protocols, but ripples had been caused, enemies had been made—a scapegoat, ultimately, would be found and his reputation

> assiduously blackened in the cabals of the ambitious world of professional and semi-professional climbers.

Perrin adds an insider's footnote, gleaned from a later interview with one of the team members (though who, Perrin does not say):

> One source from the expedition has it that Don, who was always most loyal to those he regarded as friends, felt very guilty about stepping in front of Martin Boysen like this: "He didn't give a shit about Estcourt, but suggested to Martin that he team up with him and Dougal. It couldn't have worked with three, of course, and Martin was buggered at that point anyway, with all the carrying he'd done. Martin was one of the real stars of that trip, working for the team throughout. Don worked for the team too, but always with an eye to the top."

By May 19, Whillans and Haston were installed in Camp VI, halfway up the Rock Band. They still hoped to place another camp between that site and the summit, and on the twenty-fourth they set out with that intention. Under a cloudy sky, they started before dawn, but the weather quickly deteriorated until the men were engulfed in a windy whiteout. Both Haston, who wrote the summit chapter of Bonington's book, and Whillans left accounts of that day, and it is fascinating how they differ.

Haston, in the lead, strung out a 300-foot spool of fixed rope. "There was only one thought," he later wrote, "and that was to reach the end of the gully and pitch the tent for Camp VII." Yet having ripped off his goggles because he couldn't see through them, he felt his eyelids freezing in the storm. Then "the whole outside of my left hand had gone numb." In a kind of trance, Haston realized that the two men were in "a nightmare climbing situation," with all kinds of disasters on the verge of happening: a fatal fall, getting lost in the whiteout, or succumbing to the elements.

At the only half-level spot on the slope, Whillans tried to dig out a tent platform, while Haston, waiting and watching, got colder and colder. As Haston later put it, "Slowly it dawned on us that things were serious. Retreat and defeat were right there with us. Still our minds would hardly let the thoughts begin to flow. We were so keyed up for the upward push. Down we had to go."

Whillans, on the other hand, told his biographer,

> We had shovels and a tent so we thought we'd fight it a bit. We got to the bank of snow at the foot of the rock and started digging. About a foot down, it was ice.
>
> "That's it. Get out of here. Back down the ropes . . ."
>
> "We'll find a place," Dougal said.
>
> "No chance," I said. "It's going dark."
>
> "Can't we bivvy?"
>
> "Christ, no!" I said. "We'll be back down those ropes in half an hour and in the tent." We were up there at 25,000 feet in a blizzard. Absolutely lunatic idea to stay. We dumped the gear and went back down the ropes.

Self-serving or not, Whillans's account sounds more plausible. If so, his canny mountaineering judgment saved the day. To bivouac at 25,000 feet in a blizzard with an unpitched tent as the only shelter might well have cost the men their lives. It may have been this strong-willed common sense that Haston later alluded to when he told his friend at the Leysin School that "Don saved his skin."

Still, the setback could well have ended the expedition. Bonington especially was worried about the arrival of the monsoon, hypersensitive to the warming weather that seemed to be setting off avalanches all over the south face. He was eager to get the whole team down safely before a catastrophe struck. But after two months of heroic toil, he wanted success as badly as any of his teammates.

On May 27, Haston and Whillans made a second attempt—not to pitch a Camp VII but to go all out for the summit, some 2,500 feet above Camp VI. And this time they decided to climb without bottled oxygen. The weather was markedly better than it had been three days earlier. With Whillans in the lead, the two men front-pointed unroped up the gully beside the Rock Band and onto the steep slopes above.

They made slow but steady progress. Haston's account of the climb in Bonington's book is strangely dreamy:

> The wonderful thing was that there was no breathing trouble. I had imagined great lung-gasping effort at 26,000 feet but I was moving with no more difficulty than I'd experienced four thousand feet lower down. Likewise Don was having no such problems. He picked a beautiful line through towards the summit ridge. Then he disappeared over the edge and I was alone for a brief spell. The final fifty feet needed care.

The line of the route was so clean and direct that Whillans emerged from the south face to find himself only 30 feet below the very summit of Annapurna. Haston joined him, and they plodded to the apex of the great mountain. It was 2:30 P.M. To both men's amazement, there was no wind. (I'm amazed, too, since in my experience Annapurna is one of the windiest of all the 8,000ers. Whillans and Haston were blessed with a rare calm summit day.) Haston managed to shoot a single out-of-focus picture of his partner on the summit. To both men's disappointment, clouds had started to gather on the surrounding mountains, blocking them from view, and threatening the onset of a storm.

The men did not linger on top. And in Haston's telling, the victory was almost anticlimactic:

> We didn't speak. There was no elation. The mind was still too wound up to allow such feelings to enter. Besides the supreme concentration was needed to get down. . . . The greatest moment of both our climbing careers and there was only a kind of numbness. But we knew the elation would come when we unwound.

By late afternoon, Whillans and Haston had regained their tent at Camp VI. Bonington came on the radio: "Chris calling Camp VI. Did you get out today?"

"Aye," Haston answered. "We've just climbed Annapurna."

As Bonington writes in *Annapurna South Face,* "It should have been over." The expedition had accomplished its titanic goal, even if only two men got to the top. But now Mick Burke and Tom Frost pleaded for a chance to make a second bid. Bonington agreed, then spent a sleepless night agonizing over his decision.

On May 29, having regained Camp VI, Frost and Burke got up early to make their attempt. Frost was exhilarated and feeling fit, but Burke was lethargic and pessimistic. In his book, Bonington quotes long passages from Frost's diary. One paragraph from that day sounds like a rebuke based on Frost's Mormon faith: "Here is a graphic example of the blessings that come from the obedience to the Word of Wisdom. A smoker for fifteen years, Mick Burke was failing with the altitude while I, not naturally strong at altitude, was still pulling at 24,000 feet." To this judgment, Bonington cannot resist appending a bracketed comment: "[*One must remember that Don Whillans, who had smoked for at least twenty years and drunk an average of three pints a night, was going even more strongly than Tom.*]"

Somewhat curiously, Frost today believes that while he and Burke were among the strongest technical climbers on the team, they were the weakest pair in terms of stamina. In any event, the two men got off before sunrise, but Burke managed to climb only a short way up the gully before he felt his feet go numb. It was an obvious decision for him to turn around and head back to camp.

Frost continued alone, jumaring up the rope Haston had fixed in the gully, then front-pointing onto the summit snowfield. Unfortunately, as he ascended the gully, "a tremendous wind" (in his words) began to roar down the gully, pelting him with gusts of airborne snow. Frost felt his own feet go numb, and "for the first time my fingers are desperately cold."

At 25,000 feet, he stopped to take stock. As he wrote that evening in his diary:

> After a couple of hours of indecision, . . . I realized the jig was up; that I could not reach the summit and survive. The only alternative was to turn back.
>
> Was it the Lord's will that I reach the top? Unthinkable! I have prayed sincerely and repeatedly that the Lord's will and not mine should be done.

Looking back on that pivotal moment forty years later, Frost remembers, "All that was left was the fifteen-hundred-foot summit snowfield. It would have been a slog, but through almost waist-deep snow. I could see the summit. I told myself that I could probably make it to the top, but I wasn't sure I could get back down. So I spent an hour at my high point, just trying to enjoy being there."

Frost regained Camp VI at noon. He and Burke radioed the news of their defeat down to Bonington, whose relief that his teammates were safe and sound was immense.

I have the highest admiration for Frost's decision to turn back. Not getting to the top of Annapurna would be one of the sorest disappointments of his long and illustrious mountaineering career. (As he recalls today, it took him two years to recover physically from the strain of the south face expedition.) But he made the right choice, thanks to clearheaded thinking. Frost's turnaround is a classic illustration of the motto that has centered my own climbing career: *Getting to the top is optional. Getting down is mandatory.*

It is characteristic of Frost's modesty that in the article he wrote about the expedition for the *American Alpine Journal,* he does not even mention his own May 29 attempt to go for the summit. Instead, good soldier to the end, he cheers Haston and Whillans's performance: "Victory! The pair returned to Camp VI at five o'clock. Fantastic—a 2,500-foot summit day without oxygen and in bad weather. This was a superhuman performance. And it was our passport to head home."

In the fact that eight climbers, six Sherpa, and three supporting crew members all worked their tails off for two and a half months just to get two climbers to the summit, the Annapurna south face expedition stood near the end of a grand tradition of similar Himalayan ventures. Only Herzog and Lachenal had reached the summit on Annapurna's first ascent, just as only Tenzing and Hillary topped out on Everest in 1953. On the first ascent of K2 the next year, only Achille Compagnoni and Lino Lacedelli reached the summit. The startling exception to that pattern came on the first ascent of Makalu, in 1955, when the French team performed so skillfully that they got all nine climbers to the summit.

To find true gratification in making possible a first ascent when you don't get to the top yourself requires self-sacrifice and team solidarity of the sort that seems to be increasingly rare in recent years. The French had it in 1950, as did the British on Everest three years later. As to whether the other members of Bonington's south face expedition felt genuinely fulfilled by Haston and Whillans's success—well, it's hard to say. Even Tom Frost, the most loyal and uncomplaining of all the eight, felt that the comradeship of the party had been irreparably damaged by the dispute on May 13 when Bonington sent his chosen pair leapfrogging past the others into the lead. In his *AAJ* article, Frost confessed his dismay and confusion about that development:

> Strategy. Personal relations. Expediency. Compromise. Why are we here? Really here? It is becoming questionable.
>
> The "Row" punctured the relatively good feeling that had existed. The ideal of teamwork suffered a setback. We did not endure to this particular end. When will there be a big expedition that has members who are all of one mind and individual desire is that of raising up one's companions rather than oneself?

I count it among my blessings that I've never been in a comparable situation on any of my thirty-one expeditions to 8,000-meter peaks. The only trip that could have taken on such a shape was the International Peace Climb on Everest in 1990. Our leader, Jim Whittaker, called the shots on that expedition in much the same style as Bonington had on Annapurna. It was an accepted fact that Jim had the right to make the major decisions—that's what we all had signed up for. In early May, after we'd spent eight weeks building up camps on the route on the north side, our team was ready for a summit attempt. Jim chose me to pair up with Robert Link in the first summit bid. But he also insisted that the climbers on that first try use supplemental oxygen, to bolster the team's chances of making the ascent. That ruled me out, since I was determined to climb Everest without bottled Os. I told Jim as much, but he was stubborn. "Go to bed and sleep on it," he pleaded.

I was adamant. "Jim," I said, "I'm not going to change my mind. There's nothing to sleep on!"

In the end, however, I didn't lose anything by backing out of the first summit team. Our expedition was so successful that we got no fewer than twenty Americans, Soviets, and Tibetans to the top in several successive waves. And I climbed my second 8,000er in the style I'd vowed to pursue: without supplemental oxygen.

While Mick Burke and Tom Frost had been making their last try for the summit, the rest of the team was dismantling the camps and carrying supplies down the mountain, in preparation for the hike out. Bonington could not quell his lingering anxiety that the party had stayed on the mountain too long, pushing too close to the onset of the monsoon. On May 30, through binoculars from base camp, he watched Burke and Frost descend. Martin Boysen said to him, "Relax, Chris, it's all over. Nothing can happen now."

"I don't think I'll be really happy," Bonington answered, "till everyone is down."

Only a little while later, as Bonington sat in his tent composing news dispatches to announce the triumph to the world, one of the members of the supporting team came running up, frantically calling his name. "It's Ian," the man gasped. "He's dead; killed in an ice avalanche below Camp II."

On his last trip down the mountain, as he wended his way unroped through the crevassed glacier below Camp II, on easy terrain, Ian Clough had been in the wrong place at the wrong time. A serac chose just that moment to collapse, sending an avalanche down the wall of the subsidiary ridge that loomed above him on the right. Clough had tried to run for it, but the avalanche swallowed him. Several Sherpa and the supporting team member who brought the news to Bonington had barely escaped themselves. They dug through the debris and found Clough's body. It was apparent that he had been killed instantly.

As Tom Frost recalls, "I was the last one coming down the

mountain. I took my time. As I descended, I marveled at how the route had changed. Everything was melting, there was lots of falling ice. In places, the fixed ropes were buried in snow or ice. The temperatures must have skyrocketed. The route was falling apart. Then Chris and the Sherpas came up to tell me what had happened to Ian."

The team buried Clough just a hundred yards from base camp. "I said a few words of tribute," Bonington later wrote; "Tom said a prayer and we filled in the grave. It was a very short, simple ceremony and yet it had a beauty and dignity, enhanced by the depth of feeling of all who were present."

The few pages that close the book end with the tragedy that marred an otherwise brilliantly executed ascent. In them, Bonington tries to capture the other members' sorrow as well as his own, but he remains on some level inarticulate. "As we walked down the Modi Khola we felt a mixture of grief at the death of a friend and an extraordinary elation, not solely from our success, but also because we had managed to become such a close-knit team."

Perhaps. But that summation sounds a little pat, a little too determined to find useful meaning in a meaningless accident. There is just a hint of an "I told you so" in those pages, as if staying too long on the mountain, as the team did by his indulging Burke and Frost in their second attempt, had somehow made Clough's death more likely. ("It should have been over.") But a serac is just a serac. Terrain such as the glacier where Clough met his end figures for me as some of the scariest places on big mountains, because you have no warning of and no control over the random movements of ice teetering above you. A serac falls when it wants to; its collapse is pretty much independent of the time of day or the season of the year.

In the *AAJ* article, Tom Frost's reflections on Clough's death strike a different note: "It was a tragedy which completely changed the complexion of the expedition. . . . For the first time values began to take on a proper perspective. Those things that we had supposed to be of value, and had worked for all along, were compared to values having a more eternal weight of significance."

In those thoughts, Frost seems to me to plumb the most fundamental question about mountaineering: How can we justify the risks of an endeavor that ends up taking the lives of so many of our closest friends? It's not a question with an easy answer. In fact, given the number of friends I've lost in the mountains, it's not a question for which even now I've found an adequate answer.

At least the Annapurna team did not have to face the wrenching dilemma of having a teammate killed early on in the expedition. That happened in 1963, on the American Everest expedition, when Jake Breitenbach was killed by a collapsing serac on one of the team's first pushes through the Khumbu Icefall. The rest of the members mourned Breitenbach's loss, but decided to continue the expedition, which eventually resulted not only in the first American ascent of the world's highest mountain, but in Tom Hornbein and Willi Unsoeld's astonishing west ridge traverse.

Eight years after Annapurna, in 1978, Bonington led an expedition to K2 to attempt the unclimbed west ridge. On only the twelfth day on the mountain, Nick Estcourt, who had performed so tirelessly and selflessly on Annapurna, was killed in an avalanche similar to the one that ended Clough's life. Despite an exhaustive search, his friends never found his body.

The K2 party was smaller and closer-knit than the Americans on Everest. The members deliberated whether to abandon the attempt or continue it. Feelings were mixed. Bonington himself was in favor of keeping on, but in the face of objections by four of his comrades, he yielded. The men packed up and went home.

Despite the dissension within the team, and the tragedy that took the life of the partner Bonington had called the "kindest and least selfish" he had ever roped up with, the ascent of the south face of

Annapurna ranks today as one of the greatest deeds in Himalayan history. In that respect, it demonstrates that a team need not be perfectly harmonious to pull off a stellar feat. Jim Perrin, Whillans's biographer, goes so far as to call the climb "the most momentous ascent to that date in the history of mountaineering."

When Veikka Gustafsson and I finally reached the top of Annapurna in 2005, one of the first things we did was to peer down the south face. I think I involuntarily blurted out, "Oh, my God!" The face was so unbelievably steep. We couldn't see all the way down, because mists had shrouded the bottom of the wall, but in that moment, we both were stunned by the discovery of such a dark, mysterious precipice. It was obviously gnarly, funky, dangerous, and huge. And I thought once again about what an amazing team Bonington had assembled at its base in 1970.

The great Polish climber Krzysztof Wielicki, with whom I would pair up on Gasherbrum I in 1995, had led a team up the British route on Annapurna four years earlier, in 1991. In his memoir, *Crown of Himalaya,* Wielicki salutes his predecessors:

> Thus we accomplished the third ascent of the celebrated route of Chris Bonington from 1970. The twenty years that span British and Polish climbs witnessed a great mountaineering progress, owed mainly to improved climbing gear, bivouac equipment and clothing. From this perspective the British climb seems almost incredible.

In the decades following 1970, Annapurna would serve as the arena for other breakthrough ascents by brilliant climbers from several different countries. And the mountain would prove again and again that it was one of the hardest peaks on earth to climb, and one of the deadliest.

FOUR

SO CLOSE TO THE DEAD

It was not simply the fact that the British climb of the south face was bold beyond its time; it also marked only the third ascent of the mountain. Bonington's team missed, in fact, nabbing the second ascent by a mere week. On the summit on May 27, 1970, Whillans and Haston found the footprints in the snow of their compatriots Henry Day and Gerry Owens, the two members of the army expedition who had pushed up the north face, following the French route, to top out on May 20.

It was not until 1978 that any American climbers turned their attention to Annapurna. That year, Arlene Blum, a biophysicist with mountaineering experience on Everest and Denali, put together a team of ten women—eight of them Americans, one British, and one Czech—to attempt the north face. The route the team chose was not the eternally perilous French line through the Sickle, but the safer Dutch Rib to the left of it, an alternative that had been pioneered the year before by a party from the Netherlands that succeeded in placing one Sherpa and one Dutchman on top.

Blum conceived of her expedition not only as an adventure, but also as a feminist manifesto. As she has claimed throughout a long career as a motivational speaker and climber, "There were many expeditions I was not allowed to go on"—because, according to Blum, of the entrenched sexism of the mountaineering establishment. With her all-women expedition, Blum wanted to demonstrate that female climbers could perform every bit as well as males on an 8,000-meter peak. To help raise funds for the trip, the team printed up T-shirts that read "A Woman's Place Is On Top . . . Annapurna." These items proved so popular that sales of the T-shirts furnished three-quarters of the team's $80,000 budget.

The book Blum wrote after the expedition, *Annapurna: A Woman's Place,* is regarded today by many as a mountaineering classic. After Herzog's *Annapurna,* it is by far the best-known narrative of any exploit on the world's tenth highest mountain. But both the book and the expedition fanned a controversy that still simmers more than three decades later.

The team of ten varied widely in skill and ambition. The strongest climber was the Czech, Vera Komarkova, thirty-five years old as the team headed for Nepal. Alone among the ten, she had pioneering big-wall experience, having put up a stellar new route on the southeast face of Alaska's Mount Dickey in 1977, in a twenty-six-day effort with a single male partner. Some of the more junior members of the Annapurna team, however, were intimidated by the seriousness of the mountain from the moment they reached base camp; psyched out (as Blum's account candidly divulges), they played almost no part in advancing the route. Blum herself, who had no ambition to go to the summit, never climbed above 22,000 feet.

Nor was the team united in supporting Blum's feminism. One of the youngest members, Annie Whitehouse, irked her leader by getting romantically involved with a Sherpa during the expedition. (The two were married the following year.) Whitehouse later went on record as declaring, "I can't remember a single time that I was prevented from doing what I wanted because I was a female, either on the rock or in the mountains."

To give a succinct summary, in September and October 1978, the women and the Sherpa climbers supporting them built up a pyramid of supplies and camps on the Dutch Rib, placing a highest Camp V at 24,200 feet. On October 15, four members—Vera Komarkova, Irene Miller, and the Sherpa pair of Chewang Rinzing and Mingma Tsering—reached the summit. Blum's account, based largely on Miller's and Komarkova's diaries, does not disguise the fact that the Sherpa broke trail virtually all the way to the summit, just as Sherpa on the team had earlier almost single-handedly pushed the route above the Dutch Rib and established Camp V. On the summit day, the women used bottled oxygen, while the Sherpa did without.

Two days later, Alison Chadwick-Onyszkiewicz (the British member) and Vera Watson set out on a second summit bid, unaccompanied by Sherpa. When the two failed to make their prearranged radio call that evening, the other members grew deeply alarmed. Eventually, the body of one of the women was spotted through binoculars. The pair, climbing roped together from Camp IV to Camp V, had apparently fallen to their deaths from a steep snow slope below Camp V.

The controversy that erupted after the expedition focused on the role the Sherpa played in the achievement. Blum's detractors argued that you could hardly call the effort an "all-women expedition" when male Sherpa played such a crucial role in the women's getting to the top. The most vehement of her critics were incensed that after realizing their teammates were dead, none of the women made an effort to reach their bodies, recover precious belongings, and perhaps bury their friends in a crevasse. Instead, Blum all but ordered the Sherpa to carry out this extremely dangerous mission. Once again, her book frankly confesses that none of the women was physically or psychologically up to this dolorous task. In the end, two Sherpa—including the exhausted summiteer Mingma Tsering—got within fifty feet of the one visible body (apparently Chadwick-Onyszkiewicz's) but were stopped by a crevasse too dangerous to cross.

Blum's defenders argued that Sherpa had played much the same role in the achievements of all-men's expeditions to the 8,000ers—usually without receiving their due credit. In 1939 on K2, for instance, three Sherpa, including the indomitable Pasang Kikuli, lost their lives in a heroic effort to rescue Dudley Wolfe, stranded in a high camp, when none of Wolfe's American teammates was physically able to carry out that last-ditch mission.

I have my own thoughts about the women's expedition, but I prefer to keep them to myself. I've never been comfortable pointing fingers or criticizing others' decisions on big mountains. How you climb—with or without supplemental oxygen, with or without Sherpa support, in slow expedition style or fast alpine style—ultimately comes down to a matter of personal choice. And no matter how you slice it, climbing 8,000-meter peaks is an extremely demanding business.

At the same time, it would be wrong in this book to ignore the 1978 expedition altogether. One way or another, it was a landmark in Himalayan history. Komarkova and Miller did indeed make the first American ascent of Annapurna (allowing for the fact that the former was a Czech who had settled in the United States only in 1970). The second American ascent of the mountain would come a full decade later, when Steve Boyer joined an all-star international team (the rest of the climbers were French, Italian, and Czech) to make the second ascent of Bonington's south face route.

Komarkova, a plant biologist, was perhaps the unsung hero of the 1978 expedition. Six years later, on her last Himalayan venture, she made the first women's ascent of Cho Oyu. She thus stands as one of only two women to claim the first female ascents of two 8,000ers. The other is the Japanese Junko Tabei, who was the first woman on the summit of Everest in 1975 and the first on Shishapangma in 1981.

Komarkova died of breast cancer in 2005, at the age of sixty-two. In a moving obituary for *The Independent,* British climbing historian Stephen Goodwin cast an illuminating light on the internal disputes of the "all-women" Annapurna expedition. Goodwin writes,

> Blum wanted the enterprise to be as advertised—an all-woman effort—but accepted the practical need for Sherpa support. The purist line was taken by the one British member of the group, Alison Chadwick-Onyszkiewicz, who did not want Sherpas on the climb at all. The Sherpas took this role reversal as both an affront to their dignity and a denial of a chance to earn more money in the future with an 8,000-metre peak to their credit.
>
> As the ascent via the Dutch Rib wore on, with brushes with avalanches and the usual debilitations of high-altitude mountaineering, Sherpas were taking a share of lead climbing and trail-breaking, and lobbied for two places on the first summit bid. Blum resisted; the first party would be three women, Komarkova, Irene Miller and Piro Kramar, with two Sherpas to be included in any second attempt.
>
> Komarkova had a close rapport with the Sherpas and favoured their presence on a first ascent. As the summit bid unfolded, she and the Sherpas got their way. The party that left the top camp shortly before 7 AM comprised Komarkova and Miller, plus Chewang Rinzing and Mingma Tsering. Kramar had dived back into the tent after her right index finger froze while she was putting on her crampons.
>
> Blum, who was 3,000 feet lower down the mountain, was dismayed—not only had the all-woman ethos been lost, but so had Sherpa support for a second bid. In the event, though, an effective unit had emerged; Mingma and Chewang did much of the trail-breaking while Miller struggled. She and Komarkova began using supplementary oxygen 1,200 feet below the summit.

For an hour after gaining the windy crest, the four climbed over and around a succession of cornices and bumps, unable to decide which was the real summit. Finally there at 3.30 PM, they planted the Nepalese and American flags and one bearing the "woman's place" slogan. Komarkova took the summit photos. "The view was deeply fulfilling," she wrote in her diary. Meanwhile, at the lower camps with a clear sight of the summit, other climbers were dancing and shrieking with delight. Most of all, recalled Blum, was the "joy in knowing that a woman's place was indeed on top."

Among the many outstanding deeds performed on Annapurna during the last sixty years, one of the very finest was pulled off by two Swiss mountaineers in the autumn of 1984. Surely no great Annapurna "first" remains so little known, at least within the English-speaking climbing world, as the ascent of the east ridge by Erhard Loretan and Norbert Joos.

The members of Bonington's team in 1970 were not the first climbers to explore the southern side of Annapurna. In 1964 a Japanese expedition entered the Sanctuary and made the first ascent of Glacier Dome, a 23,191-foot subsidiary peak that stands about five miles from Annapurna along the high east ridge. Then two German expeditions, in 1965 and 1969, used the Sanctuary as an approach to the east ridge of Annapurna itself. Their intent was not simply to put up a new route, but also to find a line that was less dangerous than the French route on the north face. But to reach the east ridge, you must skirt the whole of the massive south face on the right. Then, if you attain the crest, you face a gauntlet almost without parallel in the Himalaya: a four-mile-long ridge, much of it razor-sharp and corniced, all of it wildly exposed, all of it above 24,000 feet, with three intermediate summits to be traversed before you reach the top of Annapurna itself.

The 1969 expedition succeeded in placing a high camp at 24,550 feet on top of a gendarme of rock and ice called Roc Noir. But there they were hammered by an eight-day storm. It was all the men could do to hang on, then retreat at the first sign of good weather. The two leaders of that bold attempt, Günter Hauser and Ludwig Greissl, generously gave Chris Bonington the best advice they could about the south face, as Bonington planned his 1970 expedition.

It was not until 1981 that another party tried the east ridge. That year, a ten-man Swedish expedition reclimbed Glacier Dome and gained the ridge. The two strongest climbers eventually skirted beneath Roc Noir by traversing a dangerous snow slope (a place I would come to know well in 2002!). They pushed on, establishing a camp on the ridge. The next day, they made a last-ditch try to finish the route, but had to turn back 700 feet below Annapurna's east summit, which itself is still more than a mile away from the true apex of the mountain.

The idea of a Swiss expedition to the east ridge was the brainchild of a mountain guide named Jöri Bardill. Yet before he could assemble a team, Bardill was killed in an accident in the Alps. The project had enough momentum, however, that it was picked up by other ambitious Swiss mountaineers, among them Norbert Joos. Joos invited his good friend Erhard Loretan. As Loretan would later write about the weeks the Swiss spent beneath the south face and on the east ridge of Annapurna, "Because of the atmosphere that reigned throughout our two months, this expedition was one of the sort that reconciles you to humankind."

In 1984, Loretan was twenty-five years old. Born in the city of Bulle in the French-speaking Gruyère region of western Switzerland, he started climbing at age eleven, when a cousin who was a professional guide took him up such relatively serious peaks as the Fründenhorn. At the age of twenty-one Loretan went on his first expedition to the Andes. The next year, he became a mountain guide himself, though he would earn his principal income as a cabinetmaker.

Fearless and talented, Loretan turned his attention to the high Himalaya in 1982. In only a year and a half he reached the summits of five 8,000-meter peaks. In June 1983 he pulled off an unprecedented and astounding "threefer" (as I call such enchainments) when he topped out on Gasherbrum I, Gasherbrum II, and Broad Peak in a span of only two weeks.

Perhaps because their country is relatively small (population only 7.8 million in 2010), the Swiss have often been overlooked among the powers of European alpinism, but over the decades their top climbers have held their own with their French, Italian, German, and Austrian counterparts. It was a Swiss team that made the first ascent of Lhotse in 1956, and a Swiss-Austrian team that claimed Dhaulagiri, the world's seventh highest mountain, in 1960. The greatest Swiss climber of the generation before Loretan was Raymond Lambert, who spearheaded the two Swiss expeditions to Everest in the spring and fall of 1952. Not only did those teams pioneer the route that would lead the Brits to the summit the next year, but on May 28, 1952, Lambert and Tenzing Norgay reached 28,210 feet on the southeast ridge before having to turn back. It was the highest point on earth anyone had verifiably reached. (We will never be sure how high Mallory and Irvine climbed before vanishing in 1924.) Had the pair been able to surmount the mere 800 vertical feet that rose from their high point to the summit, Raymond Lambert might well be today the most famous mountaineer of all time, instead of Sir Edmund Hillary. (To his credit, after 1953, Hillary gained additional fame for his campaign to build schools and hospitals for the Sherpa people who had been so instrumental in the first ascent of Everest. In the public eye, Tenzing, being a Sherpa, will always lurk in the shadows of his Western partners.)

By 1984 the race to become the first man to climb all fourteen 8,000ers was under way. The two leading rivals were the northern

Italian Reinhold Messner and the Pole Jerzy Kukuczka. Loretan had no thought of entering that competition, but as it would turn out, in 1995, he would become only the third mountaineer to accomplish the feat, as he won a head-to-head race with the Frenchman Benoît Chamoux—a race even more frenzied and intense than that between Kukuczka and Messner. (Of this remarkable and sometimes bitter rivalry, more later.)

Loretan's partner on the "threefer" was Marcel Rüedi, the younger climber's mentor. Though twenty-one years Loretan's elder, Rüedi had become Loretan's partner of choice in the mountains. With his ascent of Broad Peak in 1983, Rüedi in fact was a force to be reckoned with in the quest to be the first to bag all the 8,000ers, for he now had eight under his belt. In the spring of 1984, Loretan and Rüedi teamed up to attack Manaslu, the world's eighth highest mountain. The pair stood on the summit on the surprisingly early date of April 30, but on the descent, something went wrong. Engulfed in a blinding windstorm and whiteout, the two men crept down the mountain, with Loretan in the lead. Focused intently on keeping his balance, as gusts of wind threatened to wrench him loose from his crampon-and-ice-ax purchase on the steep slope, Loretan eventually looked back to check his partner's progress. Stunned, he saw only a bare slope. Was it possible that Rüedi, blinded by the storm, had made a misstep and fallen to his death?

Loretan continued down, reaching Camp III, where he spent a miserable night alone, "haunted," he later wrote, "by the specter of Marcel." The next day, on reaching Camp II, Loretan learned from teammates who had been in radio contact with Camp IV that Rüedi had turned around in the storm and regained the higher camp. It took another desperate effort for the man to complete the descent, but now he had nine 8,000ers on his résumé.

That close call in no way diminished Rüedi's ambitions. Two years later, with the Pole Krzysztof Wielicki, Rüedi reached the top of Makalu, his tenth 8,000er. But on the summit day, he lagged far behind his younger, stronger partner. On the way down, Wielicki passed Rüedi still heading up. As Wielicki later described the events,

> He looked well. I gave him all the liter of tea and chocolate. I told him, "I'm going down to the tent and will prepare hot drinks for us." He answered, "OK, I'm going to the top." I didn't see him again as the couloir was hidden. It was four P.M. When I reached the tent at seven o'clock, it was nearly dark. I prepared drinks, but Marcel didn't come. It was a horrible night.

The next morning, Wielicki descended to the Makalu Col, where, as luck would have it, he ran into Reinhold Messner and his perpetual partner Hans Kammerlander, who were making their own attempt on Makalu. Peering through binoculars, Kammerlander shouted, "I see Marcel. He is at eight thousand meters coming to Camp III." Rüedi's teammates realized that the man must have bivouacked below the summit, but now there was hope.

Later that day, however, a pair of Sherpa descending from Camp III reported that they had found Rüedi dead, sitting upright in the snow only 100 feet from the camp, but with his tent unopened. He may have died of exhaustion and hypothermia, or he may have been afflicted by pulmonary or cerebral edema, as he had once before on Dhaulagiri, where he had climbed his first 8,000er.

Wrote Wielicki, "I had known Marcel only a few days, but I felt he was an old friend. I can't forget him and his optimistic face. Maybe it was my fault, but I couldn't tell him, 'Stop! Come back!' He was for me one of the biggest Himalayan tigers."

The Swiss team that entered the Sanctuary on the south side of Annapurna in September 1984 was made up of six professional guides. The leader was Frank Tschirky. Norbert Joos and Erhard

Loretan would turn out to be the strongest climbers, and it was Loretan who would end up being the driving force on the east ridge.

Before I attempted the east ridge myself in 2002, I tried to learn everything I could about the 1984 Swiss expedition, but I came up with only scraps of information. The *American Alpine Journal* published a deadpan, almost perfunctory one-paragraph note by Loretan summarizing the expedition. Reinhold Messner's book *Annapurna: 50 Years of Expeditions in the Death Zone* added further details. But most of the "beta" for the route (as climbers call advice culled beforehand from veterans who have already done a given climb) came via my partner Jean-Christophe Lafaille, who knew Loretan and had asked him about the east ridge.

The main reason such a great mountaineer as Loretan remains so little known and so uncelebrated in the United States and Britain (and probably, for that matter, in Europe outside of Switzerland) is that he is at heart a modest man unwilling to blow his own horn. Not for him the high-profile public persona of a Reinhold Messner.

In 1997, Loretan collaborated with a Swiss journalist, Jean Ammann, to write his memoir of becoming only the third climber to reach the top of all fourteen 8,000ers. Titled *Les 8000 Rugissants* (The roaring 8,000ers), it was published by an obscure press in Loretan's native Fribourg canton of Switzerland. The book is exceedingly rare in the United States—in fact, I'd never seen a copy until last year. The memoir has never been published in English. Even if I had come across a copy of the Swiss edition, it wouldn't have helped me prepare for the east ridge, since my French is nonexistent.

As I did my homework for this book about Annapurna, however, I enlisted a couple of cronies who read French (one of them a native Frenchwoman living in the United States) to translate key passages from the chapter in Loretan's book about the ascent of the east ridge. Those passages blew my socks off. It was immediately apparent that Loretan (or Loretan plus Ammann) was a very good writer. He also had a wry, dark, but brilliant sense of humor. It seems that at the core Loretan is an absurdist, for he narrates his dangerous and visionary climbs on some of the world's most difficult mountains in a tone worthy of Albert Camus or Samuel Beckett. Instead of striving earnestly to explain why he climbs (as Messner does in book after book), Loretan takes it for granted that his obsession is crazy, indefensible—in a word, absurd. The closest parallel among climbing memoirs in English that I can think of is Scot Tom Patey's posthumous collection of articles, *One Man's Mountains,* which has become a cult classic. In the words of one American admirer, Patey "milked all his best effects out of what really amounts to a single conceit: the climber as Don Quixote, tilting at Nordwands." The same could be said about Loretan. Take, for instance, the latter's riff on the mishaps of the hike up the Modi Khola:

> Two porters fell into the river the first day. Once they had dried off, they confirmed the fact that it's hard to swim with 30 kilos on your back. Our doctor, Bruno Durrer, played Albert Schweitzer: the porters passed one after another through his clinic, followed by almost the total population of the local villages. In this region, the lack of hygiene encourages infections. Microbes love Nepal at least as much as the tourists do. . . . The fifth and sixth days, our column traversed a veritable jungle. The leeches rejoiced that the trekking season was early as they threw themselves upon us. I established the absolute record: 34 bites. The fact that I hiked in sandals may have played a role in this exploit.

Yet along with the buffoonery, Loretan keeps a clear view of the magnitude of the challenge of the east ridge. As he did not in his deadpan *AAJ* note, he makes no bones about just how "out there" he and Joos were during the critical days of the ascent. He begins his account by saying, "Annapurna, which for others [i.e., the French in 1950] was the first 8,000er, came very close to being the last for me."

For three weeks the team pushed a string of camps up Glacier Dome and onto the east ridge. On October 6, Joos and Loretan excavated a snow cave for a Camp IV at 24,600 feet, just beyond the top of Roc Noir. Some of the climbing just to reach the ridge was highly technical, and Loretan led most of it. The crux was a dead-vertical 230-foot wall of "mediocre" ice that took him two hours to conquer, jabbing with a pair of ice tools and stabbing with the front points of his crampons. After leading each pitch, Joos and Loretan strung fixed ropes on them, to aid their teammates' load hauling.

A series of storms halted the expedition for ten straight days. During this lull, Joos and Loretan took a break from the serious business of climbing. Even in 1984 a side loop branching off from the trekking route on the south side of Annapurna passed into the Sanctuary. On October 9, Joos and Loretan needed only to "cross the glacier" (as Loretan later wrote) "to get news of the real world." They paid a visit to a pair of ramshackle bamboo trekking huts grandly calling themselves Hotel Annapurna. (The place has been upgraded considerably since 1984. By 2002, when we visited, the two huts had been replaced by a spacious but rustic lodge, the center of a small village, and by then it bore the name Annapurna Base Camp.) "We even found some women there," Loretan remarked, "although for the last six weeks we had begun to fear that the 'species'—by which I mean the feminine gender—had disappeared. This inquest reassured us about the survival of humankind."

Back at base camp, morale rose and fell with the barometer. Reading between the lines, you get the sense that by now the other four members of the team were starting to lose heart for the project. After October 16, various climbers made trips all the way to Camp III, but the east ridge itself had barely been explored. One morning—Loretan does not give the date—he and Joos set out from Camp II on a summit bid. "After a few hundred meters," he writes, "we had set off three avalanches!" This unpromising start triggers another witty reflection: "Alpinists freely adhere to the following theory: each individual is given a quota of luck. He stays alive only until that quota is used up. Three avalanches for two persons in one hour—this was a big dent in our quota."

The two men glumly returned to Camp II, where they waited out a storm. "A candle lit up the interior, we listened to sweet music [presumably on their Walkmans or a tape recorder], outside, the storm raged. This ambiance was magical, but at the same time, it exasperated me."

There follows a passage in *Les 8000 Rugissants* that gives a key clue to Loretan's makeup:

> Such tranquility for me is almost unbearable. My soul torments itself, I even start to ask myself if everything that we do, all of our efforts, all this agitation, makes any sense. . . . For me, such thoughts are the daughters of inaction. The ascent of an 8,000er, I tell myself, is worse than a turbulent love affair. Failure and happiness each hang from a thread, and this thread—I am not sure that we can or know how to choose the right one.

In a way, I can identify with Loretan's anguish. When I'm stuck in a tent, waiting out a storm, trying to fill up the useless time, I sometimes start brooding, *Why do I do this? What does it actually prove?* But at the same time, my doubts, I think, are less existential than Loretan's. Those gloomy down hours have never made me fundamentally question the whole point of climbing a mountain. For me, it's simply the inactivity as the hours tick by that drives me crazy. When I look back after an expedition, however, the memory of those storm days tends to vanish into the backdrop of weeks of meaningful work.

On October 21—disturbingly late in the short autumnal Himalayan season—Joos and Loretan set off on a second summit bid. They had been preceded three days earlier by two teammates who had reopened the route to Camp III, clearing fixed ropes that had been buried in the ten-day storm. Yet during only those three days, some of the fixed ropes had refrozen into the slopes. On the vertical ice wall, the crux of the route, stretches of the vital fixed rope were entombed in ice. During his climb Loretan several times had to unclip his ascender from the rope, make a few completely unprotected moves, then clip in again where the rope emerged from the ice.

I've had to do the same thing sometimes on 8,000ers. In the radiant heat of high altitude, the ropes melt into the snow and ice in the daytime, then freeze at night. If they're buried deep enough, there's no hope of digging them out. You have to unclip your ascender, make those dicey free moves, then clip in again. It's a pain in the ass, besides being scary. Then, to safeguard the descent, once you reach the next anchor, you have to string another hank of fixed rope down the pitch. On the descent, you're sure as hell not going to want to have to downclimb those unprotected moves.

The two men spent the night at Camp II. Their teammates Bruno Durrer and Ueli Bühler were ensconced above them in Camp III. At 4:30 A.M. on the twenty-second, Loretan suddenly revealed his "blitzkrieg" plan to Joos. As he described it in *Les 8000 Rugissants*: "To recover all our lost days, we would climb directly to Camp IV, at 7500 meters [24,600 feet]! Norbert was surprised, but he acquiesced. Around 6:00 A.M., we started, motivated by the magnitude of the stakes."

It took the pair only two and a half hours to reach Camp III, where they caught up with Durrer and Bühler. Loretan hoped their teammates would join the blitzkrieg assault, but at this point Durrer, the expedition doctor, decided to descend. In his memoir, Loretan treats the man's retreat with his usual wry humor:

> It was at this moment that his professional conscience reminded Bruno Durrer of his duties: on November 4, he was supposed to be in Switzerland, working at his office, and if everybody frittered away his energy climbing summits from which you had to go down anyway, the gross national product of Switzerland would not be what it is.

Loretan and Joos pushed on with Bühler. But almost at once another calamity struck the team. Again, Loretan narrates the spooky event as comedy: "I passed Ueli. And there, he uttered some gibberish that surprised me. I turned around: . . . He was green! I did not like it; I did not like it at all. Once again I remembered Peter Hiltbrand on Nanga Parbat, and at no price was I willing to relive a comparable tragedy." (On Nanga Parbat in 1982, Loretan's first 8,000er, at a high camp, Hiltbrand had succumbed suddenly in the night to pulmonary edema. Babbling incoherently, he kept saying, "It's going to be all right," but then, in the morning, he moaned, "Let me die." In the next moment, he expired. Weeping, his teammates, including Joos and Loretan, lowered his body into a crevasse. Now, on Annapurna, it was obvious that Bühler was in the early stages of pulmonary or cerebral edema.)

> Ueli was still lucid, which meant that he hadn't lost any of his character: he didn't want to hear any talk about descending, he wanted to push on to Camp IV, which was only 100 meters above us. His square head understood nothing of the roundness of psychology. Finally, we had to threaten him: "If you insist on sleeping here, we're going to have to carry you down in the middle of the night, the expedition will be wasted, and no one knows what sort of state you'll end up in."

At last Bühler acquiesced. Bravely, he turned around and started solo down the track in the snow printed by Durrer. Joos and Loretan pushed on to Camp IV. (In his *AAJ* note, Loretan records the departure of Durrer and Bühler in a laconic sentence: "The latter two descended from Khangsar Kang [Roc Noir].")

I had a very similar experience in 2005 on Cho Oyu when, just minutes after we left our high camp at 23,300 feet, my teammate Jimmy Chin nearly collapsed. His speech was slurred and he couldn't catch his breath. Like Bühler, Jimmy insisted at first on pushing on; all he needed, he claimed, was a short rest. But I was pretty sure he was suffering from either cerebral or pulmonary edema. With the same kind of forceful language, Veikka Gustafsson and I convinced Jimmy he had to go down at once. I went with him, to make sure he was all right. Veikka continued solo to the summit, but I didn't greatly regret the loss of the peak myself, since I'd already climbed Cho Oyu in 1996.

I suppose there are those who would argue that it was irresponsible of Joos and Loretan to send a teammate suffering from edema down by himself, especially on such a technical route. After fifty-two days on Annapurna, were the two lead climbers too hungry for the summit? This is not a conclusion I'm willing to come to. Whatever exchange took place up there on the east ridge on October 22, I suspect that Bühler convinced his teammates he could make it down solo. Allowing someone to head down alone is always a judgment call. With fixed ropes in place to ensure Bühler's safety, the decision seems to have been a reasonable one. And in the end, the man completed the descent without mishap.

Loretan and Joos reached the snow cave above Roc Noir, settled in, and prepared for a summit push in the morning. More comedy:

> My feet were damp, and that worried me on the eve of starting out on a ridge that culminated at 8,000 meters, a ridge lashed by perpetual wind. So I tried to dry them over the stove. I had more success with Fritz's sleeping bag [Fritz Hobi, another team member, had lent his bag to the

summit pair], which I managed to set on fire on the first try. The snow cave now resembled a chicken coop.

The men managed to patch the holes in the sleeping bag with Sparadrap, a kind of Band-Aid known for its insulating qualities, and contain the storm of down feathers. They ate a "gastronomic" dinner of mashed potatoes and cheese, then snuggled in, trying to sleep, but were too wired with anticipation of the great day they hoped the morning would bring to nod off easily.

At 4:30 A.M. on October 23, the sky was blue and the wind had dropped. Skipping breakfast, Loretan and Joos set out at 5:30. After only half an hour, they came face-to-face with an imposing wall. At this point in the account of the climb in *Les 8000 Rugissants,* Loretan's writing becomes so metaphorical that (so I'm told) it's virtually untranslatable. "It wasn't truly steep," he says of the wall, then, in French, *"mais il a 'sale gueule,' une vraie tête à claques."* A literal translation would be, "but it had an ugly mug, a face so annoying you wanted to slap it." I can't imagine using such metaphors for a passage on a mountain; the phrases just don't work in English. But you get the idea: it was a nasty little cliff.

Unroped, Loretan started up it, then backed down. "It was too dangerous," he writes, "and I had no desire to leave *ad patres* with a rope neatly coiled in my pack." This time the witty phrase is Latin: *ad patres* literally means "to [my] fathers," i.e., [gathered] to the land of the dead. As always with Loretan, the jocular tone camouflages the terrifying reality: on that nasty, ugly little cliff, he didn't want to come off and fall to his death without even having roped up with Joos.

The pair got out the rope, and Loretan gave Joos what we call a "psychological belay" (one that had only a small chance of holding him if he fell), as his partner made a second try on the ugly wall. The rope made the difference: Joos led the scary pitch, and Loretan followed.

At 8:30 A.M., the two men reached the col below the east summit. They would have to traverse not only that peak, but also a second one, called the central summit, before heading for the true top of Annapurna. The east summit looked close, Loretan reported, but it took five and a half hours for the men to climb the 1,650 feet between the col and that high point. The men were carrying fifteen kilograms each in their day packs. That's almost thirty-five pounds, which is a hell of a lot to lug at such an altitude. The reason Joos and Loretan were so burdened was that they realized they might need another camp between Camp IV and the summit, probably one they'd have to occupy both on the ascent and on the way down, so they had to take with them a tent, sleeping bags, a stove, fuel, and food.

Loretan complains about the weight of his pack: "Fifteen kilos that crushed us and disturbed the fragile alignment of our vertebrae. I had terrible back pains. This slope was interminable." Once more unroped, Joos and Loretan adopted different styles of progressing, which Loretan renders slyly:

> He advanced quickly, then rested, I moved slowly, stopping as little as possible. Norbert the hare, Erhard the tortoise. . . . In the end, our rhythms were comparable. But I could feel my strength weakening: a sudden pang of hunger reminded me that we had climbed for nine hours on empty stomachs.

At 2:00 P.M. the men stood on the east summit. The wind, so calm at dawn, had sprung up, and now it whipped violently across the east ridge.

Loretan's writing almost never inclines to the mystical, but at this point some kind of magical trance fell over the pair.

> Something incredible now happened: as if the question had never been posed, we plunged toward the col that separated

> the east and the central summits; as if our two energies were programmed for the conquest of the main summit, we pushed on across this incredible traverse. We had not exchanged a single word, because our thoughts were in unison.

I've had the same sort of uncanny sync with Veikka. We'll be moving along without saying a word. An idea will come into my head. At last, I'll speak, "I've been thinking of doing such-and-such." And Veikka will answer, "Yeah, I already thought of that." It's that kind of unconscious rapport that makes for a perfect partnership on an 8,000er.

It took the men only an hour to reach this second col. But there, close to exhaustion, they decided to bivouac. Now, in his account of the climb, Loretan drops a comment that still deeply puzzles me: "A last radio call [to base camp] during which we announced our intention of descending by the north face after having reached the principal summit . . ."

What's so puzzling about this statement is that descending an 8,000er blind by the opposite face from the one you've ascended is a desperate last resort. Preparing for our own 2002 expedition, we knew about Loretan and Joos's monumental traverse, but we assumed that it had been forced upon them by a rappel they had made on the way down from the central summit toward the final col. That rappel, we thought, had cut the men off from returning by the way they had come. J.-C. Lafaille explicitly asked Loretan what had gone into making that decision.

We were so sure that the sinister trap of the rappel had forced the two Swiss to opt for their traverse that we had made sure to bring enough rope to leave it in place if we had to repeat the rappel of the 300-foot cliff. That way, on the descent, we could reach the bottom end of the rope and use ascenders to climb it. The one thing we had agreed upon from the start was to return via the east ridge, and not to descend by the north face.

But it's clear from Loretan's account that he and Joos had already decided to make the traverse and descend the north face even before they made the rappel that cut them off from a return along the east ridge. From *Les 8000 Rugissants* alone, however, one would conclude that that decision was made on the spot in the late afternoon of October 23, as the two men prepared their bivouac on the col below the central summit.

In 2002, I met Loretan very briefly in a restaurant in Kathmandu. He was leading a trekking group. J.-C. introduced me to him, but we had no time to chat. Just this year, however, I managed to get in touch with him by e-mail, reaching him in the tiny town of Crésuz (population 274 in 2008), where he lives in semi-seclusion not far from where he grew up. I asked him about the traverse. To my astonishment, he answered, "In fact the original plan was to make all the traverse S to N as we did. After all the wind was very strong and for us the safest way was Dutch Pillar."

I'm still flabbergasted by the decision. Some might wonder whether Loretan had planned to accomplish the traverse just to increase the magnitude of the splash that such an exploit would make in the mountaineering world. Yet that doesn't seem to have been the man's style. He was no seeker of publicity. In my e-mail to him, I had written that his 1984 traverse was one of the greatest feats ever accomplished on Annapurna. He wrote back, "I think you are a bit exaggerating about our climb!!??" For Loretan, in my opinion, the traverse was purely a practical decision.

Into a plate of windslab on the col, the two men excavated a claustrophobic burrow that passed for a snow cave. It may have been too windy to pitch their tent in such an exposed place. The sleeping quarters were grim:

> Finally, toward 6:00 P.M., we were able to install ourselves. We were at about 8020 meters [26,300 feet], it was cold,

> and we shivered with every bone in our bodies. . . . It was my first night at 8000 meters, and I feared the outcome of a bivouac. We were at the point at which the tiniest mishap could turn into a catastrophe.

But just as Loretan's account starts to evoke the razor's edge onto which he and Joos had thrust themselves, he spins the wildest riff of all, the one that gives structure to his whole Annapurna narrative. When this passage—a kind of meditation on the absurd—was first translated for me, I couldn't help laughing out loud, it so perfectly captures the crazy "what am I doing here" thoughts that assail you in such extreme survival plights as that bivouac above 8,000 meters.

As they were digging the snow cave, Loretan could not get out of his head the song by Sade, the Nigerian-born British singer who had burst upon the scene in the early 1980s, that begins "Tell me why." And apparently the song was echoing through Joos's head as well. (Talk about thinking in unison!) I used to listen to Sade's music in my headphones on expeditions. She's this sultry, smoky beauty, but her music is gentle and relaxing. "Tell Me Why"—actually titled "Why Can't We Live Together?"—begins with a hypnotic, syncopated instrumental introduction that lasts a full two minutes. Then Sade's sweet, sad voice comes in:

Tell me why, tell me why, tell me why
Why can't we live together?
Tell me why, tell me why
Why can't we live together?
Everybody wants to live together
Why can't we be together?

Loretan titles the Annapurna chapter of his book " 'Tell Me Why,' Says the Song." In their bivouac, he writes,

> Go find out why, cycling non-stop through our heads, came the song by Sade, "Tell Me Why." It's a good question: tell me why we were here, at 8020 meters, in this cold that our bodies tried to ward off by shaking uncontrollably, as dogs shed their fleas. . . . I would have been very happy if this refrain had stopped turning in my head: "Tell me why."
>
> Tell me why on this Wednesday, October 24, we crawled out of our sleeping bags covered with powder snow, why we poured out of our boots a volume of snow equal to that of our feet, tell me why we continued toward the main summit even though the wind was more violent than yesterday, and surely less violent than tomorrow.

It was that morning, after traversing the central summit, that Loretan and Joos ran smack into the 300-foot rock cliff that blocked their descent to the final col. "I thanked the gods," Loretan writes, "that had made me bring two pitons, two worthless pitons, two invaluable pitons." Pounding in one for each anchor, Loretan and Joos made two rappels to clear the cliff, pulling their fifty-meter rope down after each.

It was these rappels that, we were convinced in 2002, forced the Swiss pair into the desperate expedient of climbing down the north face. Once you pull the rope, you can't return by the way you came. To add to the puzzle, Loretan writes in *Les 8000 Rugissants,* "Why didn't we return by retracing our steps? Because that rock cliff had cut off our retreat." Yet today he insists he concocted the traverse as part of his "original plan."

On the final col, the two men dropped their packs. Unburdened, writes Loretan, "It seemed to me that I had wings." After only an hour's climbing, the two men reached the summit of Annapurna at 1:30 P.M.: "We fell into each other's arms. A great happiness spread through me." (How different from the complete absence of joy Dougal Haston reported that he and Don Whillans felt on the same summit in 1970, and that Louis Lachenal felt in 1950. And as always, that other puzzle: why does such a triumph give some climbers a piercing, lasting sense of fulfillment, while leaving others simply numb?)

One thing that impresses me about Loretan and Joos is that, no matter their reason for choosing to descend by the north face, even as they stood on the summit, they were fully aware that the climb was only half over. *Getting down is mandatory.* Once again, in his account, Loretan treats this as an existential joke:

> The statistician in me told me that we had succeeded today on a new route on Glacier Dome, the third ascent of the Roc Noir, and the first of the east ridge of Annapurna with its three summits (east, middle, and main), and perhaps the first traverse of a Nepalese 8,000er. [Loretan seems to have overlooked Hornbein and Unsoeld's traverse of Everest by the west ridge in 1963.] You will have noticed that I say "perhaps." A wise literary precaution, for to celebrate that first Nepalese traverse, it would be necessary to arrive at the north-side base camp alive, and that, as the one-armed say, is another pair of sleeves.

In French, the last phrase reads, "*comme disent les manchots, c'est une autre paire de manches.*" The play on words of "*manchots*" ("one-armed") and "*manches*" ("sleeves") is untranslatable. But the meaning is clear: getting down alive would be a serious challenge.

To navigate their way down the north face, which neither man had ever seen, they had only a postcard that Loretan carried in his pocket. "We had just pulled off a fabulous thing," Loretan writes, "and yet I had a strong feeling that the adventure was just beginning." After only ten minutes on the summit, the men headed down. From the col between the central and main summits onward, the terrain before them was unknown to them. Now, at last, Loretan admits just how strung out he and Joos were:

> We advanced with great care, as if we were fording a river, and the next step could be our last. It was as if the torrential emptiness of this wall was going to carry us away. During the whole descent, which lasted two and a half days, we were three: Norbert, myself, and fear.

Earlier in his account, Loretan had summed up the exploit in another memorable phrase: "Never have I pushed my limits so far as during that traverse of Annapurna, never have I felt myself so far from the living and so close to the dead."

The two men had decided to try to downclimb the Dutch Rib rather than the more dangerous Sickle route of the first ascent. The primary problem, as they stumped down the relatively easy but vast summit slopes, was to find the top of that route. Loretan evokes the anxiety of that search:

> As poorly as we could see it, the face looked like a huge pile of seracs, interrupted by vertical rock cliffs. It would be exaggerating to say that death was certain, but it would also be false to say that life was guaranteed. In fact, we had to navigate through the zone that separates life from death: that forms, I think, a perfect definition of survival.

At around 22,300 feet the men stopped for another bivouac—their fourth in a row, as Loretan counts them, starting with the snow cave above Roc Noir. As they unwrapped their tent, one of the poles slipped through their hands. They saw it fall, then fetch up a hundred meters below, but on a ledge too dangerous to reach. Loretan retains his sense of humor about this setback: "You have to acknowledge that nowadays tents are carefully designed: all the poles, without exception, are necessary for the stability of the edifice." Using a piece of cord to shore up the sagging tent, the men got inside, where Loretan brewed up two liters of tea and bouillon. "During the last 36 hours," he writes, "we had drunk almost nothing, and all we had eaten was two Ovosports [Swiss energy bars] per day." All night a strong wind battered the men's inadequate shelter. In another metaphor, Loretan compares his and Joos's plight to a pair of seagoing vessels: "It was not the raft of the *Medusa,* but at the same time it wasn't quite the *Clemenceau.*" (The raft of the *Medusa,* portrayed in a famous painting by Géricault, commemorated a terrible survival ordeal that ensued in 1816 after a French frigate ran aground off the coast of Mauritania. The *Clemenceau* was the best aircraft carrier in the French navy from the 1960s through the 1990s.)

On the morning of October 25 the men waited for a sunrise that never came. Poking their way downward, consulting the postcard, Loretan and Joos were appalled by the conditions underfoot: the windslab snow was loose and rotten, and seracs that looked ready to topple surrounded them. Suddenly, however, Loretan spotted the upper end of a fixed rope about 300 feet below. That glimpse gave the pair a surge of hope: "Proof that someone had already tried this route, that the region was not totally unknown to humankind!"

Yet trying to figure out how to descend those 300 feet filled Loretan with horror: "Everything was vertical; we were prisoners of the vertical." He and Joos briefly considered abandoning the Dutch Rib and climbing back up to try to find the top of the French route, where it emerged from the Sickle, but they knew they were too exhausted to accomplish that herculean task. For technical gear, the men had only a thin 50-meter rope (five millimeters, or two-tenths of an inch, in diameter, far less than a standard climbing rope), an ice ax apiece, and one ice screw.

The descent of those 300 feet would turn out to be the most

desperate passage of the whole traverse. Joos gave Loretan his ice ax, took the screw, and put his weight on the rope as Loretan lowered him like a haul bag. The hope was to reach a platform less than 200 feet below, where Joos might plant the ice screw to anchor the next pitch. But after only 15 or 20 feet, Joos shouted up that the wall below him was overhanging.

The men had no choice. Loretan lowered his partner into thin air, as Joos struggled for balance, his thirty-pound pack threatening to tip him upside down. After swinging back and forth, he finally reached a marginal ledge, but without his ax, he could not keep his balance on the wall while he freed his hands to place the ice screw.

Loretan took Joos off belay, climbed down several meters, and somehow slid an ice ax down to him. After planting the ice screw, Joos was able to return the ax to his partner. Loretan's account of this sketchy operation is unclear, but one imagines that the lowering and raising of the ax was accomplished with the rope.

Now Loretan had to get down the overhanging wall himself. "It was my turn to play this game," he writes jocularly, "which squeezed my guts." He found a block of ice that looked more solid than any of the others, passed the rope around it, and let Joos lower him with an improvised "slingshot" belay. If the block pulled loose, both men would fall to their deaths; but it held. "In a game of Russian roulette," Loretan writes about this maneuver, "there comes a moment when the player must pull the trigger." Backing off the edge above the overhang was Loretan's trigger.

Because the rope was too short for the full cliff, Loretan had to stop partway and carve a bollard—a prong of snow or ice, used as a rappel anchor in only the most desperate straits. In the end, it took the men four separate rappels to get to the base of the formidable pillar, where they reached the upper end of the old fixed rope.

The going was easier below, as fixed ropes intermittently poked out of the snow, but on sixty-five-degree slopes, the men were terrified of setting off an avalanche. They unroped because, Loretan writes, "If you had to slide and die, it was better to do so alone and divide the number of victims by two."

Finally, at 4:00 P.M., the men reached the plateau at the base of the Dutch Rib. As Loretan writes, "It was not the end of our fears, however, for it was here that all the avalanches pouring off Annapurna came crashing down. To think that there were expeditions that wanted to climb Annapurna by this face! You would have to be tired of life itself." (My sentiments exactly after we bailed in the face of avalanche after avalanche cascading down that gigantic wall in 2000. Yet somehow I would rationalize returning to that face in 2005.)

The rest of Loretan's account reads like something out of Edgar Allan Poe:

> We perceived the ruins of a camp. We approached it, hoping to find something to eat, no matter what, as long as it was more substantial than our Ovosport bars. Instead we found the body of a Sherpa, whom a team from the year before had abandoned. Without any coffin except a sarcophagus of ice, without any roof except the sky.

On the spot, Loretan and Joos arranged yet another bivouac. In the middle of the night, they awakened to the roar of a huge avalanche pounding down from above. Instead of trying to look out of their drooping tent or make a run for it, the men simply burrowed deep inside their sleeping bags and awaited fate. The avalanche ground to a chaotic halt just upslope. The wind cloud driven before it buried the camp under three inches of spindrift.

At 1:00 P.M. on October 26 the men finally stepped off the glacier onto a lateral moraine. "The doors of hell had just closed behind us," Loretan writes, "enclosing inside them our fears, our doubts, and our anguish." In the last paragraph of his account, he celebrates surviving the traverse in yet another absurdist conceit:

> On solid earth, we learned all over again how to transcend the present instant, and we surprised ourselves by conjugating certain verbs in the future tense: the word "tomorrow" was no longer automatically linked to the word "if": "Tomorrow, if the seracs hold . . . Tomorrow, if we can find the route . . . Tomorrow, if we can pass the overhang . . ."

An hour after stepping onto the moraine, Loretan and Joos stumbled, like "starving zombies," into the base camp of a Japanese-Czech expedition. Stunned at the arrival of these refugees from nowhere, the team members gave them food and drink and congratulated them heartily on their achievement.

Loretan ends his narrative, "In ten days, we would be reunited with our expedition teammates in Kathmandu. But the Garden of Eden existed: it was here and now."

There is absolutely no doubt in my mind that the 1984 traverse of Annapurna was one of the greatest feats in Himalayan history. It was also self-evidently a really close call. There were so many ways those two guys could have died on the mountain, from the Roc Noir camp all the way down to their last bivouac below the Dutch Rib.

You might think that after such an ordeal, Loretan would have been tempted to take it easy for a while, or even to ratchet down the pitch of his mountaineering ambitions. After venturing, in his own words, "so far from the living and so close to the dead," he had earned the right to a nice long rest. But no, by the next summer he was on the Baltoro Glacier in Pakistan, trying an equally demanding new route on the unclimbed south face of K2.

Throughout the next nine years, in fact, Loretan plugged happily on, climbing 8,000ers, and the stamp of his expeditions was more often bold new routes than repeats of the first-ascent lines.

Today the Annapurna traverse is not even the feat for which Loretan is best known. That honor belongs to his lightning 1986 ascent with another Swiss climber, Jean Troillet, of the Hornbein Couloir on Everest: alpine style, without bottled oxygen, forty-three hours round trip from bottom to top to bottom again. That deed electrified the climbing community worldwide.

It also seems to me a great loss to mountaineering literature that Loretan's bravura account of Annapurna—at times bizarre, at others brilliantly clever, and in the end supremely modest—survives only in the pages of an obscure Swiss edition, long out of print. That chapter of *Les 8000 Rugissants* strikes me as one of the finest short accounts ever written by any climber about any expedition to any of the world's highest mountains.

When I think back about that brief meeting with Loretan in the restaurant in Kathmandu in 2002, I now feel wistful regret that it didn't last longer. Despite the language gap, knowing what I know now, I would gladly have sat there and listened while this extraordinary mountaineer relived the 1984 traverse. At that moment, Loretan was busy with his clients, so the opportunity for a long conversation didn't present itself. Also, I was somewhat in awe of meeting such a legendary climber. But if we'd had the chance, it wouldn't have mattered how long it took Erhard to tell us about the east ridge. In fact, now that I've had a peek through the screen of his French plays on words and his riffs on the eternal themes of climbing, as I saw the outline of the story that lay beneath, I'd have been happy to sit there for hours and hear every last detail of such an amazing adventure. With a guy like Erhard Loretan, the longer the telling, the better.

FIVE

THE DOOR TO THE LAND OF THE LIVING

Climbers are fond of insisting that theirs is not a competitive game. Few among our ranks have ever overtly admitted to trying to beat their rivals in a race to the summit of a mountain. An alternative theory that climbers often espouse is that if we're competitive, the only competition is with ourselves. We push ourselves so hard not to snatch the prize from anyone else, but to test our skills and nerve against a worthy challenge.

When I started amassing successful ascents of 8,000ers, all kinds of people (mainly journalists) asked me if I was determined to become the first American to reach the summit of all fourteen. There was a handful of other guys who might have been seen as in the running, notably Carlos Buhler, who's five years older than I am. By the end of 1997, when I had eight 8,000ers under my belt, Carlos had six. And he'd done some of his climbs on really tough routes, including the Kangshung Face on Everest and the north face of K2. But Carlos publicly announced that he wasn't in a race with me, as he turned his attention to peaks such as Menlungtse and Ama Dablam, which don't reach 8,000 meters. A media rumor also spread that the British climber Alan Hinkes and I were racing to become the first Anglophone to climb all fourteen 8,000ers. As for me, I can honestly swear that becoming the first American, or the first Anglophone, to collect all fourteen played no part in my motivation as a climber. Yes, I focused on 8,000ers, but Endeavor 8000, as I christened my "project," was strictly a personal quest. If some other American or Englishman had "beaten me" to the fourteenth, that would have been fine with me.

That said, there are episodes in mountaineering history that can be seen only as fiercely competitive. Perhaps the most famous (or the most notorious) was the race for the summit of the Matterhorn, which culminated in 1865, when a team led by the great English climber Edward Whymper, on his eighth attempt, surged up the formidable peak by the northeast ridge, while another team led by the Italian guide Jean-Antoine Carrel—Whymper's former partner, now his chief rival—stormed the opposite southwest ridge. When Whymper reached the top on July 14, his men were so overjoyed that they rolled rocks down the other side to lord their victory over Carrel's party below. Only hours later, Whymper's triumph turned to ashes as a man slipped, the rope broke, and four of the team of seven fell to their deaths.

By the end of 1984, after Loretan and Joos completed their landmark traverse of Annapurna, there was no getting around the fact that a race was on to become the first climber to top out on all fourteen 8,000ers. Reinhold Messner was well in the lead, with ten summits to his credit, but Loretan's close friend and partner Marcel Rüedi, the Pole Jerzy Kukuczka, the German Michl Dacher, and Loretan himself had six apiece. Publicly all five men disavowed the competition. Rüedi died on Makalu in 1986; Loretan interrupted his campaign on the 8,000ers while he tackled severe technical challenges in the Alps and on such sub-8,000ers as Nameless Tower in Pakistan; but Dacher (Messner's teammate on several 8,000ers) and Kukuczka plugged on.

Thanks to his incredibly dogged determination, Kukuczka almost caught up with Messner. But the famous mountaineer from the South Tyrol closed out the race on Lhotse in October 1986.

Only a year later, Kukuczka claimed second place by topping out on Shishapangma. (For the details of that rivalry, and of Messner's and Kukuczka's own brilliant performances on Annapurna, see chapter 6.)

Surprisingly, eight more years would pass without another mountaineer completing the cycle of the fourteen 8,000ers. By the end of 1994, Loretan had topped out on twelve of them, lacking only Shishapangma and Kangchenjunga. Another climber, the Frenchman Benoît Chamoux, also had twelve: only Makalu and Kangchenjunga had eluded him. Chamoux was a strong climber capable of dazzling feats, such as his solo ascent of the Abruzzi Ridge on K2 in only twenty-three hours in 1986. But his career was also dogged by controversy. Elizabeth Hawley, the Kathmandu-based arbiter of all Himalayan achievements, refused to recognize Chamoux's claim to have gone to the top of Shishapangma, since she was convinced he had stopped on a subsidiary summit. (Chamoux's ascent of the world's fourteenth highest peak is not the only one that that grande dame has called into question, listing it officially as "disputed.")

That mountain's a kind of booby trap for 8,000er aspirants. In 1993, I'd reached the central summit, only 100 yards away from the main summit and a piddling 20 feet lower. The heavily corniced knife-edge ridge between the two peaks, however, seemed far too dangerous for me to traverse solo. I turned back.

It would have been tempting to claim an ascent of Shisha, but I wouldn't have been able to live with myself if I had, and besides, Miss Hawley (as everybody calls her) would have called my bluff. Instead, I had to wait eight years to return to Shishapangma and climb the mountain all over again, finally knocking off that scary knife edge to the true summit.

In *Les 8000 Rugissants,* Loretan admits to his own ambivalence about trying to become the third climber to "close the loop" (as the French quaintly call nabbing the fourteen highest peaks).

"I would be lying," he writes, "if I said that the race for the fourteen 8,000ers never interested me. But for a long time I relegated it to the brouhaha of the media." Once Messner had succeeded, Loretan believed, the race was over. "I could not imagine," he comments, "that, eight years after Kukuczka, nine years after Messner, there was anyone on the planet—except for my brother and my mom—who could care about the third man to claim the fourteen 8,000ers."

If he had still been obsessed with the highest peaks, Loretan points out, he would not have gone off to Nameless Tower or tried K2 twice by the unclimbed west face, after having already climbed K2 by the Abruzzi Ridge in 1985.

But then, as he puts it, "I started accumulating 8,000ers, and I let myself subtly get won over by the idea." Once Chamoux had accumulated his own roster of high peaks, the media turned out to be very interested in the race for third place. In the spring of 1995, Loretan climbed Shishapangma. Five years earlier, with Jean Troillet and the strong Polish climber Wojtek Kurtyka, Loretan had put up a new route on the southwest face of the mountain. This was a major achievement, but, as I had in 1993, that trio turned back just short of the true summit because they considered the short knife-edge ridge leading from the central summit to the top too exposed. Loretan returned in 1995 just to make sure he could honestly count Shisha on his tick list of 8,000ers.

That spring, Chamoux got to the summit of Makalu. Whatever he had actually accomplished on Shishapangma in 1990, he made no bones about including it on his résumé. As far as the media were concerned, both men now had thirteen 8,000ers to their credit. And to give the race a Hollywood climax, Loretan and Chamoux would attempt their last summit, Kangchenjunga, simultaneously in the fall of 1995.

I met Chamoux in the spring of 1995, as he was coming down from Makalu, and we—Veikka Gustafsson, Rob Hall, and I—were heading up to it. Chamoux had arranged to split the cost of a helicopter with Rob: the plan was for us to fly in on the same chopper that the French team would fly out on. But as it turned out, because of bad weather, we had to land much lower than the place Chamoux and Hall had determined for a rendezvous. This wasn't anyone's fault—certainly not Rob's.

We met Chamoux as we were hiking to advance base camp. His team had lost a man on the mountain, so they weren't in a good frame of mind anyway, but now Chamoux was really pissed. We noticed that he had a bit of an attitude: "You were supposed to pick us up!" he said, or something to that effect.

As the autumn of 1995 approached, Loretan insisted that he entered the race to become the "third man" with a feeling of disgust:

> I've always found [the movie] *Top Gun* pitiful. I detest the sort of competition that grants victory to a simple addition of petty deeds. And also, since the conquest of the Matterhorn, the mountain has made it very clear to us that she doesn't like competition: she believes she's placed the bar high enough without humans having to add a stopwatch [to the proceedings].

Nevertheless, on September 1, 1995, Loretan's team established its base camp on the south side of Kangchenjunga. Ten days later, Chamoux arrived with a considerable entourage and set up his team's tents in close proximity to his rival's. Loretan had slipped under the media radar, but Chamoux had courted journalists for months beforehand. Now there were reporters at base camp hanging on his every word, and his partner, Pierre Royer, was charged with making a film about Chamoux's triumphant march to the summit of his fourteenth 8,000er. The French camp was a true media circus, with radio, TV, telephones, and the Internet keeping a huge public back in France up to date on the goings on.

Between Swiss and French alpinists, there had been for decades a sometimes bitter competition. After the first ascent of Annapurna in 1950, a small coterie of Swiss mountaineers (and only the Swiss) raised doubts about whether Herzog and Lachenal had reached the true summit.

In his memoir, Loretan exudes contempt for the media-driven "race" between Chamoux and himself:

> I was not going to play Knights of the Himalaya, I was not going to say that the competition was the concern only of mediocrities, I was not going to shout as I offered my white undershirt to the balls of my enemy, "Messieurs the French, fire first!" I was going to say only that if Benoît Chamoux dearly wanted to enter history as the third person to succeed on the fourteen 8,000ers, he should go for it! Good for him!

Loretan, in fact, was less interested in getting to the summit of Kangchenjunga than in attempting the first traverse of the mountain. It was only after September 20, when some Italians who had reconnoitered other parts of the mountain told Loretan that a traverse was unthinkable on account of snow conditions, that he lowered his ambition to a simple ascent.

> It was around that date that I understood that Benoît Chamoux was absolutely determined to beat me to the top. A tent is always poorly sound-proofed, and I didn't have to strain my ears to capture a conversation between Chamoux and some journalists [at base camp]. Sometimes I had the impression that Chamoux was sending his troops off to battle: Sunday the 24th of September, for example, his Sherpas set out for Camp III (7300 meters [23,950 feet]) even though the slopes were far from stable.

If Loretan is right about this business, it's a bit disturbing. I'm surprised that someone of Chamoux's caliber would have sent the Sherpa into the lead, especially when conditions were dangerous. As a team, Veikka and I never climbed with Sherpa, but if we had, we certainly wouldn't have thrust them into the role of breaking trail and establishing camps.

At base camp, relations between the Swiss team and the French were abysmal. As Loretan recalled, "Between the French expedition and ours, the ambiance was never cordial; it was even glacial. And I did nothing to thaw it. The competition was palpable, it thickened the atmosphere and made the air unbreathable."

By September 20, Loretan was ready to go for the summit, but bad weather forestalled him for more than ten days, as almost twenty inches of snow fell at base camp. Both teams knew the conditions up high were likely to be atrocious.

On October 3, Loretan, Jean Troillet, and André Georges headed up to the Swiss Camp III, which they had established two weeks earlier. "The snow was very deep," writes Loretan, "and I exhausted myself plowing a track." At Camp III, the men found their tents completely buried: "I needed the skills of an archaeologist to bring the camp back into view."

Chamoux and Royer, along with four Sherpa hired by the French team and five Italians, followed Loretan's track to Camp III. Now all the climbers hunkered down in "a village of ten tents," as a violent wind blasted the slopes. The plan was to head out in the middle of the night, establish a Camp IV during the day, and then go for the top on the following day. The Swiss decided to start at 6:00 P.M.; the Italians and the French at 2:00 A.M. Loretan and his partners got off on schedule, but the slopes, which they attacked first with snowshoes, then with crampons, were in terrible condition. Both Georges and Troillet were wasted, so Loretan broke trail all the way, but after two hours of climbing, the men agreed their pace was far too slow. They turned around and headed down. At

Camp III, they found that none of the others had even emerged from their tents.

Among all thirty-one of my expeditions to 8,000-meter peaks, I've climbed only three times in the autumn—on an attempt on Everest's east face in 1988 and on Cho Oyu in 1994 and 1996. In general, I prefer not to. It's a dubious trade-off: after the summer monsoon, the mountains tend to be less technical, because they're blanketed in snow, but that in turn increases the risk of avalanches. In the spring, more hard ice and rock are exposed, making the climbing more technical, but the risk of avalanches is drastically reduced. The biggest difference, however, is that in the spring, by the time you get high, it's usually May and the temperatures are warming up. In the fall, you don't get high until October, as the days grow shorter and colder, with winter just around the corner. For me, the trade-off has generally not been worth it.

On October 4 the whole "caravan" (as Loretan calls it) of fourteen climbers moved out together and succeeded in establishing a Camp IV at 25,600 feet, about 2,500 feet below the summit. (I can only imagine the tension of that day, as Chamoux and Loretan pretended to be teammates contributing to a group effort.) By now André Georges was completely done in. The Swiss summit team was reduced to Loretan and Troillet. Determined once again to make a very early start—in this respect, Loretan was ahead of his time—the Swiss planned a 10:00 P.M. departure. The jockeying among the climbers assembled at Camp IV was superficially polite. Writes Loretan, "Around 2:00 P.M., Benoît Chamoux asked us when we planned to leave. He thought that at 10:00 P.M. the cold would be too intense. We agreed instead to leave at 2:00 A.M." With everyone sharing the job of breaking trail, Loretan thought, the burden would be less onerous.

But it didn't work out that way. On October 5, Loretan, Troillet, and the strong Italian climber Sergio Martini (who had previously climbed ten 8,000ers) did all the trailbreaking. Loretan does not hide his annoyance: "The snow was deep, the effort painful. Very soon we noticed that the French were leaving all the hard work to us." The three trailbreakers decided to stop and wait for Chamoux and Royer to catch up. "It took them an enormous amount of time to reach our height," writes Loretan, with ill-concealed disgust, "but very little to make way for us, giving us back the pleasure of breaking trail."

I had a similar experience on Everest in 1996, as we made the IMAX film directed by David Breashears. During my push to the summit on May 23, I started out early and alone, as we had planned. But as I plowed my way through deep snow hour after hour, breaking trail without supplemental oxygen, I became aware of two foreign climbers pursuing me at a certain distance. Following in my tracks, they had caught up with me, but now they seemed to want to preserve our spacing, rather than join me and share the burden of kicking steps. When I stopped for a break, they stopped. When I advanced, so did they, at exactly the same pace as mine. Finally I gestured to them to catch up and help out with the trailbreaking, but they simply shook their heads. This pissed me off so much that it actually gave me additional strength and motivation to labor on by myself.

In 1995, outside observers of the race on Kangchenjunga later concluded that the Swiss were simply in far better shape than the French. Even one of Chamoux's teammates told Elizabeth Hawley, "The Swiss were much faster. Loretan is the best."

At this point the climbers learned via radio of an accident lower on the mountain. Riku, a Sherpa working for the French team, had lost his balance and fallen to his death. At once the two Sherpa climbing with Chamoux and Royer abandoned the summit push and hurried down the mountain. But the two Frenchmen headed on—making a decision for which they would later be harshly criticized. The Sherpa was already dead, so Chamoux and Royer could not save him. That was their dilemma: keep going up or turn around and go down?

To reach the summit, as Loretan had seen weeks before through a telescope, the men would have to find a way around a high pillar that he called the Tour Rouge (the Red Tower). Four years earlier, Sergio Martini had failed on an attempt to bypass that same tower, despite an all-out effort. Now, convinced that the Tour Rouge could not be circumnavigated, and that the cold and wind made it too dangerous to wait while the Swiss attempted to lead the tricky traverse, Martini turned around at 26,900 feet and descended. Loretan and Troillet pushed on alone.

Fighting against strong winds and severely cold temperatures, the Swiss pair closed in on the summit in early afternoon. Wrote Loretan later, "I hoisted myself to the top, my fourteenth summit of more than 8,000 meters. It was 2:35 P.M., the loop was closed. My feelings were strong and profound. A chapter was closed—sorry for Chamoux."

On the way down, below the Tour Rouge, Loretan and Troillet passed within a few dozen meters of Chamoux and Royer, still headed up. The rivals exchanged waves of the hand. A little later, Troillet got on the radio to offer Chamoux route-finding advice. Chamoux signed off, "Thank you, Jean." "Two words of gratitude," Loretan comments, "to close off weeks of unseemly rivalry."

Yet even as he descended, Loretan wondered if there was something wrong with Chamoux. "It didn't seem possible," he writes, "that a man who had made his reputation for speed ascents could be moving so slowly." Perhaps he was suffering from edema, or perhaps the cold—according to Loretan, on summit day the Italians reported a windchill factor of minus 63 degrees Centigrade—had taken the stuffing out of him.

Late that day, the climbers lower on the mountain learned by radio that Royer had given up and turned around. Chamoux continued solo, but turned back himself less than 200 feet below the summit. As night fell, however, there was no more radio contact with the two Frenchmen. It seemed inevitable that they had been forced to bivouac.

By the next day, Loretan was sure that Chamoux and Royer were dead. But the French team spent days holding out hope, and even managed to commandeer airplanes to make an aerial search. A huge public in Europe followed the drama with mingled horror and fascination.

According to Elizabeth Hawley, who interviewed members of both expeditions in Kathmandu afterward, the Sherpa on Chamoux and Royer's team "refused to go up to try to find them since they had done nothing to help Riku Sherpa when he had fallen." An unidentified American told Hawley, "The French were not well acclimatized. They tried to keep up with the Swiss and they killed themselves." To this day, the bodies of Chamoux and Royer have never been found.

Loretan thought that Chamoux and Royer might have fallen down the opposite or northern face of Kangchenjunga. But in *Les 8000 Rugissants* his final judgment is unsparing: "Upon reflection, I told myself that if the millions of spectators back home hadn't been living in real time through his weakening and then his defeat, perhaps Benoît Chamoux would have listened to his body and not to his pride."

Harsh words, I suppose, but to me they're right on. One of the worst mistakes you can make in the mountains is to let competition with other climbers (especially enhanced by on-the-spot media attention) trump your better judgment. Given the lateness of the day and the fatigue Chamoux and Royer were suffering from, they probably should have turned around and given up long before they did. Yet, in the final analysis, I hesitate to second-guess the Frenchmen. Who knows what went wrong up there on October 5, 1995, as Chamoux closed in on the goal of his lifetime?

I've seen this sort of competitive frenzy operate in similar ways on more than one expedition. You can call it "summit fever." A bunch of climbers from different teams will be hanging around a lower camp, while the weather looks unsettled. All at once, one team announces that it's going for it. And virtually everybody else scrambles to get ready and go themselves. Judgment flies out the window, replaced by the craven fear that others may know more than you do, and that you may miss out on the one golden opportunity to reach the summit.

After being shut down cold on the north side of Annapurna in 2000, I agonized over the next year and a half about how I might get up that dangerous mountain. I did as much research as I could on the other routes that had been pioneered on Annapurna. What I knew about the east ridge came mainly from Messner's slender history of the mountain. His six-page summary of Loretan and Joos's 1984 traverse made it clear just how bold a deed their ascent of the east ridge was, and how extended and vulnerable the two Swiss climbers found themselves during the descent. Messner hails Loretan in a passage that only intensified my curiosity about this unsung genius of mountaineering. Messner first met the "gaunt young man" at a Munich trade show in the early 1980s, when Loretan came up to the speaker's podium and asked him for Himalayan advice. Now, in 2000, Messner writes:

> Fifteen years later, this same Erhard Loretan is known as the most significant high-altitude mountaineer of his generation, but has faded forever into the background, vanishing from the scene in the same way that he appeared. Nowadays he is again pursuing his trade as a carpenter and hardly concerns himself at all with the mountaineering scene.

I had pretty much put the east ridge into my "file and forget" drawer when I ran into a French climber named Christian Trommsdorff in a small Tibetan village on my way to Shishapangma in 2001. He'd been on the east ridge in 2000, and though he'd failed to reach the summit, he was convinced that the ridge, despite being incredibly long and exposed to high winds, might be the only safe route on the mountain. Veikka and I reread Messner's account, stared at all the pictures we could find, and decided to launch an expedition for the spring of 2002.

In *No Shortcuts to the Top,* I recount my second expedition to Annapurna in considerable detail. Yet once again, another five years of hindsight and a rereading of my diary give me a new understanding of what went on that spring on the east ridge.

At the Outdoor Retailer trade show in Salt Lake City in the summer of 2001, I mentioned my plans to Bruce Franks, the general manager of Asolo Footwear, which was one of my sponsors. Bruce told me about another Asolo-sponsored athlete, Frenchman Jean-Christophe Lafaille, who had similar ideas about Annapurna and was also seeking partners. Bruce introduced us to each other by e-mail, and in that fashion, through a process I'd never before attempted—I likened it to computer dating—Veikka and I teamed up with a climber I'd never met. In Jean-Christophe Lafaille, I would discover one of the best partners of my mountaineering career.

Once we got to base camp, we met up with another team, made up of four Basque climbers, also intent on the east ridge. We decided to join forces with them, but in the end only one of the four, Alberto Iñurrategi, would go high on the mountain. Alberto, too, made a splendid companion on the climb, and he and J.-C. teamed up for many of the hard leads. This despite a kind of linguistic impasse among us: the Basques, Veikka, and I spoke no French, J.-C. and Alberto only the most rudimentary English. I was able to communicate with J.-C. by speaking very slowly in a simplified English, and I could understand most of his conversation. But as a Finn, Veikka had English only as a second language. When J.-C.

spoke, Veikka was hearing a kind of Frenchified English; he'd have to turn to me again and again and ask, "What did J.-C. say?" I often had to interpret for J.-C. as well, when Veikka said something.

Alberto had already climbed thirteen 8,000ers. If he could get to the top of Annapurna, he would become only the tenth person to claim the summits of all fourteen, and only the fourth to do so without supplemental oxygen. (Sergio Martini, who turned back on Kangchenjunga as Loretan and Troillet pushed on, became the seventh to "close the loop," in 2000.) What was even more poignant was that Alberto planned to dedicate his ascent of Annapurna, if successful, to his brother Felix, who had died on Gasherbrum II in 2000. He planned to carry Felix's ice ax on the climb.

Alberto thus had plenty of motivation to climb Annapurna. But for J.-C., the mountain had become an obsession. It was a word he unabashedly used when he talked about Annapurna.

In 1992, at the age of twenty-seven, J.-C. had gone on his first Himalayan expedition. His only partner was his best climbing friend and mentor Pierre Béghin, who was fourteen years older. At the time, Béghin was probably the outstanding alpinist in France. His superb record included many of the hardest faces in the Alps, and he had already been on twelve expeditions to 8,000-meter peaks, succeeding in reaching the summits of five. Those triumphs included a new route on the west face of Manaslu, a solo ascent of Kangchenjunga, and—perhaps most impressive of all—a direct new route solo on the south face of Makalu, during which Béghin survived a bivouac above 26,000 feet and two avalanches that he set off on the descent. This despite having lost several toes to frostbite on his first Himalayan expedition, on Manaslu in 1977!

For his 1992 campaign, Béghin had talked J.-C. into trying a new route on the south face of Annapurna. When we walked beneath that face on our approach to the east ridge a decade later, and J.-C. pointed out his and Béghin's line, I'll have to admit that it made me shudder. Instead of a protruding arête like the one Bonington's team followed in 1970, Béghin's route—several hundred yards to the right of Bonington's—climbed a series of extremely steep, unstable-looking snow flutings, then plunged into a crease-like gully of mixed rock and ice that looked like a natural funnel for avalanches and falling rocks coming from above.

Not only did the two Frenchmen plan to climb the face without teammate or Sherpa support, but they also insisted on tackling the huge wall alpine style, with almost no fixed ropes and no stocked tent camps. But the pair performed so brilliantly that by October 10 they had reached 24,000 feet, having climbed more than three-quarters of the face. There, however, they were forced to bivouac half-standing, hanging from their waist harnesses, anchored to a seventy-degree slope. They spent a sleepless night, but pushed on the next day, gaining 600 more feet, only to have a violent storm overtake them. Descent was their only option.

Since Lafaille and Béghin had carried a minimum of hardware, they had to ration their cams, pitons, and ice screws to set up rappels on ground too steep and difficult to downclimb. Typically, they used only a single "piece" as anchor on each rappel. (Anchors, by definition, are gear you have to leave behind.) On one pitch, Béghin rapped off an ice screw he hadn't been able to twist all the way home. Horrified, J.-C. sacrificed one of his ice tools to back up the anchor, planting the pick in the snow and attaching it to the screw with a nylon sling.

The two men had almost reached the bottom end of the crease-like groove—the crux of the whole route—when Béghin placed a large cam, called a "Friend," in a crack in the rock. Lafaille had doubled the anchor with a backup piton, but as Béghin got on rappel, he said, "Take out the piton. My Friend is good." J.-C. complied.

Béghin scuttled backward down several meters of snow, then fully weighted the rope as he passed onto vertical terrain. He looked up. He and J.-C. traded glances. Then all at once, there was a clattering sound. The Friend had popped loose. Before J.-C.'s eyes, Béghin plunged into the abyss.

"It was a long time before I could move," J.-C. later recalled. "Maybe half an hour. I was petrified with fear and despair."

Since the ropes and hardware had disappeared with Béghin, Lafaille was trapped in an almost impossible predicament. To survive, he would somehow have to get himself down 8,000 feet of highly technical terrain without a rope to use to rappel. The ordeal he endured during the next several days would eventually become one of the most amazing self-rescues in mountaineering history.

With infinite care, J.-C. downclimbed the 700-foot vertical cliff immediately below the failed anchor, using only two ice tools (his and Béghin's) and his crampons to keep himself attached to the mountain. After another sleepless bivouac on a small ledge, he was able to scavenge a 65-foot hank of fixed rope. With that pitifully short lifeline, he fashioned a series of makeshift rappels. For anchors, he used tent pegs and, on one rappel, a plastic bottle buried in the snow!

On the second day, a falling rock shattered his right arm in a compound fracture. Racked with pain, in danger of bleeding to death, his arm useless, J.-C. almost succumbed to his despair. *It's finished for me,* he thought. *I'm dead.*

Yet after fashioning a splint with his jacket and surviving another grim bivouac, he pushed on down, choosing to climb through the night in the hope of minimizing the risk of rockfall.

By the time he got off the wall and dragged himself across the glacier to the base camp of a Slovene expedition, J.-C. had lived through five days of terror, pain, and grief as he pulled off the astounding solo descent.

Upon his return to France, Lafaille was treated as a hero, even while the public mourned the loss of Béghin. But J.-C. was shattered by his ordeal. As he later told a journalist, "I closed up like an oyster."

At first he resolved to give up climbing for good. The psychological toll of what he had gone through cost him his marriage and a number of close friendships. In his wounded retreat, he felt as though he could trust no one. He eventually underwent numerous operations on his broken arm. At a loss for what to do next in life, he started walking, then scrambling, around the hills near his hometown of Gap. Within two years he was climbing well again. Slowly his guilt and depression about the loss of his partner coalesced in a fiery new passion: revenge. Revenge on the mountain that had killed his best friend. (Like *obsession, revenge* was a word J.-C. did not hesitate to use.)

For me, revenge and obsession have nothing to do with my motivation as a climber. The very concept of those mental states strikes me as dangerous, an invitation to push beyond reasonable limits. But I'm wired differently from climbers such as J.-C. Among all the partners I would have on 8,000-meter peaks, J.-C. was probably the most gifted mountaineer with whom I ever roped up. As I would come to see on Annapurna, he also was willing to accept a much narrower margin of safety than I was ever comfortable with. But he was a genius at calculating risk, and with his extraordinary talent as a climber, he pulled off one amazing exploit after another.

In 1995, only three years after his tragedy with Béghin, J.-C. returned to Annapurna to enact his revenge on the mountain. It took the form of an attempt to climb the Bonington route solo. Thanks to his brilliance on technical terrain, he reached 24,600 feet (halfway up the crux wall the Brits had called the Rock Band)—the same height at which he and Béghin were stopped in 1992. Then, prudently, he turned back in the face of bad snow conditions and deteriorating weather.

He returned in 1998 with an Italian team to try the Bonington route once more. But he was disappointed by the overcautious tactics of the team, whose members chose to deploy an old-fashioned expedition-style attack with continuous fixed ropes and well-stocked camps. Bad snow conditions stalled the climbers' progress, with abnormally deep drifts camouflaging the rock beneath. On April 25, J.-C. was leading up the route, half an hour ahead of his teammates, planning to place the last fixed ropes below the first camp on the face proper, and was barely aware of the catastrophe that was suddenly unfolding below him.

A huge windslab had broken loose, jolting three of the Italians, who barely kept their purchase on the mountain. As the slab plunged farther down the route, it tore loose pitons and fixed ropes and crashed into four Sherpa who were bringing up loads. The men were hurtled nearly 3,000 feet down the face. One Sherpa was killed, while two were badly injured; only through the heroic effort of the fourth were those two able to regain base camp.

Two days later a Russian helicopter picked up the injured Sherpa. The Italians were too shaken by the accident to continue their attempt. And J.-C. was ready to throw in the towel as well.

After this debacle, he momentarily decided to abandon Annapurna altogether. As he wrote at the time, "After the terrible accident of April 25, it was clear to me that I would never return to the south face. Two deaths on this mountain, that was too much!"

Meanwhile, however, he had fallen in love with Katia, a striking blonde who was a professional cyclist and a pretty good climber herself. They were married in 2000. Almost at once, Katia took upon herself the job of managing J.-C.'s career. He had always been a private man, with little interest in tooting his own horn, but now Katia single-handedly turned him into a media celebrity. And she convinced him that the best career move he could make would be to become the first Frenchman to climb all fourteen 8,000ers. (To this day, no French climber has "closed the loop," even though three South Koreans, three Italians, three Poles, and a climber each from Kazakhstan, Mexico, and Finland have.)

Of course, Katia alone could not have pushed her husband back onto Annapurna. J.-C. was assertive enough to make his own decisions, and he had his own deeply personal goals. The obsession with Annapurna never died; it merely lay dormant. More than once, J.-C. told journalists, "I would trade ten 8,000ers for ten minutes on top of Annapurna."

And he never stopped brooding about Pierre Béghin. His first mentor had been a kind of mountaineering poet, in the mold of Gaston Rébuffat, the great Chamonix guide on the team that first climbed Annapurna in 1950. Béghin had a gift for the pithy aphorism, and many of his sayings were lodged permanently in J.-C.'s memory. Eleven years after Béghin's death, in his own climbing memoir, tellingly titled *Prisonnier de l'Annapurna* (Prisoner of Annapurna), J.-C. recited some of his friend's pronouncements. They included "Daily life drives me crazy. I don't find enough salt in it," and "I have this anxiety about time passing and slipping through my fingers." J.-C.'s favorite mantra from Béghin, which he quoted in its entirety in *Prisonnier,* amounts to a romantic credo explicating the man's love-hate relationship with mountaineering:

> Up high, at the same time I taste exaltation and fear. Exaltation, because I have the feeling of dominating the whole world. Of having traversed hundreds, even thousands of vertical meters, and of dominating this light world, with its seas of clouds, its somber valleys. But at the same time, there is this fear, even this terror. I truly have the feeling of being very far away from everything, in an extremely precarious situation. Of being very far from my bases in life. Of being lost at the end of the world—at the top of the world. Of not being able even to imagine how to find the way back.

By the early spring of 2002, J.-C. and I had agreed to go to the south side of Annapurna, to attempt the east ridge together. It would be my second campaign on the peak in three years. It would be J.-C.'s fourth, stretching across a decade. If ever a man was determined to get up a mountain and lay to rest his personal ghosts, J.-C. was that man.

In *No Shortcuts to the Top,* I write that I was completely surprised and shocked to learn afterward (through a friend who translated passages from *Prisonnier* for me) that during our 2002 expedition, J.-C. harbored a secret fantasy to join forces with the rest of us only during the early stages, then break away to attempt a solo ascent of the 1992 route on the south face where Béghin was killed. But now, on rereading my diary and sifting through my memories, I remember that as we passed beneath the south face, J.-C. kept looking up at that line as he vaguely remarked, in his broken English, "I'm having thoughts of going over there." It was nothing definite—just a kind of musing: "I'm thinking of this other idea . . ."

Maybe I didn't take that musing seriously at the time. I do recall that J.-C. actually mentioned the possibility of splitting off from the rest of us and attempting a line up the south face solo. He wanted to contribute to the east ridge effort as much as possible, acclimatize, and then do his thing alone. In the end, it didn't matter, because he eventually gave up the idea of trying the 1992 line solo. The east ridge, he came to realize, was so intense that he felt it was a worthy goal.

As for me, on rereading my diary, I realize that I was in a constant state of tension during that expedition. By now Paula and I had two children, since Ella had been born in 2000, and I really missed my family. The diary is full of comments such as "Stayed up til 9 P.M. to call Paula & kids [on our sat phone]. All sounds well—they got the postcards," and, "*Can't wait to get home!!*"

By the spring of 2002, I was forty-two years old. This was my twenty-sixth expedition to an 8,000-meter peak. I'd reached the summit of eleven of them, leaving only Broad Peak, Nanga Parbat, and Annapurna to complete my Endeavor 8000. I knew already that if a single mountain was likely to thwart my best efforts, it would be Annapurna. My anxiety about the mountain was based not only on my setback on the north face in 2000, with all the risks that we encountered, but also on reading and hearing about other teams' efforts there. Annapurna was not to be taken lightly.

During my early years in the Himalaya, going off on an expedition wasn't such an emotionally wrenching transition. I wasn't leaving behind anybody who mattered to me more than any mountain, or who I knew would worry about me every single day that I was gone. But after I married Paula in 1996, and especially after we had children, leaving home became the hardest part of going on an expedition.

Paula and I decided that saying our last farewells at the airport was not the best way to make the break. Sometimes Gil and Ella wouldn't even come to the airport, or they'd stay in their car seats while Paula dropped me off. Instead, we'd have a nice dinner the night before. We'd say our I-love-yous and good-byes that evening, in the privacy of our home. Even so, it was tough. Gil was very attached, and he'd always get emotional. Ella would be tearful, but once I was gone, everything would seem to be fine for her. Ella tends to keep her emotions in check, whereas Gil wears them on his sleeve. It was actually hardest for me—leaving behind two beautiful kids, who were crying because of what I felt I had to do.

That's why the sat phone calls from the mountain were so important. Rereading my diary, I notice how often I mention those calls. Sometimes the entries are mere dutiful reminders: "I'll call Paula later and hopefully Gil & Ella," or "Called Paula right away—talked long time. Called 2xs [two times]. Updates on kids." But sometimes the entries reveal just how emotionally strung out I was: "*Really, really* miss Paula, Gil & Ella. I'd love to be home with them *right* now! Could be 20 more days til I get home—ugh!"

As much as I wanted to be back in Seattle, however, I never let it undercut my determination to give the mountain my best shot, or to stay as long as it took to have a chance for the summit. I'd seen other guys on expeditions lose all heart for their projects in midstream and start inventing rationalizations why they needed to get home early. It's a sore temptation, especially when camp life can be so full of drudgery and so uncomfortable, or when storms last so long you start to think you'll never get a chance to go for it. But if you let homesickness get the better of ambition, you've really lost the whole point of setting out on an adventure.

Sometimes I could quell the temptation by putting it in historical perspective. When great explorers such as Scott and Shackleton were trying to reach the South Pole, the men on their trips knew they would be as long as a year and a half in the cold and ice without being able to send or receive any news from home. Even earlier, in the mid-nineteenth century, as British sailors tried to force the Northwest Passage—the sea route to the Orient north of Canada and Alaska—parties could be gone as long as three or four years without any contact with their loved ones. That's hard to imagine. And somewhere I read about the mammoth Russian journey led by Vitus Bering, which made the European discovery of Alaska. His Great Northern Expedition lasted eleven years, from 1733 to 1743. Among the seventy-seven men aboard his farthest-ranging ship, only forty-six returned alive. Among the dead was Bering himself, who was buried on an uninhabited island off Kamchatka. (And we think we have it tough on a three-month expedition to the Himalaya!)

Once the other three Basques realized they were in over their heads, our climbing team was reduced to J.-C., Alberto, Veikka, and me. Through the last two weeks of April and the first week of May, we worked out a route to the crest of the east ridge. This involved some 6,000 feet of climbing up steep snow and ice slopes, with occasional "mixed" passages, fixing ropes and establishing a Camp II midway, near the summit of a subsidiary peak called Singu Chuli, then Camp III on the crest of the east ridge. We chose a route considerably to the left or west of the line Loretan and

Joos had pushed in 1984. I'm not sure, in fact, why they chose that line, for it looked more difficult than ours, was steeper overall, and required them to climb the subsidiary summit of Glacier Dome, whereas we were able to bypass Glacier Dome on the left.

It was J.-C. and Alberto who put in the crux pitches on that ascent. Climbing with the diminutive Frenchman—J.-C. stood only five feet two inches tall, so that Veikka nicknamed him the Hobbit—was a revelation. I'd always been in good enough shape so that I could keep up with the fastest of my teammates, and usually go faster than most of them. But I couldn't match J.-C.'s pace. As I wrote in my diary as early as April 18, "JC unbelievable as point man—go, go, go. Can't keep up!"

I was also impressed with the fact that both J.-C. and Alberto were so energetic and super-punctual. If we agreed to take off at 6:00 in the morning, they'd sometimes be out of the tent and moving at 5:30. This was a far cry from some of my previous teammates, who were often lethargic to a fault about getting going in the morning. In my diary on April 16, I wrote, "I am amazed at how anti-slacker these guys are. No dilly-dally, no rest. They've already packed for tomorrow & they're rarin' to go."

Before 2002, Veikka had been my teammate on eight expeditions to 8,000ers. He'd become my partner of choice, and I knew that I could always count on him to pull his share of the weight, to climb as well as I did, to pay his half of our costs, and to share the grubby chores of expedition life. But something was different this spring. Veikka wasn't performing like his usual self.

A series of relatively trivial acts on his part started to get on my nerves. I thought he was simply being lazy, but instead of asking, "Veikka, what's wrong?" I kept it all inside. That's one of my faults: I'm too nonconfrontational, I never verbalize my complaints. Instead, I took it out on my partner in my diary. Poor Veikka! When I look back on what I wrote about him that spring, I cringe—especially in light of what we learned after the expedition. Excerpts:

> Veikka offered to make platform [in the snow] if I erected tent—OK. He did a shitty job with platform. We put up tent, got inside—sloping, uneven, not big enough. I was a bit steamed—make a decent base!
>
> No cooking for breakfast although I made a pot of water last night that VG could have melted (it was his turn) as we dressed to fill our water bottles—it just did not register & I kept my mouth shut.
>
> Just as we got to CI [Camp I] yesterday I melted lots of water, filled all bottles & pots—Veikka lounged. He made no move later @ dinner to do anything, so neither did I. . . . I could've heated something up but didn't feel like accommodating VG as well so I skipped it. Maybe I'm making a big deal out of it but it peeved me anyway—but of course I did not say anything.
>
> VG makes no move to get out of his bag—his warm gear is at CII so he needs to stay in bag to stay warm! So I make the move to get the stove going, while baby bird stays snug in his bag.

The most alarming performance by Veikka that spring came one day when he descended from Camp II to Camp I by himself to bring up a load. He's normally a great route finder, but on the way back up he became temporarily lost. It took him hours to reorient himself and find the route, and by the time he stumbled up to Camp II, he was dangerously close to hypothermia.

Why couldn't I simply have asked Veikka what was wrong? The fact was, however, that he didn't know himself what was causing his weak performance. The truth came to light only a few years later, when I asked him about this business as I was writing *No*

Shortcuts to the Top. Only months after our 2002 expedition, when he underwent a thorough physical exam, did a doctor tell him he had a serious case of anemia. Veikka didn't believe it. "There's no way that I have anemia!" he insisted. "I'm a mountain climber."

Eventually the doctor deduced that Veikka had acquired hookworm on a New Guinea trek the summer before. On Annapurna the next spring, he was certainly not being lazy—instead, worms inside his body were attaching themselves to his intestines and gorging on his blood. It's amazing that with that kind of anemia ravaging his system, Veikka performed as well as he did. On the telephone years later, as he recounted this medical melodrama, we could finally laugh about the whole business instead of nursing the tensions it produced in 2002.

In May a pattern began to form, with J.-C. doing most of the leading on our route. In part that was because he was so fast and so technically gifted. But temperamentally it seemed he *had* to be out in front. For him it was almost a case of lead or don't go. In his memoir, J.-C. admits that after Béghin's death and the ordeal of his recovery, "It took me a long time to trust anybody." It may be that in 2002 he could trust only the anchors that he himself placed and the ropes he fixed.

Camp III, which we'd pitched on the crest of the east ridge at 23,000 feet, was sheltered by a small ice cliff that blocked much of the wind. As we stood there and looked west along the ridge, the seriousness of our route came home to me. We were four miles east of the summit. Four miles isn't a great distance if you're plodding through the lowlands or up a glacier. But on a ridge above 23,000 feet, it's a monstrous gauntlet, knife-edged most of the way, and constantly exposed to winds that could approach gale force. None of the four of us had ever before faced such a challenge, for the simple reason that there are virtually no ridges so long and so continuously high anywhere in the Himalaya or the Karakoram. The only thing comparable that I can think of is the ridge connecting the five summits of Kangchenjunga.

One thing we had firmly agreed upon beforehand: no matter what, we would not descend the north face, as Loretan and Joos had in 1984. To me, such an option seemed tantamount to suicide. Since we were laboring under the conviction that a pair of irreversible rappels the Swiss made descending from the central summit to the final col had cut them off from any hope of returning along the east ridge, we made sure to bring enough rope to leave in place on those rappels, so that we could use our ascenders to get back up them.

Alberto, who had a sly sense of humor, joked that he was carrying a few rupees in his pocket, just in case he was forced to descend by the north face, hike out to some village, and buy his way back to Kathmandu. But none of us seriously entertained the thought of repeating Loretan and Joos's traverse. Now that I've learned that those two superb mountaineers planned the traverse from the start, I'm all the more in awe of their achievement.

After a return to base camp for some brief R&R, we set off all four up the route. From Camp II, I made another call to Paula, getting news about the kids, and trying to keep the uncertainty and anxiety about the route out of my voice. In my diary, however, I wrote, "Hope we have decent snow or it's gonna be a bitch!"

On May 13 we got off at 6:00 A.M. on a perfect day. Even so, the 4,000-foot push up to Camp III and onward to our Camp IV on the east ridge, carrying heavy loads and trudging through ankle-deep snow, was "a hump," as I put it in my diary—"like Camp Muir to summit [on Mount Rainier]—ugh!!" I added, "Did not feel all that strong today," although I was able to keep up with the others. Once more, Veikka dragged behind.

The next day, still benefiting from great weather, we pushed along the east ridge, as we planned to go alpine style the rest of the way to the summit. Once again Alberto and J.-C. left camp earlier than our predetermined departure time, as I scrambled to get out myself. Veikka was a bit slower, following some minutes behind. All day J.-C. and Alberto broke trail, and again, to my chagrin, I could not catch up with them. Although we traversed a considerable distance along the ridge, we had gained only four hundred feet of altitude.

In midmorning I halted on the saddle just before the sharp fang of rock and ice named Roc Noir, as I waited for Veikka to join me. With growing apprehension, I watched J.-C. and Alberto push on up the steep snow face on the south side of the fang. As I wrote that evening in my diary,

> Started getting the heebie-jeebies. . . . Deep snow on the face—not good. This is when I start questioning everything—beyond this point I am stepping over the line. The 800-foot face itself seems dangerous, let alone the ridge beyond. Now my conservative side takes control & tells me to quit, go down now. Maybe we could get up, but what about coming back—w/ more snow, tired, bad weather?? That starts to freak me out and I lose it.

As I waited for Veikka to catch up, my gaze was riveted on J.-C. and Alberto above me and to the left. J.-C. was leading, as usual, plowing through snow that was sometimes thigh-deep. Some forty feet behind him, Alberto placed his feet with great care in the steps his partner had kicked in the steep slope. The Basque and the Frenchman could converse only in their limited English, and now I heard J.-C. call out, "Be careful! It's bad snow and bad condition!" There was urgency, even a strain, in J.-C.'s voice that I hadn't heard before.

To bypass Roc Noir, J.-C. had traversed left, rounded a crevasse, then headed straight up to regain the crest. But the slope was angled at fully 45 degrees, and below the soft snow, J.-C.'s crampons scraped on rotten bedrock. The whole slope looked to me as though it was ready to avalanche at any moment.

Even before Veikka came along, I decided to start the traverse. I got 50 feet out, but with each step a darker sense of dread settled over me. Some part of my brain was trying to shout to me: *You shouldn't feel this way! This goes against everything you believe about climbing safely!*

I gave up the traverse, turned around, and made my way back to the relatively safe stance from which I'd started watching J.-C. and Alberto push ahead. Finally Veikka came along. He urged me to give the traverse another go. But 50 feet out, I felt the same overwhelming doubts. I turned around again, telling Veikka, "This just doesn't feel right." He nodded in agreement.

We decided to wait until J.-C. and Alberto were out of range, so that there would be no danger of their knocking loose big balls or slabs of snow that could hit us climbing below them. But as we lingered, the day grew warmer, and the slope seemed even more avalanche-prone than before.

Finally we decided to pitch a tent and wait for night and colder, safer conditions. Once we got inside our sleeping bags and began to discuss our options, however, the tension of our predicament only escalated. I wrote in my diary,

> I was way stressed thinking about having to go up the slope and further—my heart wasn't into it. VG was having some trepidations as well. Then snow in afternoon to add to our fears. Finally @ 2 or so J.-C. called [via radio] from the ridge. Said the slope even w/ rope was bad & immediately over Roc Noir summit was a steep hard ice traverse. This was really stretching our safety to do this & have to retreat later as well.

I realized that I was in a situation I had never before faced on any of my previous twenty-five expeditions to 8,000ers. Never before had I been on the verge of turning back when any of my teammates was determined to go on. But at the same time the dilemma brought home vivid memories of the comparable predicament I'd faced on K2, exactly a decade earlier. There, on summit day, as a storm gathered around us and heavy snow began to fall, I was haunted by the conviction that what we should do is turn back at once and descend. My partners, Charley Mace and Scott Fischer, had no such qualms—they were all for bombing ahead toward the summit. And I went with them, out of a peculiar kind of inertia: minute by minute, hour by hour, I put off making a decision, and thus, by default, decided to go with them.

We reached the top of K2, but on the descent to our high camp I was convinced that we were about to be avalanched to our deaths. When we got away with it, regaining camp without an accident, I felt relief, but absolutely no gratification. I knew that I had made the biggest mistake of my climbing life, and I vowed then and there never to make the same mistake again.

It was the lesson of K2 that now gave me the guts to make a really hard decision on Annapurna. The terrible snow conditions on Roc Noir had pushed the needle on my personal risk meter into the red zone. I recorded that decision in my diary: "We both agonized but finally after hours of silence knew we would go *down*. Once that decision was made I was overcome w/ relief—we both were. The route is just too long & the safety margin gets thinner & thinner."

While we spent the night in our Camp IV at 23,400 feet, J.-C. and Alberto had managed to pitch their own tent beyond Roc Noir. Despite the relief of having made our decision to retreat, I had a lot of trouble sleeping. I suppose a certain sense of defeat was nagging at me, even though rationally I was pretty sure I'd made the right decision. How would I ever climb Annapurna? This retreat meant that eventually I'd have to start all over again from scratch.

On top of Roc Noir, J.-C. had planted a single "willow wand," a stake of bamboo with a small ribbon attached to its head. Its ostensible purpose was simply to mark the return route, but for him it had a powerful, almost symbolic meaning. As he later wrote in *Prisonnier,*

> I have had a lot of different feelings in the Himalaya, but I think I had never been more affected than at the moment when, for the last time, I turned my head forward and left that fragile bamboo stake behind me. . . . In that second, I had the reflection, "Here, truly, you are entering another world." To return alive from this adventure, we would have to force ourselves to get back to that initial ribbon, that preliminary lookout post.

After talking to me on the radio, J.-C. felt a certain disappointment that I'd chosen to turn back. As he later wrote, "I know how much that decision cost [Ed]. It's often harder to turn back than to go on. I understood his reasons. . . . Alpinism is a personal adventure."

On May 15, Veikka and I descended all the way to base camp. At Camp II, in the middle of our descent, I pulled out my sat phone and made a hurried call to Paula, telling her we were headed down. "She wanted to talk long[er]," I wrote in my diary, "but had to tell her we needed to keep moving." We were determined to descend all the way to base camp in one push, while it was still cold and the anchors were frozen solidly in place.

At base camp, for the first time, I met Katia, J.-C.'s wife. Two days earlier, over the radio from Camp III, J.-C. had been stunned to hear her voice answer him. All by herself, without telling her husband, she had flown to Kathmandu, arranged transport to the last hill town, hired porters, and hiked in to base camp. As J.-C. reports in *Prisonnier,* Katia's arrival made him "crazy with happiness." Now, during the fateful days of J.-C. and Alberto's summit attempt, she would act almost like an air traffic controller, encouraging her husband and relaying weather forecasts, but also constantly warning him not to let his guard down.

I'll admit that when I first learned that Katia had arrived, I wondered if it would make the climb harder for J.-C. While we all waited to find out what was going on high on the east ridge, Katia paced back and forth on the glacier, radio in hand. Emotionally, she was a wreck, no matter how brave and supportive she sounded in her radio transmissions.

On May 15, J.-C. and Alberto pushed on along the east ridge. They had agreed to climb unroped as much as possible, so that each man could move at his own pace. Very soon they sensed that their packs were too heavy, so they jettisoned some of their stuff—snow pickets, fuel cartridges, and a portion of their food. Upon his return to France, J.-C. would tell a journalist, "After the Roc Noir, I had the feeling of closing a door behind me. I was far from the land of the living. I had never had this feeling on any other mountain."

It's striking to me that J.-C. chose the same metaphor for the journey along the east ridge of Annapurna that Erhard Loretan had. In *Les 8000 Rugissants,* the Swiss climber writes, "Never have I felt myself so far from the living and so close to the dead." Before his fourth attempt on Annapurna, J.-C. had of course consulted with Loretan, and he must have read the man's memoir many times. It's as if he had absorbed Loretan's very way of thinking about life and death.

"The day became interminable," J.-C. later wrote about May 15. The wind rose to thirty or forty miles an hour. The going was not particularly technical, but there were always those fiendish cornices to worry about. Quite a few great mountaineers—among them the Austrian Hermann Buhl and J.-C.'s compatriot Patrick Berhault—have died when a cornice they mistook for solid ridge collapsed under their feet and sent them plummeting down the face below. But only on the trickiest passages did J.-C. and Alberto rope up.

By late afternoon both men were exhausted. They bivouacked just short of the central summit, at 25,900 feet. Once they'd hacked out a platform with their axes—*Why the hell didn't we bring a shovel?* J.-C. berated himself—and crawled inside their bivvy tent, Alberto vowed not to go outside until morning. But with his last ergs of energy, J.-C. emerged just before dusk and strung two ultralight fifty-meter fixed ropes along a steep snow-and-ice slope mixed with rotten rock.

That night, J.-C. knew, the two men had reached the crux of the whole expedition. They were so strung out that both of them seriously entertained the thought of giving up and heading down. Radio contact with base camp was poor, but Katia managed to convey the forecast she had received from the team's ace meteorologist back in Chamonix. May 16 would be almost perfect, the finest day in a week. After that, however, the conditions would deteriorate rapidly.

J.-C. and Alberto knew that the rock cliff that Loretan and Joos had had to rappel—and that they believed left the Swiss with no option but to descend the north face—lay ahead of them, just beyond the central summit. On the morning of the sixteenth they left their bivvy tent in place, knowing they would almost surely have to spend another night inside that fragile shelter. Early on they came to the cliff. Here J.-C.'s superb alpine technique came into play, as he found a way to circumvent the rappels on the rock cliff, downclimbing nearly a thousand feet on the north side of the ridge. The men roped up, and J.-C. led every pitch of the dangerous traverse required to regain the east ridge. He was effectively soloing those pitches, for if Alberto had come off, J.-C. could not have held him, and both men would have fallen to their deaths.

At 10:00 A.M. on May 16, the two men stood on the summit of Annapurna. As J.-C. later wrote,

> There, at an altitude of 8,091 meters, a deep cry of joy, of liberation, came from the bottom of my lungs, as Alberto fixed the moment forever with his digital camera. He joined me; our effusions were brief but sincere and deeply felt. We held each other in our arms. I started crying, my emotions were so strong. Alberto clasped his brother's ice ax to his heart.

The climb, of course, was not over. Like me, J.-C. was acutely conscious of the fact that on 8,000-meter peaks, more climbers come to grief on the way down than on the way up. From the summit, J.-C. radioed Katia. Both she and her husband were overcome with joy, but almost at once, she warned him, "Now, pay attention. Go slowly. It's not finished."

Later J.-C. recaptured his deepest thoughts as he and Alberto started down after only half an hour on the summit.

> Liberated from Annapurna?
>
> At that moment, I realized how isolated we were from the world, still more prisoners than free men, in a space that had more to do with the cosmos than with the earth. . . . Katia was right: it was not finished, it even seemed to me infinite, when I took the measure of what lay ahead of us.

(Here, a Francophone friend pointed out to me, J.-C., like Loretan, was characteristically playing with words. In the original French, *"Ce n'est pas fini, cela me parait même infini," "pas fini,"* or "not finished," is opposed to *"infini,"* "infinite." Those French-speaking climbers!)

By late afternoon, the men were back in sight of their bivvy tent just below the central summit. And that sight, J.-C. wrote, was "a vision of horror." The wind had torn loose three of the four anchors holding the tent to the mountain. It was flapping wildly, so J.-C. dashed ahead and grabbed the tent before it was too late. Had the shelter been blown off the ridge, both men would probably have died. J.-C. and Alberto packed up the tent and their gear and descended even farther: to save weight, they abandoned their sleeping bags.

Their last bivouac was by far the worst. Having run out of fuel for their camp stove, the men had been able to drink almost no water all day and night. They got no sleep at all, and as they headed out on May 17, the weather indeed showed signs of deteriorating. They abandoned yet more gear to lighten their loads.

By radio at base camp, Veikka, Katia, the other Basques, and I followed every step of our friends' desperate retreat. As I put it in *No Shortcuts to the Top,* it was like listening to *Apollo* 11 limp back to earth.

At last the two climbers came in sight of that single bamboo pole J.-C. had planted on top of Roc Noir. And now Alberto persuaded his partner to make a last sacrifice. They threw away their bivvy tent, even though it weighed only three and a half pounds.

There remained a single technical challenge: to back down from the crest on the south side of Roc Noir, traverse to the right, and regain the safety of the ridge where Veikka and I had pitched our Camp IV. Exhausted though they were, the two men tackled that final obstacle with excruciating care—and pulled it off.

Once past Roc Noir, as J.-C. later put it, "At last I had reopened the door I closed behind me four days earlier. I had once more entered the land of the living."

The next day, May 18, I hiked up the glacier to meet J.-C. and Alberto as they came down, bringing with me food and a thermos full of hot tea. We hugged as we greeted each other, and I told them what a great thing they had done. J.-C. later wrote about how much that simple gesture of mine meant to him.

Several friends have asked me whether it wasn't a bitter pill to swallow to have my teammates succeed on a route from which I had turned back. In all honesty, I felt nothing but pride and admiration for J.-C. and Alberto's ascent. In my diary, I wrote, "They walked the razor's edge for sure! Awesome achievement!" To this day, I consider J.-C. and Alberto's climb one of the greatest deeds ever performed in the Himalaya. And in *Prisonnier,* J.-C. calls the summit push and descent "the eight finest days of my life as an alpinist."

I didn't get back to Seattle and Paula, Gil, and Ella until late May, more than a month and a half after I'd left home. In my own way, I was almost as exhausted as J.-C. and Alberto. Among all the trips I've taken to 8,000-meter peaks, Annapurna in 2002 ranks with only K2 in 1992 as the most prolonged and stressful expedition experience I've ever gone through.

At least I'd come back in 1992 with the summit of K2 under my belt. Now, in terms of the summit of Annapurna, I'd come back empty-handed for the second time. If I was ever going to complete my Endeavor 8000, I'd have to face that terrifying mountain again. And I'd have to figure out a way to get up it that was safe enough to justify the risk.

Annapurna would never become my obsession, but over the next three years, it would cost me plenty of sleepless nights.

SIX

MESSNER AND KUKUCZKA

In October 1986, when he topped out on Lhotse, Reinhold Messner became the first person to climb all fourteen 8,000-meter peaks. Curiously, though, he claimed that it was not until 1982, by which point he had reached the summit of nine of them, that he even conceived of the goal of bagging all fourteen. In his memoir about that campaign, *All 14 Eight-Thousanders,* he insists that if by 1982 "closing the loop" had become for him a goal, "it was only a secondary one. Climbing increasingly harder routes, setting myself new targets, was of far greater importance to me."

Messner also appears to have been the first person to set himself this challenge. Before the early 1980s a project such as that seemed unthinkable. It was hard enough (and costly enough, in an age before mountaineers commanded full-time sponsorship) simply to get up *any* 8,000er. During the so-called Golden Age of Himalayan Mountaineering, between 1950 and 1964, when the first ascents of all fourteen were accomplished, only two men—Hermann Buhl and Kurt Diemberger, both Austrians—participated in the first ascent of more than a single 8,000er. Buhl reached the top of Nanga Parbat alone in 1953, and four years later shared his triumph on Broad Peak with Diemberger, who in 1960 was one of the three men who first reached the summit of Dhaulagiri. (Lionel Terray came close, having topped out on Makalu in 1955, five years after selflessly giving up his chance at summiting on Annapurna to work in support of Herzog and Lachenal.)

It was not until 1975 that any man reached the summit of three 8,000ers. That man, not surprisingly, was Messner, who had succeeded on Nanga Parbat and Manaslu before adding Gasherbrum I to his list. The 1975 climb of Gasherbrum I, marking only the second ascent of the peak (eighteen years after an American team first climbed it), was a Himalayan breakthrough, as Messner and Peter Habeler tackled the eleventh highest mountain in the world without porter or Sherpa support up high and in true alpine style.

As mentioned in the previous chapter, by 1984 the competition to become the first to nail all fourteen 8,000ers had evolved into a genuine race—no matter that all five leading candidates insisted that they were *not* involved in the race. It took Messner sixteen years to close his own loop. Meanwhile, the remarkable Polish climber Jerzy Kukuczka turned on the jets of his ambition and got up all fourteen in the span of only eight years. He lost out in the race with Messner by a mere eleven months.

Eight years later, Erhard Loretan was surprised that anyone would give a damn if he became the third man to close the loop. But his head-to-head competition with Benoît Chamoux to claim that honor climaxed in the dramatic and tragic events on Kangchenjunga in 1995, as recounted in chapter 5.

Nor did Loretan's achievement discourage the next men in line. The year after Loretan completed his round, the Mexican Carlos Carsolio became the fourth to accomplish the feat, and the Pole Krzysztof Wielicki became the fifth. I climbed with both men on Gasherbrum I and Gasherbrum II in 1995 and found them excellent partners. They both loved the adventure not only for the climbing itself, but for the journey to and from the mountain as well.

I became the twelfth person to get up all fourteen 8,000ers, in 2005, and only the sixth to do so without supplemental oxygen. As of the summer of 2010 the list has stretched to twenty-one, including my great friend and constant partner Veikka Gustafsson, who finished his own roster (also without bottled oxygen—only the ninth person to do it that way) on Gasherbrum I in 2009. So the goal continues to motivate some of the best mountaineers in the world, and to generate huge public interest. (In Finland, for instance, Veikka is like a rock star, celebrated above all for becoming the first Finn to climb Everest, which he did in 1993.)

In recent years, a spirited and for the most part friendly competition heated up among three women closing in on the distinction of becoming the first female climber to capture all the 8,000ers: the Basque Edurne Pasabàn, the Italian Nives Meroi, and the Austrian Gerlinde Kaltenbrunner. But then, in May 2010, the South Korean Oh Eun-sun, who came out of nowhere to catch up with the other three, got to the top of Annapurna, and snatched the prize from her rivals.

Or seemed to snatch it. A number of sources (including Pasabàn, who finished her own fourteenth only three weeks after Oh) disputed the Korean's claim to have gotten up Kangchenjunga in 2009. The evidence hinged on Oh's own suspect summit photo, and on the alleged testimony of some of the Sherpa supporting her effort. Elizabeth Hawley, the arbiter of all Himalayan records, tentatively credited Oh with becoming the twenty-first climber to close the loop, but marked her claim as "disputed" pending further investigation.

Sadly, the rewards of getting your name on the elite list of "all fourteen 8,000ers" have tempted good climbers to fudge their ascents. In the previous chapter I mentioned the dispute over Chamoux's claim to have gotten to the top of Shishapangma. Besides Oh Eun-sun, three other climbers who have claimed to close the loop of the 8,000ers have been widely discredited, their names either left off the list or marked with asterisks as "disputed."

Climbers have a long tradition of trusting each other to tell the truth about their ascents. But this has not prevented outright hoaxes from being perpetrated. The most notorious may be Dr. Frederick A. Cook's completely bogus assertion that he and a single companion made the first ascent of Mount McKinley in Alaska in 1906. Equally suspect, most observers believe—although I'm not completely certain that it was a hoax—was the Italian Cesare Maestri's 1959 claim to have climbed Cerro Torre in Patagonia, often called "the hardest mountain in the world." Since Maestri's partner Toni Egger was killed on the descent when he rappelled off the end of his rope in a storm, there was no other survivor to verify or contradict Maestri's claim. Climbers who subsequently tackled the Maestri-Egger route found no evidence that the pair had gotten even halfway up the peak.

The sorry business of fudging claims on 8,000ers may actually be escalating. It's one thing to gloss over a 100-yard knife-edge summit ridge simply to gain a mere 20 vertical feet to touch the true top of Shishapangma. But another whole order of chicanery emerges in the stunt pulled off in August 2010 on K2 by the Austrian climber Christian Stangl.

After the disaster on K2 in 2008, when eleven climbers died in a thirty-six-hour period, a full complement of skilled, ambitious mountaineers returned to the mountain the next summer. But thanks to atrocious weather and K2's notoriously dangerous snow conditions, not one climber got up the peak in 2009. And most of the summer of 2010 passed without anybody getting to the top of the world's second highest mountain, despite the efforts of some of the best Himalayan climbers in the world. Then, on August 12, Stangl returned to base camp reporting that in a blitzkrieg solo dash, he had pushed his way to the top through terrible conditions and survived a desperate descent. His deed was hailed internationally as the only successful climb of K2 in two years.

But others on the mountain doubted Stangl's claim from the start. And after the Austrian produced his only summit photo, topographic sleuths figured out that it had been taken at only 7,500 meters. Stangl had actually gotten no higher on K2 than 24,600 feet—fully 3,500 feet below the summit!

By the end of August, Stangl had caved in, making a full confession of his hoax. The apology he issued to the press, however, seemed to me deeply disturbing. I can only hope that his sort of antics—and his feeble rationalizations for why he lied to the world—don't presage a trend in Himalayan mountaineering. Stangl pleaded,

> I suppose that I came to this from a mixture between fear of death and even greater fear of failure. Achievement and success were and are the determining factors in my sport. I think that I tried to suppress my personal failure after three summers and altogether seven attempts at this mountain. My sponsors did not pressure me into doing this. This pressure came from inside me. Fear of death is bad enough, but the fear of the failure in an achievement-oriented society is worse.

Messner climbed Annapurna in 1985, Kukuczka in 1987. Both deeds represented genuine breakthroughs on this difficult and dangerous mountain, for neither climber was willing simply to repeat the kinds of ascents earlier expeditions had accomplished. As Messner writes in *All 14 Eight-Thousanders,* "Whatever I did, I wanted to push one step ahead of all my predecessors. That way I could be assured of the quality of what I was doing."

The great Tyrolean climber set his eyes on Annapurna's northwest face. On the French expedition in 1950, as detailed in chapter 2, Herzog and Terray tackled an extremely technical route on what they called the Northwest Spur, before turning back at only 19,000 feet. It was not until after that five-day failed attempt that the team focused its attention on the hazardous north face route through the Sickle.

The Northwest Pillar, as it is called today, was tried again in 1973, 1981, 1983, and 1986, by teams from Italy and France. All four attempts failed, at the cost of a total of seven lives. The route would not be climbed until 1996, when an international team succeeded in getting a Pole and a Ukrainian to the summit, after rigging 6,500 feet of fixed ropes on very difficult terrain.

In 1985 it was not the Northwest Pillar that Messner pinned his hopes on, but a route to the left of it that angled through ice bands and hanging glaciers up a scary-looking concave bowl. Messner had studied the face from an opposite slope with Friedl Mutschlechner in 1984, concluding that the route was "doable." But as he later wrote in his survey of the mountain's history, *Annapurna: 50 Years of Expeditions in the Death Zone,* "My friend Mutschlechner refused to participate in the project, however. 'Too dangerous,' he argued."

In the spring of 1985, at the age of forty, Messner put together a team of five Tyrolean comrades. The strongest of them was Hans Kammerlander, with whom Messner had paired on three previous ascents of 8,000ers. Although twelve years Messner's junior, Kammerlander would become his favorite partner in the Himalaya and the Karakoram. The rest of the team was also made up of younger climbers.

In view of the dissension that eventually marred the expedition, some of Messner's published comments about his teammates should perhaps be taken with a grain of salt. There's a very curious passage in the Annapurna survey book about Messner's own role within the team. It seems obvious that he was the organizer and leader, but he writes,

> On this expedition, I saw my job primarily as leading a small group of relatively inexperienced high-altitude mountaineers in to Base Camp and advising them during the preparations for their summit bid. Naturally, I also wished to get to the top of the mountain myself, but not necessarily as a member of the first team.

In *All 14 Eight-Thousanders,* Messner adds a somewhat critical judgment about his younger companions, even though it's couched in a kind of general pronouncement:

> In choosing members I noticed that the younger climbers viewed this sort of expedition quite differently than we did fifteen years ago. They were not just going to the face, they were also going to the "market-place." This was understandable—with a successful expedition, it was possible to increase the value of your name, and with it, your income.

From this relatively tame complaint, Messner goes off on a full-blown rant:

> So many professional climbers have sprung up recently that the competition has become harder. That is a good thing. What I don't like is a new kind of charlatanry, which peddles half-truths. There are a few people who sell their tours with dubious information, comparing their deeds to those of earlier epochs in order to appear superior to the majority of other climbers around, when in fact they cannot hold a candle to them.

It's impossible to know just which "charlatans" Messner is talking about. In any case, from early on, he has been famous for stirring up controversy. Passages such as these, which inevitably add spice to the narrative, are what you come to expect when you read his books. But they also illuminate the frictions that seem to have divided the northwest face team in 1985.

Before focusing on the northwest face, Messner took Kammerlander on a side trip east to check out the 1950 French route on the north face. Messner freely admits that the first-ascent line would serve as a fallback alternative if the northwest face proved too difficult or too risky. But he also wanted to scout the French line as a possible escape route from the summit, if climbing back down the northwest face turned out to be too dangerous. At the site that had served as the French base camp, the two men found engraved on a memorial stone the names of the dead from different expeditions over the years. This grim memento mori occasioned a dialogue between the close friends about their chances on the northwest face, as they strolled closer to the base of the French route. Fifteen years later, in his Annapurna history, Messner reconstructs the dialogue:

> "Our face has been tried plenty of times," I said during a short rest break.
>
> "Yes, but left and right of our line," Hans interrupted our climbing a short while later.
>
> "But they were all unsuccessful."
>
> "And why did they fail?"
>
> "Because they avoided the logical route."
>
> "Avalanche threat. I am worried about that too."
>
> "Me too."
>
> "There are avalanches everywhere around here."
>
> "We will just have to take care not to get caught under their wheels," Hans said, and we stamped farther uphill.

While the two men reconnoitered the French route, their three Tyrolean teammates had already started up the northwest face, fixing ropes as they went. Messner praises their effort: "These Himalayan newcomers had thus proved that they were not only skillful climbers but also had stamina and commitment."

The trio of "youngsters" came down for a rest at base camp, while Messner and Kammerlander jugged up the fixed ropes, intending to establish a Camp II somewhere on the face, "reconnoiter the second third of the face," and then decide if the team should push on or give up.

Now something went awry, dividing the party of five into two competing factions. Messner's explanation of the schism, short on concrete detail, is cryptic at best:

> Right from the start, Hans and I climbed together. We belonged together, and we formed one of two teams, an arrangement that was to remain until the end of the expedition. The fact that the other three considered themselves to be the second team was neither intended, nor was it particularly helpful for our progress on the route. Unfortunately, this situation soon led to tensions, which remained unspoken. There was a rivalry between the two teams, a rivalry that existed right up until the journey home.

Messner and Kammerlander established a small Camp II at 19,600 feet. The following morning, as the two men packed up, Kammerlander "insisted that we take everything with us, including all the gear and food, for a possible summit push. It was clever thinking." Kammerlander obviously felt that if conditions remained good and the men had enough strength, they should keep pushing upward alpine style, without descending for more supplies. This "sudden plan" may have been the source of the antagonism within the party. If you read between the lines, you can imagine that the other three may have felt that they had done all the hard work so far, leading and fixing on the difficult lower third of the face, only to have the more experienced pair leapfrog past them and use the fixed ropes as a springboard toward their own summit dash. It's conceivable that what happened in 1985 mirrors the British conflict in 1970, when the hard work of the others, especially Estcourt and Boysen, ended up launching Whillans and Haston toward the summit.

In his accounts of his climbs, Messner can be hard on others, but he's also unsparingly self-critical. In *Annapurna: 50 Years of*

Expeditions in the Death Zone, he not only admits that Kammerlander was the driving force on the ascent, but also acknowledges his own fears and doubts:

> Above all it was my own weaknesses that frightened me. . . . The fear did not diminish with increased expedition experience; it became greater year by year. And with every new expedition, it grew more and more difficult to bite the bullet and go for it, to set off for just one more attempt.

I fully empathize with that sentiment. Especially when it came to Annapurna. After my second failure in 2002, it indeed became harder "to bite the bullet and go for it."

On April 22, with the good weather holding, the men pushed upward. As Messner later wrote, "We were both ready to move now, and prepared to give it our best shot. . . . Hans, in his youthful, carefree way, had been the first to feel it and he simply said, 'Let's give it a try.' "

The climbing grew more and more difficult, delicate friction moves on rock slabs interspersed with steep snowfields. Still, the men gained height with remarkable speed. That evening, they managed to pitch their tent, as Messner puts it, "between a leaning tower of ice, a crevasse, and the abyss." By the time they had crawled inside, a storm was raging. They passed a fitful night, getting little sleep; the flapping of the tent was so loud they gave up even trying to talk to each other. In Messner's account, the only intention the two men had at this point was to wait out the storm, then descend.

But April 23 dawned clear and calm, so instead of descending, Messner and Kammerlander charged upward, covering another 1,200 feet of difficult terrain. They bivouacked again in their small tent at an altitude of 24,600 feet, only 1,900 feet below the summit.

The next day, according to Messner, the men were still uncertain whether to go up or down. They could hear the wind roaring across the summit ridge above, but on the face itself, the air was still. "Should we carry on?" Messner later wrote. "Why not?"

It was on the summit ridge that Kammerlander took over as the driving force, leading virtually every step of the way. At 11:00 A.M. the two men reached the summit. "We stood there," Messner remembered, "shivering, a little bit proud, yet at the same time still with a feeling of urgency, for we knew that in order to fully appreciate this success, we would first have to get back down, back to safety."

As Veikka and I would in 2005, Messner and Kammerlander stared down the dizzyingly steep south face. They were impressed: "With a shudder of horror, I saw where Whillans and Haston had climbed up back in 1970. It was just a steep, bottomless pit down there!"

There was no thought of descending the French route, but as the two men retreated along the summit ridge, exhaustion threatened to overtake them. "I was aware, however," Messner writes, "that at all costs we must not sit down to take a rest. We would never have gotten to our feet again." The wind was so strong that the men sometimes had to hang on to rock holds to keep from being blown off the ridge. They had lost all feeling in the tips of their fingers and the soles of their feet. And now, as they left the ridge and started down the face, Messner began to have the kinds of hallucinations that so often assailed him in extreme situations:

> I was now hearing voices more and more often, together with a repeated screeching sound as my crampons slipped on rocky slabs. . . . No, this face was not made for men. But we were there anyway, and I was having the strangest thoughts. Not fantasies about being all-powerful, but thoughts of being rewarded by fate. But what does that prove?

It's amazing to me that again and again on 8,000-meter peaks, Messner was able to hear voices, to hallucinate, and to have "strange thoughts" about all kinds of metaphysical questions, yet always keep his act together and make sound decisions. There's no doubt that he was one of the strongest high-altitude mountaineers ever—maybe *the* strongest, if you consider his whole career. Yet a key to his success was how often he was willing to turn back, rather than push on. With Annapurna, Messner had now made the ascents of eleven 8,000ers over a span of fifteen years. But in *All 14 Eight-Thousanders,* he admits that he had also "failed" (his word) ten times on 8,000ers during that period.

It's in this respect, I think, that Messner and I are most alike. It took me twenty-two expeditions to 8,000ers to climb all fourteen. Between 1987 and 2005, over an eighteen-year span, I "failed" eight times, in the sense of not getting to a summit. But that's what it takes, I'm convinced, to survive in such a treacherous domain.

For me, patience and persistence were the key components not only of success but also of staying alive. Time and again, I had to temper my ambition and be willing to wait until conditions were perfect. "Failure" on a climb never seemed to me the right word. I never gave up because I was short on training, motivation, preparation, or desire. All of my "failures"—"non-successes," I prefer to call them—were due to conditions beyond my control. This was true, I think, for Messner as well

On the descent of the northwest face, however, Messner and Kammerlander came close to the end of their tether. They had expected their Tyrolean teammates to be climbing up the route in support, and now they were so strung out that they started shouting for help. And at that critical juncture, the strongest two of their teammates, Reinhard Patscheider and Reinhard Schiestl, appeared. It was a godsend. In *All 14 Eight-Thousanders,* Messner does not stint on his gratitude to the younger men:

> They piloted us down through the relatively flat couloir in the middle of the face, nursed us into camp, and helped us pull through the long night. Avalanches poured over the tents all night long, and had Reinhard Patscheider not gone out, hour after hour, to shovel them free, perhaps in my exhausted state, I would have just let myself suffocate inside the tent under a huge mass of snow.

By the next day, Kammerlander and Messner were back at base camp, where they quickly recovered. A few days later, the three younger climbers made their own attempt on the face, but the accumulation of new snow from the storms their partners had pushed through had made the face too dangerous. At 23,600 feet, they turned back. On the descent, Patscheider slipped, then fell unroped a full 1,300 feet down the face. "At the last minute," Messner records, Patscheider "managed to brake his fall before going over a 100-meter icefall. He escaped death by the skin of his teeth." That near-tragedy spelled the end of the expedition.

There is no doubt in my mind that Kammerlander and Messner's climb up the northwest face and along the wind-blasted ridge to the summit is one of the finest deeds ever performed on Annapurna. A few grumblers commenting on the "race" between Kukuczka and Messner to become the first to claim all fourteen 8,000ers have taken Messner to task for choosing easier or less innovative routes than those that his Polish rival tackled. That canard is manifestly untrue about Messner's climb of Annapurna.

It's odd that Messner wrote two different accounts of his northwest face ascent, and that they differ significantly. The first, in *All 14 Eight-Thousanders,* published in 1988, is relatively brief, in large part because that volume is essentially a picture book, with a gorgeous selection of photos interspersed with succinct accounts of the climbs. In that account, although Messner goes off on his rant about younger, media-hungry mountaineers who "cannot hold a candle" to their predecessors, he names no names, and he levels no criticisms at the three Tyroleans who rounded out his team. Nor is there any hint of tension within the party.

It's only in *Annapurna: 50 Years of Expeditions in the Death Zone,* which was published in 2000, that Messner brings to the surface the tensions that split the team in two, and that seemed to have caused bitter feelings on both sides. By 2000, however, Patscheider and Schiestl were dead, the latter in a car crash, the former in a mountaineering accident. Whatever hard feelings tore the Tyrolean expedition asunder, they remain the private business of the climbers on that team. Patscheider's and Schiestl's complaints, if any, have gone with them to the grave. The fifth member, Prem Darshano, has never, as far as I know, commented publicly about the expedition. Neither has Hans Kammerlander.

Reinhold Messner may be, as he is often hailed, the greatest mountaineer of all time. According to friends of mine who know him better than I do, he also has a reputation for holding grudges that last for decades. After their brilliant ascent of Everest without bottled oxygen in 1978, Messner and Peter Habeler had a bitter falling-out that took twenty years to repair.

What you can't take away from the man is the audacity of his climbs, such as the northwest face of Annapurna. Messner is not only a bold mountaineer, but also a truly visionary one. It was he more than anyone else who pushed the fast-and-light alpine style onto Himalayan objectives. He climbed Everest without bottled oxygen when some of his own teammates were sure he would die trying, or suffer irreparable brain damage. Then, two years later, he climbed Everest solo, without oxygen, during the monsoon season, by the difficult Norton Couloir, one of the handful of the most stunning accomplishments ever performed on the world's highest mountain. That climb, in my view, is also the most amazing display of physical and psychological strength anyone has ever performed in the Himalaya.

And yes, let's not forget, Reinhold Messner was not only the first person to conceive of climbing all fourteen 8,000ers, he was the first to pull it off.

I've met Messner only once. It was at Outdoor Retailer, the biannual trade show held in Salt Lake City, sometime in the late 1990s. I was standing duty at the Mountain Hardwear booth, since that company was then my chief sponsor. Somebody said, "Messner is in the building!" And there he was, surrounded by an entourage. He was at another booth just across the way, looking at some mittens an outdoor manufacturer was pushing.

I would never have tried to introduce myself to the man, even though he was one of my heroes. I'd read every one of his books that I could get my hands on, starting with *The Seventh Grade,* his inspiring polemic about the future of climbing, which came out in English in 1974, when I was only fifteen. But somebody who knew Messner, and who was more aggressive than I, said, "Hey, Ed, do you want to meet Reinhold?"

"Sure," I answered. "I'd love to meet him." We walked over to the booth where Messner was examining the mittens, and my friend made the introduction. I'm not sure if Messner had ever heard of me. He seemed busy and flustered. I'm sure everybody at the show wanted to touch him, he was so famous, and I was reluctant to bother him.

I shook his hand and gushed, "I'm honored to meet you. I've read all your books."

There he was, with his bushy beard, his great head of wavy brown hair. He fixed me with his piercing eyes, then, in his South Tyrolean German accent, said, "You could not possibly have read all of my books!"

I was completely deflated. He was right, of course—a prolific author, Messner by now has written more than fifty books, and even by the late 1990s, there were some of his works—a couple of homages to his native Dolomites, a book about the Gobi Desert—that had never been published in English. I could have said something in response, to the effect that I merely wanted to express my respect for what he'd accomplished, but I was mortified. I just slunk away. Since then, I've never met him again. It seems a shame: I'd love to grab a beer with Messner and spend an hour or two talking climbing.

Among the great Himalayan mountaineers, Messner's partner on Annapurna, Hans Kammerlander, remains one of the most underrated. He's done fiendishly technical routes in the Alps, climbed the formidable spire of Cerro Torre in Patagonia in only seventeen hours up and down, and made a specialty of partial ski descents of the 8,000ers. As Messner has freely acknowledged, Kammerlander was the "engine" that got the two of them up Annapurna. In *Annapurna: 50 Years of Expeditions in the Death Zone,* Kammerlander gets the very last word on that daring ascent. As the team started to hike out from the mountain, Kammerlander took a last look at the northwest face, then said to his partner, "After a big route in the Alps, I always think I know myself, know exactly who I am. It is only above 8000 meters that I realize again and again just how little I really do know about myself and my body, myself and the mountain."

After Annapurna, Kammerlander continued to go after 8,000ers. By 2000 he'd reached the summit of eleven of them. His personal nemesis was K2, on which he'd turned back twice, the first time only 500 feet below the top, when he judged the avalanche risk too great.

In 2001 he finally got to the summit of K2. He'd set out to attack the Cesen route solo, and hoped to ski down the Abruzzi Spur. While he was on the mountain, he ran into my good friend and Annapurna partner J.-C. Lafaille, who was also trying K2 solo. They joined forces, got to the top together, and descended safely—Kammerlander having once more judged the snow conditions too treacherous to ski. (In the summer of 2010, the talented Swedish

The Annapurna 2000 team: Viesturs, Veikka Gustafsson, Dorje Tamung, Michael Kennedy, and Neal Beidleman

After an eleven-hour climb, I am finally sitting on the summit of Annapurna at 2:00 P.M. on May 12, 2005, ending my eighteen-year Endeavor 8000 project.
Veikka Gustafsson

J.-C. Lafaille, Veikka Gustafsson, and me at base camp in 2002. *Ed Viesturs collection*

J.-C. Lafaille at Camp III with the east ridge above. *Ed Viesturs*

Looking back along the ridge above Camp III as Veikka approaches at 24,000 feet in 2002. *Ed Viesturs*

Veikka in the morning at the high camp tent, preparing to descend with me for the last time at 24,000 feet in 2002. *Ed Viesturs*

J.-C. Lafaille and Alberto Iñurrategi upon their successful return to base camp. *Ed Viesturs*

The south face of Annapurna: Bonington's (red), Moro's (pink), east ridge (yellow), and Lafaille's (blue) routes.

At dawn on May 9, 2005, the Italian team and Veikka just now approaching the entrance onto the north face, which I called the Gauntlet. This was the most treacherous part of our ascent, but it was also the key to the summit slopes. *Ed Viesturs*

Veikka and the Italian team arriving at the site of our final and highest camp at 22,000 feet. We had just topped out of the north face, having climbed it in eight hours with barely a safe place to stop and rest. Above us still lie 4,000 feet of climbing to the summit. *Ed Viesturs*

A small celebration in our hotel moments after arriving back in Kathmandu. Veikka and I, tired and skinny, with our great friend Wong Chu Sherpa whose company, Peak Promotion, organized our in-country logistics. *Ed Viesturs collection*

Working my way up and around the numerous seracs while climbing the north face on the way to our high camp on May 9, 2005. Veikka and I both carried a large load of supplies necessary to establish our final camp. *Veikka Gustafsson*

The Italian team at base camp prior to our joining forces on our ascent of Annapurna 2005. Their efforts on the mountain contributed invaluably to our success. The blue food barrels behind them are loaded with Italian treats, which they graciously shared with us. *Left to right:* Silvio Mondinelli, Daniele Bernasconi, Mario Panzeri, and Mario Merelli. *Ed Viesturs*

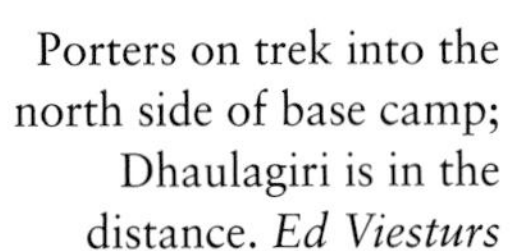

Porters on trek into the north side of base camp; Dhaulagiri is in the distance. *Ed Viesturs*

The Italian team and I taking our only break during our eight-hour ascent through the Gauntlet of the north face on our climb to high camp. There simply was not another safe place to stop during the entire day. *Veikka Gustafsson*

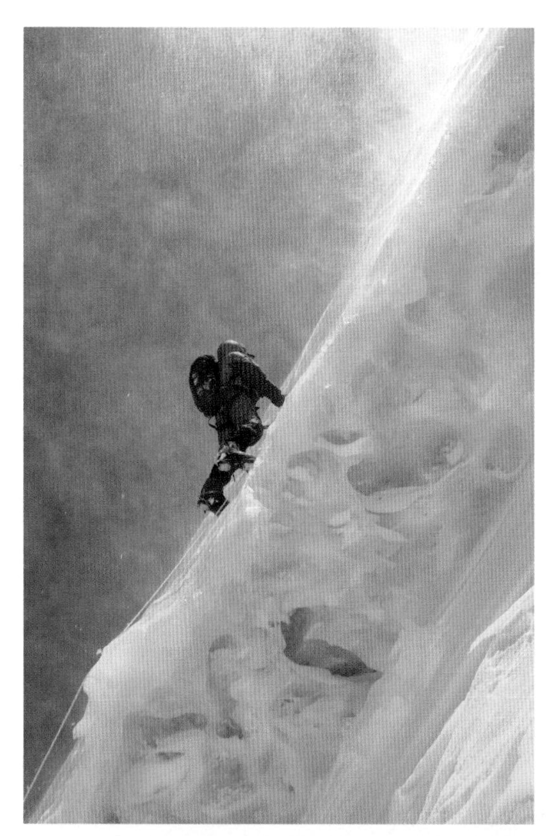

A final stretch of steep ice was our exit from the Gauntlet just below our highest camp on the north face. The Italians had fixed rope to this section on their prior foray some days earlier, which made our ascent highly efficient. *Ed Viesturs*

Climbing above Camp I with the north face ahead in 2000. *Ed Viesturs*

Annapurna's east face with the Messner route (red) marked. *Simone Moro*

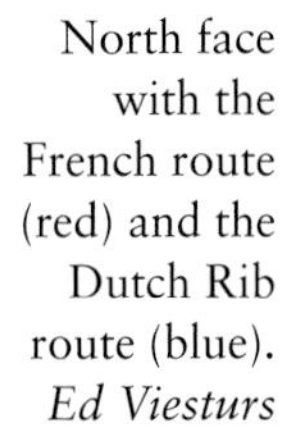

North face with the French route (red) and the Dutch Rib route (blue). *Ed Viesturs*

The view from our high camp at 22,000 feet on Annapurna in 2005. Dhaulagiri is in the center distance and the steepness of Annapurna's north face is apparent in the foreground. *Ed Viesturs*

climber Fredrik Ericsson fell to his death while climbing the Bottleneck couloir on his way to the summit. Ericsson's intention was to ski down the mountain after he'd reached the top. To this date, nobody has successfully skied the world's second highest mountain.)

With his ascent of K2, Kammerlander had only two 8,000ers to go: Kangchenjunga and Manaslu. Moreover, he climbed every one of his high peaks without supplemental oxygen. (I've never criticized climbers who use bottled Os, but Kammerlander has, publicly declaring that after Messner and Habeler showed the way on Everest, he considered resorting to supplemental oxygen "no longer acceptable in this sport.") By the summer of 2001, only eight mountaineers had climbed all fourteen, and only three of them had done so without supplemental oxygen. But rather than try to become the ninth, Kammerlander did something no other aspirant has done before or since—although I thought hard about it after my second failure on Annapurna. He turned his back on the challenge. Kangchenjunga would not likely have given this superb climber insuperable problems. It was Manaslu that was his sticking point, for in 1991, on an attempt on that mountain, he saw two of his friends die going for the summit. One of them, killed by lightning on the descent, was Friedl Mutschlechner, the same man who had told Messner that he thought Annapurna's northwest face was too dangerous to try.

On his way back from K2 in 2001, Kammerlander told a press conference, "Too many tragedies I lived on Manaslu, I will not face my bad dreams. I could go on living with thirteen tops instead of fourteen. There are so many beautiful mountains in the world I can climb now. Not Manaslu."

You have to admire that kind of integrity. The pain of the memory of losing his two good friends outweighed the promise of all the celebrity that would have come from "closing the loop" on the 8,000ers. Kammerlander climbed for the right reasons: personal satisfaction and nothing else.

With Annapurna, Messner had eleven 8,000ers. He climbed his first in 1970, an epochal ascent of the Rupal face on Nanga Parbat. During a desperate descent via the opposite, or Diamir, face, Messner's brother Günter disappeared. Jerzy Kukuczka reached the summit of his first 8,000er, Lhotse, a full nine years later. But by the end of 1985, only six years after he started his campaign, Kukuczka had nine under his belt. He was catching up—in no small part because he almost never turned back once he set his eyes on a summit.

Later, after the "race" was over, both men were magnanimous about their competition. They even traded epigraphs for each other's books chronicling their capture of the fourteen highest peaks. For the opening pages of Messner's *All 14 Eight-Thousanders,* Kukuczka wrote, "Congratulations on your grand slam!" And when Kukuczka wrote his own book, *My Vertical World,* Messner tipped his cap: "You are not second. You are great."

Kukuczka's first winter ascent of Annapurna in 1987 was every bit as much of a breakthrough as Messner and Kammerlander's new route on the northwest face. It's odd, then, that in *Annapurna: 50 Years of Expeditions in the Death Zone,* Messner devotes not a single word to Kukuczka's achievement. The Pole's ascent is not included in a dateline of notable events that serves as an appendix to Messner's history of the mountain, even though that dateline has entries for Arlene Blum's "all-women" expedition of 1978 and a routine repeat in 1979 of the original north face route by a "sensationally hyped" French expedition (the epithet is Messner's). You have to look in the fine print of another appendix, titled "Summit Successes," to find the names of Kukuczka and his partner, where they are credited with being the thirty-seventh and thirty-eighth climbers to stand on top of Annapurna.

Kukuczka's own little jabs at Messner in *My Vertical World* are not snubs of omission so much as satire spun around the Tyrolean's fame and ego. The two men first met near Namche Bazar, the hill town in the Khumbu Valley, on Kukuczka's hike out from his ascent of Lhotse, his first 8,000er, in October 1979. Lying in his tent, Kukuczka heard an outcry: "Mr. Messner is coming! Mr. Messner's expedition!" As he explains,

> Two panting Sherpas came running up. If they had known Polish they would no doubt be shouting, "Out of the way, herrings!" meaning Shift, you rubbish! . . .
>
> They pitched his tent, remaining inside for a long time, laying everything lovingly out; they hung up a lamp and prepared his bedding. We watched this unusual performance, pretending that we had seen it all before, but fascinated. After a few minutes the main body of the expedition appeared. He was coming.
>
> I saw Reinhold Messner for the first time. He behaved like a normal human being.

The Pole and the Tyrolean traded small talk. Kukuczka's mention of having just climbed Lhotse "only provoked a polite smile, neither of approval nor admiration." (Lhotse would be the very last of Messner's 8,000er summits.)

Kukuczka asks, "What are your plans?"

"Ama Dablam," Messner answers.

"I was taken aback a bit," Kukuczka writes. "Ama Dablam is only 6856 meters high." The unspoken gibe is, *What is such a great mountaineer doing on such a minor Himalayan peak?*

Kukuczka finally gains Messner's full attention when he mentions his own attempt on Nanga Parbat in 1977, during which, at an elevation just below 8,000 meters, he found a "torch" [i.e., a flashlight].

"It must be Günter's torch," Messner replies. "That is exactly where he changed the batteries."

Writes Kukuczka, "Nine years later [actually seven] I had found that torch. This created a link between us. I could not take my eyes off his wonderful equipment, including suits lighter than down, which the Sherpas were carrying up for him." The two men trade addresses, as Kukuczka vows to find the torch and send it to Messner, and also to "write a few words about how [I] found it" for Messner's upcoming Nanga Parbat book. (Despite searching through his belongings back home, Kukuczka never did find the flashlight.)

Three years later, in 1982, Messner and Kukuczka ran into each other again, this time on Broad Peak in the Karakoram—and once again the encounter generated some tense feelings. The Pole and his partner, Wojtek Kurtyka, had a permit to attempt the unclimbed east face of K2, but they decided to storm up Broad Peak by the normal route to acclimatize. Technically, this was illegal, for their permit did not cover the world's twelfth highest mountain. On the way down, at 21,000 feet, the two men ran into Messner and two Pakistani climbers heading up, also intending to climb Broad Peak by the route of its 1957 first ascent. (The presence of Pakistanis no doubt made Kukuczka all the more uncomfortable about what he called his "stolen mountain.")

According to Kukuczka, Messner's first words were, "Where are you coming from?"

> "We've been doing an acclimatization trip. We went up to the area of the summit," Wojtek answered evasively.
>
> That was not enough for Messner. He examined us for a few seconds silently, then asked directly: "So were you on the summit or not?"
>
> "We were in the area," Wojtek stressed. Messner just smiled.
>
> "Yes, yes. Understood."
>
> "And, if I may ask you, please, do not talk too much about having met us here."
>
> "Fine, fine," he made light of the situation.

Elsewhere in his Broad Peak chapter, Kukuczka rails against the very idea of permits sold by governments to climb their mountains. "[W]hen I am there on the mountain," he declares, "I feel it belongs to me. Any rules and regulations brought in to say that I am allowed to go this way but not that way are simply ludicrous. It is like trying to say: this is my air in my garden, you cannot breathe it."

Two years later, Kukuczka and Kurtyka returned to climb Broad Peak by a new route, traversing the north and middle summits—this time legally. But in 1982, after the men's return to Poland, they got hold of a copy of the book Messner had just written about climbing three 8,000ers—Kangchenjunga, Gasherbrum II, and Broad Peak—in one year, more or less back-to-back. It was the first "threefer" in Himalayan history. Kukuczka closes his chapter, "A Stolen Mountain," on a note of puzzlement and perhaps resentment against his more famous rival:

> Soon after that Reinhold Messner's book appeared, with a title something like *Three Times Eight*. . . . In it he wrote, "On my way up Broad Peak, somewhere around 6400 meters, we met Wojtek Kurtyka with another Pole, coming down from the summit. . . ."
>
> To this day I wonder. Maybe he simply forgot about our request at the time of our meeting.

By the time Kukuczka had climbed Cho Oyu, his eighth 8,000er, in 1985, he was fully aware of the media hype about his race with Messner. It's a subject he explicitly confronts in *My Vertical World,* as Messner never does in *All 14 Eight-Thousanders*. "After Cho Oyu," Kukuczka writes, "I was aware that I was now being treated as the one who could offer a real challenge to Reinhold Messner. . . . Yes, I could give him a bit of a run for his money, but for me to be able to win the race they would have to imprison Reinhold in his alpine castle." The dig about Messner's castle is no mere metaphor: by 1985, Messner had indeed purchased a historic castle in northern Italy that he converted into a mansion-like home.

Kukuczka's poverty versus the sponsored affluence of the top climbers from western Europe is a theme he returns to again and again in his memoir. Indeed, the achievements of Polish climbers in the Himalaya are all the more remarkable for the fact that they had to scrape together funds from the most arcane sources just to afford to go on an expedition. Typically, the gear the Poles bought—everything from sleeping bags and tents to ropes and pitons—was far inferior to the equipment every western European or American expedition carried into the field. To make ends meet and to fund his trips to Nepal and Pakistan, Kukuczka regularly took jobs painting industrial chimneys—dangerous and grueling work for which climbers had a natural aptitude.

In the fall of 1986, while he was on Manaslu, Kukuczka got the news that Messner had just climbed Makalu, his thirteenth 8,000er. And he knew that Messner planned to head straight to Lhotse from nearby Makalu. Kukuczka's reaction was ambivalent:

> I could not help feeling a bit sad. He was, after all, going to be the first. At the same time I felt a hint of relief. At last the excitement surrounding our "race" had subsided. Now I could continue towards my own target more calmly. I still needed Manaslu, Annapurna, and Shisha Pangma.

Later, still on Manaslu, which he was attempting by a new route, Kukuczka and his partner, Artur Hajzer, tuned in to their daily broadcast:

> One morning at breakfast, we heard over the radio: "Yesterday, the outstanding mountaineer Reinhold Messner reached the summit of Lhotse. In so doing he has become

the first person to reach the tops of the fourteen highest mountains in the world. . . ."

A silence descended on the mess tent. . . . Eventually Artur could not stand the suspense.

"So?" he burst out. "There's no need to hurry any more! We can take this mountain gently!"

Erhard Loretan's memoir of becoming the third man to climb all fourteen 8,000ers, *Les 8000 Rugissants,* has never been published in English, though it richly deserves a British and American audience. Fortunately, a British publisher brought out Kukuczka's *My Vertical World* in 1992, though it's out of print today. (Amazon lists a pair of mint-condition copies through used-book affiliates at $250 apiece!) Kukuczka's memoir about the 8,000ers is utterly different in style and tone from Loretan's, but it's an equally extraordinary book. It's hard for me to think of *any* climbing book I've ever read that is more understated. In a mere 179 pages, Kukuczka tells the stories of each of his fourteen triumphs. I think you have to be a mountaineer yourself to realize how modestly and unassumingly the Pole summarizes some of the most astounding Himalayan feats yet accomplished.

Even while he was racing Messner, Kukuczka insisted on setting himself challenges that went far beyond the deeds of his predecessors. No fewer than ten of his climbs were by new routes on the mountains (one of them solo), and three were first winter ascents. Only on that first expedition to Lhotse in 1979 did he choose to repeat a known route in a "normal" season (i.e., spring or fall in the Himalaya, summer in the Karakoram). And Kukuczka pulled off all fourteen of these monumental expeditions in a span of only eight years. There's simply no achievement that quite matches that in mountaineering history.

By the time Kukuczka turned his attention to Annapurna, he lacked only that mountain and Shishapangma to close his loop. No longer worried about the race with Messner, he decided to try Annapurna in the dead of winter. Six expeditions had previously tried the peak in winter, but all had failed. Only one succeeded in getting to the summit ridge, but on the descent, four climbers from that team died. A Japanese expedition never even reached base camp, after its porters refused to complete the difficult approach march from the north.

Kukuczka toyed with the idea of trying Annapurna by its formidable south face, weighing that option against an assault by the 1950 French route on the north. The trade-off was an easy approach march versus a very difficult one, then technical difficulty versus cold. Finally, Kukuczka settled on the north side, even though he knew that once his team was on the French route, "we would not be able to count on even one hour of sunshine during the day." The choice guaranteed that the climbers would encounter severe cold of the sort that had scarcely ever been endured by Himalayan mountaineers.

Once more, the "organisational hell," as Kukuczka calls it, of scraping together funds for a Himalayan expedition presented major obstacles. At the last minute a Polish journalist based in Italy, who had "walked across Borneo and sailed the Atlantic" but who had absolutely zero mountaineering experience, offered Kukuczka four thousand dollars if he would include him in the team. Despite misgivings, Kukuczka needed the money, so he acceded. The journalist gamely completed the hike in to base camp, but was so freaked out that soon thereafter he left the expedition.

That approach from the north, as I learned firsthand in 2000, is tough enough in April. In midwinter it's extraordinarily perilous and difficult. On the Polish team's approach in January 1987, only nineteen of the sixty porters they had hired in the lowlands succeeded in pushing through to base camp, even though the Poles had paid the men five times the rate they would earn in the "normal" season.

Despite such setbacks, the team started up the route and established a series of camps. On January 30 the four strongest climbers set out to find a site for Camp 4. They were Kukuczka and Artur Hajzer, his companion from Manaslu, joined by Wanda Rutkiewicz and Krzysztof Wielicki. As mentioned earlier, I would pair up with Wielicki in 1995 on Gasherbrum I and Gasherbrum II. By then, he was forty-five years old, but still strong as a tiger. As for Rutkiewicz, she was far and away the best woman high-altitude climber of her day. Before her untimely death near the summit of Kangchenjunga in 1992, she climbed eight 8,000ers, and nearly everybody thought that if a woman would ever close the loop, it would be Wanda.

If an American team, or one led by Reinhold Messner or Chris Bonington, had pulled off the first winter ascent of Annapurna, you can guarantee that a full-length book about the exploit would have hit the presses. In *My Vertical World,* Kukuczka devotes only seven pages to the accomplishment. He titles his Annapurna chapter "Cold Hell," and while you have to read between the lines to decipher the difficulty of the ascent, the one experience Kukuczka vividly evokes is cold:

> The cold troubled us most of all. We were climbing a mountain in perpetual shadow. The sun had one pleasant surprise for us, its rays did warm up our base camp for just a few hours every day. But this blessing was not extended to the northern slopes of the mountain. Only mountaineers can appreciate what that endless cold shade means, where it is impossible for a moment to get away from that bitter, penetrating frost, that takes away one's will and hope. In the tent it is cold, you go out and it is cold, you walk and it is cold.

The cold meant that slopes that would have been made of snow in April or May had frozen into solid ice.

> The frost continued to bother us, and the ice. In winter the mountain seemed to put on a glassy coat. We climbed on

> ice so hard that even the tips of our crampons could barely penetrate it. With every step one had to kick several times for the crampon's spikes to grip. This glass begins at 6000 meters [19,700 feet]. Our progress was becoming very slow.

Rather than dig out a proper tent platform, the climbers had to hack a bivouac ledge out of the ice with their axes. They could pitch only one of their two two-man tents, into which all four crowded. Through the night, tiny fragments of ice regularly pelted the tent, and as Kukuczka dryly put it, "It did not escape any of us that the tent could be hit at any instant by something substantially bigger." That grim bivouac site lay somewhere in the middle of the face beneath the Sickle, in the catchment basin that in 2000 seemed to us a virtually suicidal place to camp, it was so constantly swept by avalanches.

Another equally slow and dangerous day of climbing followed on January 31, culminating in another bivouac, at 22,300 feet. This time, however, the foursome was able to pitch both tents.

The plan was to descend in the morning all the way to base camp, rest up, then make a summit push. But that evening, Kukuczka was surprised to find that "I was feeling in very good shape." He deliberated for long moments, then, as he put it, "threw down my challenge."

> "I'm going up tomorrow! Who'll come with me?"
>
> Silence, I saw manifest surprise written on Wanda's face, and a good few seconds passed before someone answered from the other tent. It was Artur.
>
> "Me!" he said.

Rutkiewicz declared that she was not sufficiently acclimatized; she would go down. After a few minutes, Wielicki said, "Fine. Then I will go down with Wanda. We will make a summit attempt next time." Throughout the rest of the expedition, and for months afterward, Kukuczka would agonize over the fear that he had "dumped" Wielicki. But that selfless mountaineer never uttered a word of reproach.

So, on February 1, Hajzer and Kukuczka pushed on, while the other two descended. By that evening, the pair heading upward had reached 24,600 feet, where they camped again. Now, however, the weather started to deteriorate. "I was beginning to feel that this push was not doing me much good," Kukuczka wrote. "I was beginning to move like a fly stuck in tar. But I was optimistic."

As February 2 dawned, the tent was shrouded in "an impenetrable mist." Starting to get dressed, both men felt weak and lethargic. Kukuczka proposed a rest day. "Artur grunted something and with obvious joy burrowed himself back into his sleeping bag."

It was not until early on February 3 that Hajzer and Kukuczka set out for the top. They were still in semi-whiteout, but the wind had dropped somewhat. They plodded on up the seemingly endless snowfield, tantalized by one false glimpse of the summit after another. At last, at 4:00 P.M., they stood on top.

Kukuczka writes that back home, whenever he recounted his ascents of 8,000ers, people would inevitably beg to know just what his feelings were on the summit. About Annapurna, he answers indirectly: "Often one just feels nothing. One just concentrates on breathing."

Four P.M. is a late hour to arrive on a Himalayan summit in May. In early February, it was desperately late, for both men knew they had only an hour of daylight left. Getting down would be the all-consuming challenge.

It is at this point that Kukuczka's narrative outdoes itself in terms of sheer understatement. Night fell before the pair was anywhere near their highest camp. They staggered on.

> We were now moving by torchlight. The route I had tried to memorise on the way up was useless. By nine it was

> pitch black and we were still trying to find the tent. It should be somewhere nearby. Maybe it was a bit lower. Our legs were buckling under us from exhaustion, but our search was futile.

Kukuczka never mentions willow wands, those green garden stakes that I believe are essential to place in the snow every fifty or a hundred yards on the way up, so that you can find your way back down in whiteout or darkness. I doubt that the Poles used any; most European expeditions don't.

Then the miracle happened. "At ten, ploughing through the snow, and losing confidence in the point of this search, I suddenly stepped on something soft. Our tent!"

Man, talk about a close call!

By the next day, Hajzer and Kukuczka had regained base camp, where they found some twenty inches of new snow had fallen. Wielicki and Rutkiewicz made a second attempt, but the conditions were atrocious, and Wanda was suffering from some kind of bronchial ailment. They turned around at Camp IV. The expedition was over.

If in fact Kukuczka "felt nothing" on the summit, he also resisted all temptations to gloat about his amazing climb afterward. He closes the short, spare chapter called "Cold Hell" with a deadpan assessment: "We left behind us Annapurna which had succumbed to its first winter ascent. True, by only two climbers. But we had not added any names to the long toll of those who have contributed to the tragic reputation of the mountain."

On September 18, 1987—eleven months after Messner won the race for the fourteen 8,000ers—Kukuczka reached the top of Shishapangma, claiming his own fourteenth summit. Once again his partner was Artur Hajzer, and once again Kukuczka completed a new route, in this case the west ridge.

It ought to have been an occasion for supreme happiness, "the last bead on my Himalayan rosary," as Kukuczka called it. Yet it was not. The account of the summit of Shishapangma in *My Vertical World* breathes not triumph, but letdown:

> I just could not fully express my joy at this significant moment. I was simply overcome by it all. A person is not designed to be able to express his joy in every imaginable circumstance. Only once, on Nanga Parbat, had I had the urge to express my feelings by jumping up and throwing my arms in the air, and a miserable jump it had been. Never again.
>
> But why was I unable to be spontaneously, simply and genuinely happy at this moment? That this was my fourteenth summit no longer seemed important. It could quite well have been the third or the seventh.

This whole business is deeply puzzling to me. How is it that some of the world's best climbers can feel not fulfillment but emptiness as they finally achieve the goal of a lifetime? For me, when I at last got up Annapurna in 2005, the sense of fulfillment was radiant, even explosive. And it lasted and lasted after I came home.

Kukuczka's emptiness on top of Shishapangma reminds me acutely of Louis Lachenal's feelings upon climbing Annapurna. But Lachenal knew he was going to lose his toes, and the horror of that prospect outweighed any transcendental rapture of the sort that seized his partner, Maurice Herzog. Atop Shishapangma, Kukuczka had lost nothing . . . except the goal that had driven him for eight years.

This most self-effacing of memoirs ends in an appropriately ambiguous mood. Looking back on his quest, Kukuczka writes, "Has something really come to an end? No, the vertical world never comes to an end. It is there. Waiting. I'll come back."

Kukuczka was as good as his word. When I finished my own Endeavor 8000, the last thing I wanted to do was go off on another expedition. I wanted to be home with Paula and the kids and to bask in my satisfaction. I knew that I wouldn't be tempted to go after another 8,000er anytime soon, and as it turned out, I would be drawn back to Everest only in 2009, a full four years after Annapurna. After he'd topped out on Lhotse in 1986, Reinhold Messner went on only one further expedition to an 8,000er—an attempt on a new route on Nanga Parbat in 2000. He did, however, pull off other notable feats, such as skiing unsupported across Antarctica.

Kukuczka hardly slowed down. In the fall of 1989 he attempted Lhotse again, not by the route pioneered by the Swiss in 1956, but by its unclimbed south face. That gigantic precipice, almost 10,000 feet from base to top, was fast becoming a Last Great Problem of the Himalaya, having turned back many of the world's best climbers, including Messner. It was as if climbing Lhotse by the first-ascent route in 1979 was the one blemish on Kukuczka's otherwise perfect record. Getting up the south face would correct it.

With a single Polish partner, Kukuczka set out in late October to go for the summit. After the men endured two bivouacs above 8,000 meters, Kukuczka was leading up a nearly vertical headwall. The summit ridge was in reach, less than 20 feet above. But something went wrong, and he fell. His partner tried to stop the fall, but when the sudden jerk came on his belay device, the rope broke. Kukuczka plunged the whole length of the face.

Rumor had it that the rope the two Poles were using was a cheap secondhand line Kukuczka had bought somewhere in Kathmandu. If so, the perpetual poverty that left Polish mountaineers no choice but to go to the Himalaya with inferior gear contributed directly to the death of one of the greatest climbers of his generation. At the same time, I think Kukuczka was smart enough to realize that relying on a used rope on such an extreme climb was not a good idea. Even a new rope, subjected to all the wear and tear the climb must have inflicted, perhaps including a bad nick from random rockfall, might have broken under the strain of his fall. In any case, sheer bad luck tragically ended the life of an amazing person and mountaineer.

Among all the men and women who have made their sterling marks on Annapurna, the character of Jerzy Kukuczka is one of the hardest for me to fathom. There are scant clues to it in *My Vertical World.* He was obviously a deeply driven person, an idealist and a purist. It may be that, as J.-C. Lafaille wrote of Pierre Béghin, Kukuczka was the kind of man who could barely endure domestic everyday life. He left behind a wife and two children, but they are barely mentioned in his memoir. The one vignette of his wife, Celina, comes as she gives birth to the couple's second son in 1985. The infant was "radiantly happy," Kukuczka writes. "When I bathed him he smiled blissfully." But the birth created complications. Kukuczka was about to head off for Dhaulagiri but was afraid that his departure would upset Celina. When he finally broached the question, she meekly agreed that he ought to go on yet another expedition. "As for me," Kukuczka writes, with no apparent irony, "any feeling of guilt about the desertion of my fatherly duties evaporated as I launched myself into a whirl of preparations."

I never met Kukuczka, but I suspect that he and I were about as unlike as any two climbers could be. My family has always been one of the most important things in my life—no, *the* most important thing. Rather than wanting to flee Paula and the kids to go off on my next expedition, those departures became for me increasingly difficult emotionally.

Yet what shines through in Kukuczka's dazzling career is his absolute dedication to climbing the highest mountains in the world not to compete in a race against Messner, but to tackle them by some of the hardest routes, in the purest of styles. That integrity, combined with the man's evident modesty, the understated plainness of his accounts of his climbs, and the subtle sense of humor that peeps through here and there, sets a standard few can match. I admire Jerzy Kukuczka as highly as I do any mountaineer whose exploits I've ever contemplated.

SEVEN

COMET ON ANNAPURNA

I was on Mount Everest in the spring of 1996 when the disaster of May 10–11, made famous (or infamous) by Jon Krakauer's *Into Thin Air,* struck the many climbers heading for the summit from the South Col. Our IMAX team, headed by David Breashears, was at Camp II, having retreated from our initial summit bid to wait for better weather, when the sudden storm caught the climbers high on the southeast ridge, eventually killing five of them, including my good friends and former partners Scott Fischer and Rob Hall.

No one will ever know exactly what happened during that storm. In the aftermath of the tragedy, however, a considerable share of the blame fell on the shoulders of Anatoli Boukreev, the Russian superclimber who was serving as one of Fischer's guides. Anatoli insisted on going to the summit without supplemental oxygen. That day, he was the first to top out, and he then descended quickly all the way to Camp IV on the South Col—obeying, he later claimed, Fischer's endorsement of his plan to brew up hot drinks for the slower climbers straggling down the ridge and to gather up oxygen bottles in case they were needed to get exhausted men and women back to camp.

Krakauer is especially hard on Boukreev, in effect accusing him of abandoning his clients in a selfish sprint for the top; he also claims that Anatoli's decision not to use bottled oxygen meant that he could not linger on the way down to help save the climbers who were in trouble. (Without bottled Os, you simply get too cold to stand or wait very long in one place.) Krakauer does give Boukreev the highest praise for later going out in the storm and bringing such moribund clients as Sandy Pittman and Charlotte Fox back into the safety of Camp IV.

Boukreev responded to *Into Thin Air* through a co-writer, G. Weston DeWalt, who tells Anatoli's version of the story in a memoir titled *The Climb*. In fact, quite a pissing match ensued between DeWalt and Krakauer, as Jon answered the journalist's attacks on his veracity with counterattacks in a postscript to subsequent editions of *Into Thin Air*.

Krakauer was not the only well-respected climber to criticize Boukreev's decision to guide without oxygen. David Breashears went on record as calling Anatoli's choice "incredibly irresponsible." "The only place an Everest guide should be," Breashears amplified, "is either with his clients or right behind them, breathing bottled oxygen, ready to provide assistance." Reinhold Messner also weighed in: "No one should guide Everest without bottled oxygen."

On the mountain that spring, I crossed paths with Boukreev several times, often as we traveled in opposite directions: he would be climbing up as I headed down, or vice versa. I first got to know Anatoli in 1987, in the Pamirs. I was guiding on Peak Lenin, while he was one of the "camp guides," strong Soviet climbers assigned to the various teams from other countries to help coordinate their logistics and, if need be, support their ascents of unfamiliar peaks. During those years, Soviet climbers had a hard time obtaining decent climbing gear, so they would trade their homemade titanium ice screws for whatever Western equipment they could get their hands on. The "camp guides" were polite and patient as they waited until we were done with our climbs. Then they would circle in like vultures and start the bartering process. I recall a long evening in my tent with Anatoli during which I got rid of quite a bit of gear in exchange for some shiny new ice screws, the negotiations softened with shots of vodka. One item that Anatoli particularly coveted was a purple JanSport bomber-style hat. After I traded it to him, he wore it for years on most of his ascents.

Anatoli was obviously a fantastically strong and talented climber, but how responsible a guide he may have been on Everest in 1996, it is hard to say. The Soviets had their own style of guiding, which to those of us trained in a different style of leadership may have given the impression that Anatoli was lacking in compassion. He was much tougher on his clients than most Western guides are. It's a style that I consider valid and sane, especially on the world's highest peaks. My style as a guide was always closer to Anatoli's than to that of other Westerners, and in the aftermath of 1996, I've become even more demanding of my clients. In my opinion, it's better to empower them with the skills they need to be self-sufficient than to coddle them to the point of making them almost helpless without the constant presence of a guide.

Something else may have been taking place on Everest that year. Anatoli's English was sketchy at best, so it wasn't easy for non–Russian speakers to communicate with him. There may indeed have been a language barrier between him and Scott that caused fatal misunderstandings on the descent on May 10.

I did, however, find Anatoli's decisions on Everest a bit problematic. Although I climbed all fourteen 8,000ers without supplemental oxygen, when I guided Everest, I used a mask, a regulator, and bottles of oxygen, just so that I'd have a reserve in case any of my clients got in trouble. As for Anatoli's dashing to the summit and back down to the South Col, I felt, as I write in *No Shortcuts to the Top*, that his actions didn't make sense: "You stay with the group to prevent a disaster; you don't leave the group to prepare for a disaster." That said, it was indisputable that even without supplemental oxygen, Anatoli was stronger than anyone climbing *with* oxygen on Everest that spring.

In retrospect, I feel that Anatoli never got a full, fair hearing in public. That unfortunate outcome may have been the direct result of what happened a year and a half after Everest, on the southwest face of Annapurna.

DeWalt was not an experienced climber, and he spoke only a very rudimentary Russian that he had learned in college. His interviews with Boukreev took place in Anatoli's halting English, or through interpreters. All this, I believe, did a disservice to Anatoli. His ghostwriter rendered the account of the crucial hours when Anatoli went out into the storm to rescue the clients lost in "the huddle" as a verbatim Q&A transcript. In the wee hours of May 10–11, ensconced at Camp IV, Anatoli saw Lene Gammelgaard, Klev Schoening, and Martin Adams come stumbling through the storm with news that others were out there, helpless in the dark. In *The Climb,* Anatoli recounts his urge to attempt a rescue thus:

> Yes, I gave some oxygen from like what I have, three bottles—one Martin, one Klev, one Lene. From tent. And I give for people this, and this is situation. I understand I need to be ready. I began take my shoes, but it is not so easy. Also I tried to find the shoes, I found the shoes, take over my shoes, big shoes. It was before I was without the shoes. And then was ready to go out.

No doubt this is exactly what Anatoli said, trying to explain that desperate night to DeWalt in his halting English. Yet such writing not only confuses the reader, but also contributes to the widespread caricature of Anatoli as an immensely strong but inarticulate and unfeeling mountaineer.

I've always told people, "If you want to understand Anatoli, don't read *The Climb*. Read *Above the Clouds*." The latter book, less well known than DeWalt's ghostwritten memoir, was posthumously published in 2001. The passionate project of Anatoli's girlfriend, Linda Wylie, *Above the Clouds* collects Anatoli's mountaineering diaries and other short pieces, professionally translated from the Russian, including his account of Everest 1996 and its aftermath. The Boukreev that emerges from this book is a thoughtful, articulate, even poetic man whose philosophy of life and mountaineering was uniquely his own.

Above the Clouds offers Anatoli's own explanation for his decision to descend fast to the South Col on May 10, rather than escorting the clients down.

> I knew that when our people ran out of oxygen during their descent, they would experience a sudden drop in strength and ability. Physically assisting anyone at such high elevation is hard if not impossible; the best help in those circumstances is to provide a resupply of oxygen. Talking to Scott, I expressed my desire to descend, to reach the Col quickly so I would be available to bring oxygen and hot drinks up from the assault camp to anyone who was exhausted. I knew that I was strong enough to do that. Scott listened to me; he said descending was the right thing for me to do. He told me to go down.

Who are we to dispute this account? If Anatoli suggested a plan that Scott fully supported—whether or not other experts consider it foolish—who can blame Anatoli for descending? Scott was the boss, he told Anatoli to do just what he proposed.

On the other hand, Scott was extremely sick on summit day. He was moving exceedingly slowly, and though he tried to hide his debilitation, he may not have been thinking clearly when Anatoli passed him on the way down. It's possible that Anatoli told Scott that he was heading down to the South Col, and Scott, in his seriously impaired mental state, simply acquiesced.

In his journal, as published in *Above the Clouds,* Anatoli denies that he was making a selfish decision that day: "I did not think I was choosing the easiest option for myself. It would have been much easier for me to stay with the group, slowly continuing the descent." Indeed, to climb from the South Col to the summit without supplemental oxygen, then back down to Camp IV, and still have the reserve to head back up the route to aid others, takes superhuman fortitude. Except for Anatoli and Neal Beidleman, Scott's other assistant guide, every climber that day who regained Camp IV immediately collapsed into his or her tent.

Others on the mountain, however, including Jon Krakauer, didn't believe Anatoli's claim that it would have been easier for him to descend slowly with the clients. According to these critics, Anatoli simply couldn't stand to go at a slow pace and babysit his clients. They insist that earlier on the expedition, Scott frequently admonished Anatoli for rushing down ahead of his clients—but Anatoli persisted in doing so.

Above the Clouds also reveals how deeply hurt Anatoli was by the controversy that swirled around his deeds on Everest. Back in Santa Fe, his adopted hangout in the States, he was besieged by reporters.

> In America my actions were misinterpreted and my descent from the summit was condemned. . . . I can look in anyone's eyes and say I did the best I knew how to do for our team.
>
> Basically I spent the summer engaged in stormy discussions and arguments stirred up by the slant put on events by the publicity in America. My critics were either people who did not have a professional understanding of the situ-

ation or those professionals who had not endured such circumstances.

Anatoli never mentions Jon Krakauer by name among his critics, but one remark is clearly aimed at the author of *Into Thin Air:* "I do not know how a person climbing above eight thousand meters for the first time can hope to assimilate the experience a guide has acquired over decades."

In *Above the Clouds,* Anatoli also cogently pinpoints a delusion built into the very phenomenon of clients paying big bucks to be guided on Everest:

> The realm above eight thousand meters is a world unto itself with rules inherent only to itself. The right to go there is not available for a price. You can pay for a guide's experience, experience he has accumulated during decades of work, but to use it correctly and to survive when the situation becomes critical at eight thousand meters depends on the strength of the individual. In the worst case a guide is able only to die, having assumed impossible responsibility for a client's survival.

Anatoli received an important vindication in December 1996, when the American Alpine Club awarded him its David A. Sowles Memorial Award, bestowed, in the club's language, on "mountaineers who have distinguished themselves, with unselfish devotion at personal risk or sacrifice of a major objective, in going to the assistance of fellow climbers imperiled in the mountains." The award recognized Anatoli's heroic efforts in going out in the night to guide the storm-bound clients back to camp, and in subsequently climbing back up the southeast ridge to try to rescue Scott Fischer.

I recently learned, however, that two of Scott's clients, Pete and Klev Schoening, were furious at the AAC for giving the Sowles award to Anatoli. They considered Anatoli's actions on summit day an unforgivable dereliction of duty. Pete Schoening's opinion is not to be taken lightly, for in his prime, he was one of America's foremost mountaineers. In my K2 book, I laud Schoening's "miracle belay" on the Abruzzi Spur in 1953, which saved the lives of four of his teammates.

At base camp in May 1996, after the last climbers from the May 10–11 disaster were off the mountain, we all gathered for a memorial service for those who had died. Anatoli spoke in his halting English about Scott Fischer. I would have liked to say something myself—after all, Scott and Rob Hall were two of my closest friends in mountaineering—but I couldn't get a word out. I was too choked up. In the end, I just sat there on the edge of the service, listened to the others, and kept my thoughts to myself.

Then Anatoli did something that later earned him further criticism. On May 16, only three days after the last refugees from the catastrophe had been shepherded down to base camp, he set out on a lightning solo attempt on Lhotse, Everest's neighbor and the fourth highest peak in the world. In a feat of remarkable fitness and endurance, he reached the summit in only twenty-one hours.

His climbing Lhotse, however, left Neal Beidleman, the only other surviving guide from Scott's Mountain Madness team, with the doleful task of tending to the shattered clients on the hike out. To some, Anatoli's peak-bagging seemed simply callous: how could he have wanted to notch another personal triumph in the immediate wake of such a disaster? *Above the Clouds* offers Anatoli's rationale for climbing Lhotse:

> In early March, Scott had put my name and that of several interested clients on a Lhotse permit and paid for our share of the cost. The impulse that compelled me to climb after such a tragedy may be impossible for some people to understand. It may seem a vain and ambitious act. It

> is difficult to explain. Mountains are my life. At the time I remembered the standard that Scott had set for all of us when he'd climbed Lhotse and Everest back-to-back. Repeating his achievement, demanding of myself the price in effort he had once paid, was a way I could express my respect for him as a mountaineer. I wanted to say farewell to him that way.

This is a moving passage, and it sounds sincere. There's only one problem with it: Scott never climbed Lhotse and Everest back-to-back. He *was* the first American to climb Lhotse, in 1990, but he never climbed any pair of 8,000ers back-to-back. (I climbed Lhotse and Everest as a "twofer" in 1994, reaching the summits only seven days apart, but I don't think Anatoli was confusing me with Scott!)

The relevance of all this "back story" is simply that it raises the question of whether Anatoli headed off in late 1997 for a truly perilous objective on Annapurna in part as a way of getting back at his critics. Other observers have suggested as much. But on further consideration, I think the answer is no.

There's no mistaking the fact that Anatoli was a very ambitious mountaineer. By 1996 he was in headlong pursuit of all fourteen 8,000ers, which helps explain his sudden bid on Lhotse. Despite the controversy that centered on him through the summer after Everest, Anatoli was determined not to miss a single Himalayan season. In fact, as he writes in *Above the Clouds,*

> By the middle of August the pressure of these arguments became an intolerable weight. I felt defenseless and was psychologically exhausted by the accusations. I knew the best medicine for me would be hard physical labor. I needed to breathe the oxygen-depleted air surrounding the giants that prop up the Tibetan sky.

In the fall of 1995, Anatoli climbed Cho Oyu and Shishapangma back-to-back. That September, guiding a group of clients, I ran into Anatoli at Cho Oyu base camp. As we chatted during our rest days, Anatoli seemed quieter and more reflective than usual.

In the summer of 1997 he pulled off another "twofer," on Broad Peak and Gasherbrum II. By then he could claim eleven 8,000ers. He was lacking only Gasherbrum I, Nanga Parbat, and . . . Annapurna.

By the summer of 1997 there were still only five climbers who had closed the loop on all fourteen. Messner, Kukuczka, and Loretan had been followed by the strong Mexican climber Carlos Carsolio and the equally strong Pole Krzysztof Wielicki, both in 1996. As I mentioned before, I had paired up with Wielicki on Gasherbrum I and II in 1995. I'd also gone to the summit of GI that July with Carsolio. Both men were fine companions and teammates you could count on in a pinch. I wish I could have climbed other big mountains with them.

Reaching the top of all fourteen 8,000ers would have transformed Anatoli's career and life. As a Russian climber, he had risen steadily through the ranks of the Soviet mountaineering bureaucracy, setting speed records on peaks such as Mount Elbrus and Communism Peak. He had won awards such as Honored Master of Sports in his own country. But he was still, by 1996, as impoverished as most of his rivals in Russia and Eastern Europe. For Anatoli, as it had been for Jerzy Kukuczka, just scrounging up the funds to go on another Himalayan expedition demanded a major effort.

It was not until May 2009 that a Russian first climbed all fourteen 8,000ers. Topping out on a new route on Cho Oyu, Denis Urubko became the fifteenth person to close the loop, and only the eighth without supplemental oxygen. Though born in Russia, Urubko moved to Kazakhstan when he was seventeen, one year after the collapse of the Soviet Union. Urubko has always climbed as a Kazakh, not a Russian.

By 1997, however, Anatoli's record on the 8,000ers sported an asterisk or two. On Shishapangma in October 1996, he reached only the north or "central" summit, turning back on his solo attempt in the face of the corniced knife-edge ridge that leads to the true summit, only about 20 feet higher. It was the same turnaround in the face of horrendous snow conditions that I had made in 1993, and that I remedied only in 2001, when I traversed that final ridge and got to the true summit. In *Above the Clouds,* Anatoli freely admits that he did not reach the true summit of Shishapangma. He made no attempt to conceal the truth, even though many other climbers have claimed success after reaching only the central summit.

As it happens, I was on Broad Peak with Veikka Gustafsson in the spring of 1997, at the same time as Anatoli. On the way up the mountain, we were a day behind the Russian, who was again climbing solo. The morning that Veikka and I climbed to our high camp, we passed Anatoli's tent. He greeted us warmly, invited us to stop and visit, and brewed up coffee and tea for us. We assumed he was descending from a successful summit bid. The next day, on our summit push, we followed the windblown traces of the footsteps he had made the day before. Then, just as on Shishapangma, we were stopped cold only a hundred yards short of the top by a nasty ridge, corniced on one side, avalanche-prone on the other.

Anatoli's footprints stopped exactly where Veikka and I halted. We even said to each other, *If Anatoli turned back here, then we're making a smart decision.* Being that close to the summit, we could easily have claimed that we had been successful—no one was there to witness our ascent. But upon our return to Kathmandu I admitted publicly that we had stopped short of the top. I knew that eventually I'd have to return to climb all the way to the true summit.

In *Above the Clouds,* Anatoli's diary treats this possible discrepancy somewhat evasively. He writes,

> Near the top a cornice broke off under my feet. Jumping off the falling island, miraculously I landed on solid rock. At four-thirty, from the peak I surveyed the relief around me. The other end of the dangerously snow-burdened ridge looked to be about the same elevation as where I stood, give or take a meter. For me, I was on the summit.

Granted, Anatoli wrote his diary for himself, not for publication. And he never got a chance to clarify this somewhat strange declaration. Linda Wylie, editing the diaries, gives him unequivocal credit for topping out on Broad Peak, as she salutes his accomplishment: "He had summited four 8,000-meter peaks in eighty days—never before had anyone achieved those results in such a short time." But Wylie's making the claim is not the same thing as Anatoli crediting himself for the summit. I like to think that in the end, Anatoli would have recorded for posterity only exactly what he actually did. If so, by late 1997 he actually had five 8,000-meter summits still to visit, not three.

As if anticipating future criticisms, or still smarting from the Everest controversy, Anatoli ends his Broad Peak diary with a defiant manifesto:

> No one keeps track of records on these mountains. Each climb is different because the conditions are different. You might say the competition is held and each person achieves a personal result. Mountaineering is a struggle with yourself, a struggle to face a natural situation and take what comes.

As if Anatoli's year and a half in the mountains between spring 1996 and autumn 1997 weren't hectic enough, he also accepted a job as the chief guide for an expedition to Everest composed of soldiers from the Indonesian army. These clients were fit men but virtual novices as mountaineers. Anatoli signed on, he admits, because he needed the money, but he also won a pledge from the team leader that he, Anatoli, could call off a summit attempt at any time if he thought the risks were unreasonable. He also persuaded the Indonesians to hire two of his fellow Russian climbers as assistant guides.

The Indonesian expedition reached its climax at the end of April 1997. Curiously, Anatoli carried out his role as chief guide in a fashion diametrically different from what he had done on Everest in 1996. This time he used bottled oxygen for himself above the South Col. He established a camp around 27,500 feet, midway between the conventional Camp IV and the summit, following a tradition established by the first attempts on Everest in the 1950s. This was a very smart move, in my opinion, because Anatoli knew the Indonesians might not be strong enough to surmount all 3,000 feet of climbing from the South Col and get back down to camp in a single day's effort.

In the end, the most determined of the Indonesians barely made it to the summit, "doggedly running in slow motion," as Anatoli put it, "falling and embracing the tripod that is the official top of the mountain." But Anatoli ruthlessly turned around the other two Indonesians who had persisted thus far, one when he was less than 300 feet below the top, the other a mere 65 feet short.

I totally endorse this style of guiding, rather than the practice of "nurturing" as many clients as you can to the summit so that you can claim a higher success percentage. Anatoli realized that someone staggering to the summit on his last fumes would be making a grave mistake. Any climber who did so wouldn't have enough strength left to get down safely, except with a huge amount of help from the guides.

The intermediate camp served its purpose, saving the lives of all three clients. No one died on the Indonesian expedition. Perversely, however, Anatoli's critics used this success further to discredit his behavior on Everest the year before. This time Anatoli had gotten it right, they implied: he had used bottled oxygen himself, and stayed with his clients when they were in trouble, rather than rushing down to a lower camp to prepare for trouble. Had he done the same in 1996 as an assistant guide to Scott Fischer, the critics hinted, fewer lives would have been lost. These commentators, however, seemed to overlook the fact that in 1996, none of Scott's clients died, even though Scott himself did.

In 1997, Anatoli insisted on being called a "consultant" rather than a guide. "I can be a coach and an adviser," he explained in *Above the Clouds;* "I will spend my strength as a rescue agent. But I will not guarantee success or safety."

In an almost rueful tone, he concludes his account of the Indonesian adventure: "Our team descended to the sweet embrace of victory . . . , but above all, we were lucky in playing our game of Russian roulette. The expedition had an ending that does not burn in my heart."

By the autumn of 1997, Anatoli was thirty-nine years old. It would be tempting to attribute the frenzied drive of his climbing through 1996 and 1997 to a determination to silence his detractors by the sheer excellence of his performance on the world's highest mountains. But I think that misses the point. I think Anatoli would have climbed just as hard if the Everest tragedy had never happened.

In the epilogue to his later editions of *Into Thin Air,* Jon Krakauer reports a meeting between two great mountaineers at the end of summer 1997 that, in Krakauer's view, had everything to do with Anatoli's ambitions on Annapurna. Anatoli invited Reinhold Messner to join him in the Tien Shan Mountains near the border of western China and Kazakhstan for some relatively laid-back climbing, and Messner accepted. According to Krakauer,

> During Messner's visit, Boukreev asked the legendary Italian alpinist for advice about his climbing career. Since first

visiting the Himalaya in 1989, Boukreev had accumulated an amazing record of high-altitude ascents. All but two of these climbs, however, had followed traditional, relatively oft-traveled routes with few technical challenges. Messner pointed out that if Boukreev wanted to be considered among the world's truly great mountaineers, he would need to shift his focus to steep, very difficult, previously unclimbed lines.

Boukreev took this advice to heart.

Jon had this story directly from Messner, and I'd heard a similar version of that meeting from someone else. Yet I wonder if Anatoli's audacious plan for Annapurna was really spurred by Messner's stern injunction. It may simply have come about because Anatoli happened to fall into the company of another climber who was every bit as ambitious as he was, with a kindred dream for the future. That other man was a thirty-year-old Italian named Simone Moro.

I climbed with Simone in 2003 on Nanga Parbat, when J.-C. Lafaille and I joined up with a small Italian team he was leading. By then Moro was a legendary mountaineer, and I was honored to share an 8,000er with him. In person, I found him warm and friendly. He was evidently a great raconteur, for at base camp his shaggy dog stories invariably had his teammates in stitches. Immediately after rendering his tales in Italian, Simone was kind enough to translate the jokes into a passable English for the benefit of J.-C. and me.

On Nanga Parbat, unfortunately, Simone began to contract pulmonary edema during our final push to high camp. Wisely, he turned around. The next day, J.-C. and I succeeded in reaching the summit. It was my twelfth 8,000er, leaving only Broad Peak (which J.-C. and I climbed ten days later) and Annapurna to complete my

Endeavor 8000 quest. Despite a partial recuperation, on a second attempt several days later, Simone was not able to climb above Camp III. Bad weather contributed to his defeat.

For some reason, on Nanga Parbat, although we briefly discussed it, I never asked Simone to tell me the full details of his expedition to Annapurna with Anatoli Boukreev in the winter of 1997–98. I had only a rough idea of what happened on that momentous adventure. The *American Alpine Journal* ran a short note by Simone about the expedition, but by and large it had passed under the radar of the English-speaking climbing world.

Meanwhile, Simone wrote a book about the expedition, which he titled *Cometa sull'Annapurna* (Comet on Annapurna). Published in 2003, it has yet to appear in an English edition. But when I e-mailed Simone last year, I learned that he had commissioned his own English translation, which he was happy to send to me electronically. For the first time, I was able to read the full account of that ill-starred attempt on Annapurna, recounted in vivid detail by the expedition's leader.

Simone met Anatoli on Shishapangma in the fall of 1996. Leading a nine-man Italian team, Simone set out ahead of his partners in a last-ditch attempt on the peak, after weeks of storms and high winds defeated their previous efforts. He was startled to see a solitary climber trudging ahead of him carrying an "enormous rucksack." The gap closed. The stranger said hello in English; Simone answered, "Ciao." Then, in English, Simone offered to take over the grueling job of breaking trail. The stranger gratefully accepted.

At the next camp, the man with the monstrous pack unzipped Simone's tent, stuck his head in, and said, "Thank you for today's work. Forgive me, but I had an extremely heavy rucksack and wasn't able to take my turn."

"Heavens!" replied Simone. "Don't mention it."

In *Cometa,* Simone adds, "That was how one of the greatest

Himalayan climbers in history introduced himself. By saying thank you."

During the next few days, climbing solo, Anatoli pushed ahead of the Italians, breaking trail all the way to the north summit. Simone was awed: "I personally felt like a midget compared with the strength and incredible determination shown by that man up there."

The next day, Simone led five teammates to the north summit. Like Anatoli, they balked at traversing the knife-edge ridge to the true summit.

As it turned out, Anatoli and Simone shared the twenty-mile hikeout from base camp. "I walked alongside Anatoli and that was where our friendship really began. . . . We talked about all kinds of things, not just mountains. We asked each other a lot of questions and after a few hours decided to try pairing up for future expeditions."

The conversation evidently took place in English, which of course was neither man's native language. One might imagine all kinds of halting pauses and misunderstandings between the Italian and the Russian, yet deep friendships can be forged in the mountains despite such language barriers. I'd guess that the communication between Anatoli and Simone was on about the same level as mine with J.-C. Lafaille—and that never got in the way of one of the best partnerships of my life.

In *Cometa,* Simone titles the chapter about Shishapangma "The Giant from Kazakhstan," in tribute to not only Anatoli's height (well above six feet) but his strength and endurance, too.

A few months later, on a detour from a ski trip to Aspen, Simone rented a car and drove to Santa Fe to spend time with Anatoli and his girlfriend, Linda Wylie. Shortly after Simone's arrival, Anatoli took him on a training run through the foothills back of Santa Fe. The rigorous run lasted three hours, and it was all Simone could do to keep up with his new friend.

One morning that January, at Wylie's house, Simone was awakened at sunrise by loud thumping noises. The vignette he recorded, as he looked out the window of the bedroom, bears witness to the Spartan intensity of the Russian's regimen:

> To my amazement I saw Anatoli stark naked, with his bare feet in the snow and an axe in his hand, chopping wood. I rubbed my eyes like a sleepy child and saw him put down the axe. He took two paces and put his hand in a saucepan full of water that had been standing outside since the night before. With his hand he removed the three centimeters of ice that had formed on the surface because of the cold and threw it on the snow. Then he took the saucepan and tipped it over himself. He began scrubbing himself all over with snow and then went indoors to get dry and dress.

In Santa Fe, the two men concocted a wildly ambitious project. After Anatoli was finished guiding the Indonesians on Everest that spring, he and Simone would attempt an unprecedented feat: a traverse of Lhotse and Everest, beginning at base camp below the Khumbu Icefall and ending on the north side of Everest, in Chinese Tibet.

As it turned out, Anatoli was finished with his Indonesian expedition by the end of April. Ideally, that would have allowed Simone and him to spend the full month of May attempting their Lhotse-Everest traverse. Instead, Anatoli and his two fellow Russian guides had to fly to Kathmandu and wait for two and a half weeks to get paid by the top brass of the Indonesian army. It was a dispiriting interlude for Anatoli, who sank, he reported, into "the lethargy that characterizes my physical rehabilitation after hard climbing." He added, "The capital city, with its polluted atmosphere, is not the best destination for a rest." Meanwhile, Simone arrived at the Khumbu base camp and tried to get himself acclimated in preparation for the traverse.

Descending with the Indonesians from Everest in April, Anatoli had left a tent pitched on the South Col in support of the planned traverse. According to Simone, his Russian friend was "physically stronger and more experienced than me," while Simone considered himself technically more expert than Anatoli. Thus the two men had agreed that Simone would lead the difficult descent of Lhotse's north ridge to the South Col, a route that, for all the traffic over the years on the two peaks, had never been climbed. (The normal route on Lhotse follows the standard Everest track to a point high above the Western Cwm before diverging from it to climb toward the top via gullies and ledges on the northwest face. The true north ridge is a technically far more difficult route.) On the descent of Everest's northeast ridge, Anatoli would take the lead, since he had climbed the mountain from the Tibetan side in 1995.

The permit for Lhotse actually belonged to Vladimir Bashkirov, one of the two Russian guides who had helped Anatoli shepherd the Indonesians on Everest. Leading a Russian team, Bashkirov would climb Lhotse in conventional fashion, while giving logistical support to the duo trying the bold traverse. But it was not until May 15 that Bashkirov and Boukreev flew back to Lukla to start the hike in to base camp.

As it would turn out, the stay in Kathmandu did neither Russian any good. Back on the mountain, Anatoli felt rundown and even ill. The plan was for Bashkirov and his comrades to string a series of three camps up Lhotse. Anatoli and Simone would depart a day later and climb through the camps to bag the summit ahead of the main Russian team.

Catching up to Bashkirov on the second day of the ascent, Anatoli recorded an exchange that would presage trouble.

> "How are you, Volodia?" I asked.
>
> "I didn't sleep well. I had a low fever during the night, and now I feel a little tired," he responded.

> Nothing in his demeanor made me worry. He spoke normally. I confessed that my own condition left me wanting for better.

On top of his own fatigue, Anatoli had developed a persistent, hacking cough.

On the day planned for their summit attack on Lhotse, Anatoli and Simone left Camp III in the middle of the night. At first, Anatoli led in the footsteps of his Russian friends, with Simone just behind him. Then, abruptly, he made a suggestion that surprised and puzzled the Italian. In Simone's telling, Anatoli turned to him with a plea:

> "Simone, I'm feeling tired. What do you say if we cross over to the left and leave my rucksack on the ridge? We have to come back that way anyway on our way down to the South Col."
>
> I was taken aback by this statement. While on the one hand this was possibly a good idea, on the other hand it was extremely unusual for Anatoli to be tired.
>
> "Okay, Anatoli. No problem!"

After making the traverse left and depositing Anatoli's pack on the north ridge (which unburdened him of a load of food, a stove, and pots), the two men pushed on toward the summit. Both of them grew anxious as the sky clouded over and "a threatening gray mantle" swallowed the summit of Everest. Now Anatoli pleaded, "You go on, Simone. Go up as fast as you can. All hell is going to break loose in a minute. Last year the storm started just like this. I'll follow at my own speed. I don't know why, but I can't go any faster."

It's evident in *Cometa sull'Annapurna* that Simone is reconstructing dialogue from memory. The men's rudimentary shared

English was no doubt less fluent than this. But what happened that day is pretty clear.

Despite the ominous weather, Simone pushed on, reaching the top of Lhotse at 12:30 P.M. Anatoli arrived half an hour later. "He was visibly weary," Simone recalls, "and paused frequently up the last stretch of the climb." The men clapped each other on the shoulder, but then, after sitting down to rest, Anatoli spoke in a way that alarmed his companion.

> "Where are we? I'm not well, I'm going down. Ah, sorry, what do you want to do?" These three sentences are a summary of a much longer speech, but his meaning was abundantly plain.
>
> "Anatoli, we must look to ourselves and I agree with you. We must go down. The traverse is impossible in these conditions."

Anatoli's account in *Above the Clouds* of the decision to give up the traverse is terser and more succinct than Simone's, and he refuses to blame the weather: "Simone arrived at the summit first, then I came up. My illness was progressing rapidly. I advised him that I would not be able to attempt the traverse. We began to descend."

On the way down, the two men met Bashkirov only 100 feet below the summit. Once again Anatoli asked his friend how he was feeling. "Not too well," Bashkirov answered, "but as a leader of the expedition I need to wait for the slower ones."

Bashkirov never made it down from the top of Lhotse. In Simone's summary, "He died of exhaustion at around 8,100 meters [26,550 feet] after battling all night for his life, assisted by his companions." According to Simone, in subsequent weeks "Anatoli became increasingly convinced that he and Bashkirov had caught an infection, perhaps from something they had eaten [in Kathmandu], which had slowly debilitated them and left Vladimir without his proverbial ability to survive."

Anatoli's own verdict, characteristically, was more unsparing:

> Too much time at altitude weakens your defenses and you are more susceptible to illness, yet your body has no energy available to fight disease. That day I had a simple sore throat, a cough, but I knew that I could not make the traverse. I did not feel sick necessarily; I simply felt that if I fell asleep, I would never wake up.

My own experience in the Himalaya bears out Anatoli's observation. In 2003, after we had climbed Nanga Parbat together, J.-C. Lafaille and I made a dash for Broad Peak. Prior to Nanga, J.-C. had summited Dhaulagiri, so now he was attempting a rare "threefer." But all that exertion at altitude must have taken its toll on his body. He got slower and slower as we climbed the final ridge of Broad Peak, and confessed to feeling so tired he wasn't sure whether he should go on. J.-C. made the summit, but on the descent, he needed the aid of the Kazakh climber Denis Urubko and me to get back to camp. It turned out that J.-C. was suffering from the preliminary stages of pulmonary edema, even though he'd never before had any kind of mountain sickness.

For Anatoli, the tragedy of losing Bashkirov was one more reminder of the stern indifference of the mountains, and of the necessity to guard against all the things that can go wrong there.

> High-altitude mountaineering is the most dangerous kind of sport; it has the highest rate of fatal consequence. Most of these tragedies happen because human response is so unpredictable at high altitude. Though I have enormous potential at altitude, I am not protected. I know that if I get sick, I, too, can perish. You can't accurately

calculate all the odds; maybe God is unhappy with you one day.

Fourteen years after Anatoli and Simone's failed attempt, the traverse of Lhotse and Everest has yet to be accomplished. More than ever, it has entered the empyrean realm of a Last Great Problem of the Himalaya. Yet even after mountaineers finally pull off that daring project, there will be an even greater Last Problem still staring them in the face. Though climbers have started talking about it, no one has yet attempted it. The so-called Horseshoe Traverse—the complete traverse of the linked ridges of Nuptse, Lhotse, and Everest, starting below the Khumbu Icefall and ending at the foot of the northeast ridge of Everest in Tibet—is truly a challenge for the next generation.

The setback on the Lhotse-Everest traverse only whetted Anatoli and Simone's hunger for Annapurna. Six months after retreating from Lhotse, the two men arrived in Pokhara, the hill town at the end of the road south of the mountain.

The plan, which was the joint brainchild of both men, was to make the third winter ascent of Annapurna, and the first by a new route. (As recounted in chapter 6, the first winter ascent, by the original French route, was accomplished by Jerzy Kukuczka and Artur Hajzer in February 1987. The second winter ascent came ten months later, as four Japanese climbers repeated the Bonington route. On the descent, however, two of the summiteers, exhausted by their ordeal, fell to their deaths in separate accidents.)

The new route that Anatoli and Simone set their sights on was a line attacking the fiercely glaciated southwest flank of Annapurna, well to the left of all the south-face routes. If the men succeeded in reaching the crest of the southwest ridge at 20,700 feet, they would still need to climb almost 6,000 vertical feet along that immensely long, unexplored ridge, traversing over or beneath a daunting rock tower called the Fang, before reaching the true summit.

The style of the assault, moreover, was to be purist in the extreme. Only two other climbers would round out the team—a Kazakh mountaineer named Dimitri Sobelev, who hoped to film the ascent, and Andre Starkov, another Kazakh, who was an artist and photographer, and who had no ambition to go higher than the lower flanks of the mountain. Although the team would use a helicopter to fly in to base camp, their Sherpa support would be limited to a cook named Phurba, and they would employ no porters. If Anatoli was heeding Messner's injunction "to shift his focus to steep, very difficult, previously unclimbed lines," he was doing so with a vengeance!

By December 1997, Anatoli had become somewhat famous, though mostly as the fulcrum of the acrimonious debate about the Everest disaster of May 1996. (Simone, at the same time, was highly regarded within the European climbing community, but virtually unknown in the United States.) The caricature of Anatoli as the strong, unfeeling guide unfortunately prevailed.

All the while, however, he was writing not only diaries on his expeditions, but short set pieces that laid out his mountaineering philosophy. Sadly, none of these works was published in his lifetime. If they had been, in decent translations from the Russian, another Anatoli might have emerged.

Thus, in a meditation on the Everest disaster, Anatoli wrote:

> The incommensurable value of mountaineering experience, it would seem, exists alongside the danger. Why? For me, though I have devoted myself to climbing mountains as objects of passion for twenty years, this has always been a straightforward question. What is it that pushes a person to climb? . . . Of course, inside each one of us is the ambition to reach the summit, to realize that you are stronger

than obstacles, that it is within your power to do something uncommon and indeed impossible for most people. But one must be prepared to face those obstacles.

To a Kazakh journalist just before leaving for Annapurna, Anatoli mused:

> Speaking honestly, I do not feel fear climbing high; rather, my shoulders straighten, square like a bird stretching its wings. I enjoy the freedom and the height. Down below, when I become immersed in the problems of ordinary life, there is fear sometimes, or the pettiness of human behavior can weigh heavily on my shoulders.

Anatoli even wrote poetry. On his way off to Annapurna, he gave a poem titled "Summit" to Linda Wylie. Among its lines:

Next to me, climbing with me were a troop of men
Their past lives marching.
Lives cut short by love that was true.
Songs left unfinished
They could not tell you why love
Sacrificed life for the blue mountains.
I came down to see you
Bearing thoughts and dreams
To live their unfinished melodies
So you would hear and understand them.

I've never attempted an 8,000er in winter, but I've gotten cold enough, especially on Annapurna, in the "normal" seasons so that I can fully imagine the rigorous challenge of attacking a Himalayan giant in December, January, or February. Oddly enough, the shock of starting such a climb is only intensified if you fly in to base camp, rather than hike in. There's no transition. You step out of the chopper, and suddenly you're plunged into the heart of a high-altitude winter.

On December 2 the team flew in a big Russian helicopter into the basin below Annapurna's south face. The pilot tried to put his craft down on a shelf at around 13,000 feet, only to have the chopper sink into powder snow up to the doors. Anatoli jumped out, then Phurba. The snow was so light and soft, the five-foot-three Sherpa sank in almost to his neck. After Phurba, the other three team members jumped out. In a state of controlled panic, the pilot and his flight engineer dumped cargo as fast as they could. Fighting for balance in the snow, the climbers caught parcels of food and gear as they were tossed out of the helicopter. Then, with a roar of its rotors, the lumbering machine climbed back into the thin air and sped down the valley.

Wrote Simone later, "We seemed to have landed on another planet, in some surreal world with no color, no smell, and no noise. There was not a sign of life and the sense of desolation aroused by the place was overwhelming." Yet, only a few minutes later, a number of Nepalis appeared—workers who staffed the trekking lodges in tourist season, and who had been trapped in them by a sudden storm 2,000 feet above their winter houses. These locals, Simone noted, "looked at us in amazement, trying to understand the reason for our visit. They probably dismissed the idea that we were climbers, since they had never seen any in the area during the winter season."

The first days were spent struggling to build a base camp in the cold and the snow. "I was in the company of three Russians," wrote Simone, "well used to the difficulties and harsh weather, and every time something went wrong they repeated, 'It would be even worse in Siberia,' and burst out laughing."

The proximity of the tourist lodges proved to be an unexpected blessing. One of the proprietors, a seventy-year-old named Dibi

Gurung, decided to linger on, in the hope of serving these strange visitors who had arrived out of nowhere. Since the lodge was only a five-minute walk from the team's squalid tent-and-tarp city, the temptation of a tin roof and a hot meal was hard to resist. As Simone recounts,

> [Dibi] had taken a liking to me and as soon as he saw me would ask, "Pizza?" and each time I would answer, "Yes, thank you!"
>
> And so once again that day he would earn two or three thousand rupees, which made him feel like a "businessman," too.

During the first days at base camp, Phurba turned out to be a disaster as a cook. Anatoli grew particularly exasperated by the Sherpa's feckless efforts in the kitchen. "Where on earth did you get this cook?" Anatoli demanded of Simone. "You should never have brought him along!"

Simone rejoined, "Well, then, next time you can find a cook and I'll be the one to judge how he's doing." But the Italian agreed with Anatoli's assessment. As he noted one morning, "Phurba had prepared an awful breakfast in bowls that could no longer remember the date when they were last washed."

After a few days, Dibi Gurung announced that he was going to close his lodge and head down to his village. Simone asked him if the expedition could rent a couple of rooms. "To my amazement, Dibi immediately agreed to my request and asked only a thousand rupees (around 17 U.S. dollars)." The next few days were occupied in packing up base camp and moving it into the lodge. The arrangement even served to improve the culinary situation, as Phurba "began cooking just as he had said he knew how to." Of the team's new base camp, Simone wrote, "It felt like being in a five-star hotel. Four beds, candles, a tidy kitchen and a tin roof over our heads had turned our lives around and lifted morale. Even Anatoli began smiling more often."

Progress on the mountain, however, was negligible. During the first two weeks, it snowed every day. Breaking trail toward the foot of the southwest face, Anatoli, Simone, and Dimitri Sobelev routinely sank in up to their waists. The men could have used snowshoes, Simone noted, although virtually no one ever had on an 8,000er before. The wands they placed at regular intervals to mark the route were in constant danger of being covered up in new snow. The accumulation in places reached an incredible thirteen feet of powder.

A short spell of better weather deteriorated quickly into the usual pattern. After weeks spent just trying to get to the base of the proposed route, Simone summed up the mood of discouragement that hung over the team:

> From that day on we learned to live with these new weather conditions: clear skies in the morning, cloudy in the afternoon and snow overnight. And we got used to not counting on the effectiveness of the trail-breaking done by day. We spent a good many days doing the same job over and over again and it was frustrating to realize it was not possible to proceed with the climbing proper. Like idiots, we continued to go backwards and forwards along the same path: the only advantage was that we were now perfectly acclimatized and could manage to work faster and longer.

Despite the weather, Andre Starkov satisfied his artistic urges by making a number of moody paintings of the stunning landscape. On December 18 he left the expedition and started a long hike out through the native villages. He carried with him a letter from Anatoli to Linda Wylie. In it, Anatoli wrote:

> Tomorrow we are going back up. My expectation is to finish the expedition about January 16, be back in Almaty [Kazakhstan] by the twentieth, and America before February 20.
>
> First I must survive this. If possible we will summit, but it is more important to come back with my sticks. This expedition has cost a lot of money so I will be fighting until the last drop of strength is spent.

By "my sticks," Anatoli meant his ski poles. It was a jesting metaphor for coming back with his life intact. Those sentences were the last words from Anatoli that Wylie would ever receive.

Eventually the three climbers got a depot of supplies cached at 14,100 feet, still on the glacier below the southwest face. Then they pushed on to a shelf the team called the Korean Base Camp, at 16,400 feet, where they found the debris left behind by the first team to attempt an ascent of the Fang. At last the men were on the lower flanks of the southwest face proper. Digging in the snow, they uncovered a low stone wall built by the Koreans. They pitched a single tent in its lee and spent a night there. The next day, they marked the site with tall wands topped with flags, in case more new snow should drift the camp over.

A few days later, Anatoli and Simone returned to the Korean Base Camp. Their worst fears were realized: there was no trace of the stone walls or the tent, but only endless billows of new snow. "Anatoli!" Simone cried. "It just has to be here!"

"I think so too," Anatoli answered, "but we can't clear the whole plateau!"

For the next half hour the two men wandered across the shelf, probing with their ski poles, hoping to feel the soft give of tent fabric. At last Simone's crampons dislodged a loose rock—part of the Korean wall, he guessed. After a number of further probes, his ski pole found the roof of the tent. It was buried under ten feet of new and drifted snow!

The same thing happened to Neal Beidleman and me on K2 in 1992. At Camp III at 24,000 feet, we'd pitched two tents. But when we climbed back up after a storm, we saw only a smooth slope of snow. I'd even anchored the upper end of the last fixed rope to an ice hammer that I'd buried right at the tent site. But the newly drifted snow was so thick and heavy it was impossible to pull the rope free as we approached the camp, so that gave us no clue as to where the tents lay. It took us quite a while, probing with our axes and digging with a shovel, before we found both tents. Then it took a longer while to clear out all the snow and free up our camp. Fortunately, the tent poles were only slightly bent from the weight of snow.

During the last daylight hours, Anatoli and Simone frantically dug out their tent, which had filled up with snow, which had even sifted its way inside the men's sleeping bags. They had to remove every piece of gear, sweep the tent clean, then rearrange their belongings in the claustrophobic pit that was now their camp. The worn-out climbers had finally gotten themselves fed and hydrated and drifted off to sleep when the mountain launched what Simone called its "terrible ambush."

> While we were soundly asleep the sky clouded over again and out of the dark sky the first flakes of snow started falling. The most fearful of enemies seemed to have waited till night to strike and this time he decided to do it with unheard-of violence. For three nights and three days a snowstorm lashed the whole valley and the Annapurna mountains and, like a crippled submarine, we sought desperately to surface from under the mass of snow.

At only 16,400 feet—more than 10,000 vertical feet below the summit—and without having come to grips with any of their route's technical obstacles, Anatoli and Simone were forced to fight just to survive. The terrible conditions took their toll on the men's morale. In a reflective moment, Anatoli told his friend, "I think this is going to be the hardest of all my expeditions." He amplified, "I've never seen so much snow and there are only two of us. . . . On Manaslu [which Anatoli had climbed in the winter of 1995], the only problems were the cold and the wind, but the surface we moved over was as hard as concrete. Usually winter in the Himalayas is like that. That's why it must change, it has to!" In saying "only two of us," Anatoli indicated that he thought the route on Annapurna would be too difficult for Sobelev. When the weather finally cleared, it took a major effort for the two men simply to stagger down to base camp, as they took turns plowing a trough through the snow that had fallen during the previous three days.

Deeply discouraged, and in dire need of a respite from their ordeal, in the third week of December the three climbers and Phurba decided, as Simone phrased it, "to leave Base Camp and go down the valley to rest, breathe oxygen-rich air, see people and colors and smell the perfume of the forest. In short, to rediscover the joys of living." Anatoli knew of a hot spring in the lower valley, and in the village of Gandrung, Dibi Gurung's home, there was even a telephone, the only one in the whole region.

The several days of R&R worked wonders on the men's depleted spirits. In a lodge in the village of Kyamrung, the men ate pizza after pizza, washed down with vast quantities of Sprite and hot lemonade. They bathed and basked in the hot spring, marveling at the warmth, though, Spartan to the core, Anatoli insisted on alternating dips in the hot spring with plunges into the icy river nearby. In Gandrung, he hoped to call Linda Wylie, but discovered that the telephone was out of order.

On their last day in the lowlands, in a tourist lodge near the hot spring, the climbers ran into "a very attractive girl sitting by herself at a table, reading a book." Her name was Cecilia and she was from Argentina. She had been traveling around the world for the better part of a year, most of it with her boyfriend. When he left for Argentina, she spunkily resumed her wandering alone, until she found herself the last tourist of the season in the Annapurna Sanctuary. The climbers invited her during the coming days to hike up and visit their base camp. "Anatoli then added," Simone wrote, "that she would be a guest of the expedition and if she wanted she could also help with the cooking." In the end, Cecilia would play a vital role in the expedition's denouement, as would the initially hapless Phurba.

The shortest day of the year came and went. It was not until December 23 that the three climbers regained their Korean Base Camp site. To reach that shelf, the men had to plow a track through the deep snow all over again. At the camp at 16,400 feet, they found their tent "torn and bent by the weeks of storm it had had to endure."

Dimitri Sobelev planned to climb only to 19,700 feet, then film his comrades through a zoom lens as they pushed on upward toward the crest of the southwest ridge, a thousand feet higher. The next day, the three men started climbing on new terrain. At last, twenty-two days after being dropped off by the helicopter at base camp, as Simone writes, "we were beginning to gain height and make headway on a route we were doing for the first time." As the men moved upward, they snaked out spools of fixed rope and anchored them to the snow, to facilitate their passage in the coming weeks. To Anatoli and Simone, fixing ropes all the way to the crest of the ridge at 20,700 feet seemed a prerequisite for tackling the fiendishly long and difficult ridge between the crest and the summit. The men guessed that that high gauntlet was every bit as long and difficult as the four-mile-long east ridge that Loretan and Joos first solved in 1984.

Roped to Anatoli, Simone led nearly all the pitches that day, while Sobelev trailed behind, filming his teammates. That afternoon, the men established what they called Camp I at 18,000 feet. All day the route had wound through a maze of seracs and gullies, but the slope relented briefly as it leveled off in a shelf that Simone estimated as a hundred meters wide by fifty meters deep. Here, they pitched their tent.

Late that evening, Anatoli produced a small bottle of vodka and offered a Russian toast. The men lingered over their meal "like three friends in a pub." Later, Sobelev announced the terminus of his effort on Annapurna. "Guys," he said, "for me tomorrow will be my last day with you. I've already done more than I ever dreamed of. I'll come up to 6,300 meters [20,700 feet], take shots of the whole of the long ridge you'll be doing over the next few days, film you digging the snow hole and then I'm leaving."

The men discussed the division of labor for the next day. Simone offered to lead again, while Anatoli and Dimitri handled the fixed ropes. To manage the complex process, the men would have to unwind four 200-meter ropes from the big reels they had come on. Simone would tie into one end of the first rope; as he climbed, the other two would ensure that the line paid out without getting tangled in snarls. At the end of the first 200-meter rope, Anatoli would call to Simone to stop while he tied the end of the second rope to the first. And so forth. The division of tasks for the morrow that the men agreed upon that evening would prove to be a fateful one.

After Simone had fallen asleep, he was awakened by a kick from Anatoli. As he later recalled that moment,

> "*What's happening?*" I asked.
>
> "*Merry Christmas!*" Anatoli replied, lighting a candle.
>
> It was midnight and the coldest Christmas of my life. Anatoli was Orthodox and therefore used to celebrating on January 7th, but he had remembered about me and my faith.

"*Thank you, Toli. Thank you.*"

He let the candle burn for a few seconds and then as he blew it out said: "So good night then and sleep well, because you'll have a lot to do tomorrow."

In the morning, Simone led up the steepening face, trailing a fixed rope from his harness. The climbing grew more and more difficult: "Sinking into the snow on an almost vertical surface produced a feeling of insecurity and greatly increased the technical difficulties." But Anatoli and Dimitri handled the rope management to perfection.

After several hours and nearly 3,000 feet of ascent, with almost all the fixed rope paid out, Simone neared the crest of the ridge. His view was blocked by a large boulder, which he managed to work his way around. As soon as he gazed up at the nearby crest, "a rush of adrenaline swept through my body, taking my breath away." In *Cometa,* he vividly describes the sight that met his eyes:

> Above my head there was a terrifying, gigantic cornice of snow and ice stretching out like an ocean wave. Death was hanging right over our heads, and only some strange combination of forces had kept it from crashing down on us. It was impossible to see from below, which was why I was even more stunned and disoriented at finding myself just a whisker away from this time bomb. And it was there, at that precise moment, that the signal came that there was no more rope and I would have to make some sort of a belay to fix this desperately long umbilical cord linking me to my two friends. I was 6,300 meters [20,700 feet] up. I identified a possible way up through an overhang to the right of the huge cornice, but it would need a partner to belay me. Anyway I had no choice, I had to wait where I was.

After kicking a stance in the snow, Simone built an anchor with a pair of ice screws. Then he untied the rope from his harness and tied it in to the anchor. He also took off his rucksack and dangled it by a carabiner from the screws. He was so nervous about the cornice above him that he signaled to Anatoli to come up, rather than shouting—the very sound of his voice, he feared, could make the hanging mass of ice cut loose.

Anatoli understood the signal. Quickly he jumared up the fixed ropes. When he was partway up, Dimitri got out his own jumars and clamped them to the same 800-meter-long chain of rope. Then he, too, started up.

The cold was intense. Simone tried to keep moving, to ward off hypothermia. He got out a video camera to film his friends as they ascended. Then, because his hands felt clumsy, he took off his gloves and stuck them in the rucksack. After only thirty seconds of filming, his hands went numb. He turned off the camera and put it back in his pack. Instinctively, he glanced up. Simone later wrote:

> A fraction of a second later a deafening roar announced the end of that gigantic cornice, and with it our lives.
>
> "Anatoliiiiii . . ." That desperate cry was all I could manage before the explosion of ice and rock started pouring down on me. I had just time to turn towards him and I still remember his eyes. I don't know how, but despite the hundreds of meters separating us I can remember the expression in his eyes just as though he had been standing right in front of me.
>
> It is difficult to put into words what those blue eyes said to me. If I had to interpret that look, Toli's last look, I think it showed a mixture of fear and determination to make it.

In an instant, Anatoli grasped the situation. Without hesitating, he did what experienced climbers always do when an avalanche or collapsing serac bears down on them from above. He tried to run sideways to get out of the path of the tons of falling debris.

Praying that "death would pass me by," with his bare hands, Simone grabbed the fixed rope he had just anchored.

> I managed to hold on for a second, maybe even less, and then I felt myself being torn from the face by an indescribably powerful force. I began falling at supersonic speed with the rope running through my hands. Then a few seconds later I had the impression that the rope was falling with me and that my hands—at last—were holding on to something.
>
> After that there followed an interminable phase of bouncing, sliding, spinning round and round at great speed as though in a vortex, then falling again and the violent impact of all the different parts of my body against the various protuberances of the face. I banged my face, rebounded into the void and then again knocked first my legs, then my back and began sliding again.

As he fell, knocked from side to side by the tumbling blocks of rock and ice, Simone had the sense of being in a whiteout: he could see nothing, and could not even tell up from down. The fall seemed to last forever, until "I finally came to a stop [and] found myself in a sitting position, and everything around me was silent as the grave."

One of the first things Simone did was to look at his altimeter watch. The time was 12:36 P.M. on Christmas Day. His altitude was 18,000 feet. Incredibly, battered by the debris of the collapsed cornice, Simone had survived a tumbling descent of 2,600 feet.

Even before looking at his watch, he had stared at his hands.

"They were cut open right down to the bone," he later wrote, "and burnt flesh marked the edges of the deep gouges made by the rope. I was losing blood and had difficulty focusing on what was before my eyes."

It remains unclear whether the anchor had come loose with the cornice debris, as implied by Simone's "impression that the rope was falling with me," or stayed attached to the mountain so that the static rope whipping through his bare hands cut the flesh down to the bone. In either case, if only he had had his gloves on at the moment of the accident—had not taken them off to work the video camera—he might have prevented the terrible injuries to his hands.

Slowly and awkwardly, Simone clawed himself free from the snow and a tangle of rope that ensnared his right leg. He checked and was astounded to realize that he had broken no bones. Then, only moments after the long fall ended, he looked around for his teammates. He shouted their names into the void.

> Nobody answered . . . nobody! I saw a piece of cloth, perhaps a rucksack, in the snow. I went closer, but realised it was only, terribly, a piece of cloth. I wandered about for ten, maybe fifteen minutes, but there was no clue, I did not know where to start. I was powerless.
>
> "They're dead!" was the stark conclusion I came to. "They really are dead!"

Though alive himself, Simone was in a truly desperate situation. He was losing blood from the gouges in his palms, and one eye had swollen shut. The temperature, he guessed, was 30 below Centigrade (minus 22 Fahrenheit). He was also, as he put it, "half naked," because the violence of the fall had torn gaping holes in his high-altitude suit. No one, not even Phurba, was stationed at base camp, for Simone had urged the cook to spend the days in the lowlands while the men were on the climb. "Time was running out," he later wrote, "and the hour of my death inexorably approaching."

Still, in that instant, Simone rallied himself, shouting out loud, "No! I don't want to die! You stinking bastard of an avalanche, you'll have to strike again if you want to kill me! You're not going to get me. Yes, you heard me. I'm getting back down even if it means crawling like a worm."

Thus began one of the most amazing self-rescues in Himalayan history, a feat in many ways as impressive as J.-C. Lafaille's desperate retreat from the south face of Annapurna in 1992.

In an avalanche, whether one lives or dies often depends simply on luck. The disaster of Christmas Day 1997 on Annapurna would bear a striking similarity to a tragedy that would unfold on another 8,000er, Shishapangma, a little less than two years later. On October 5, 1999, Alex Lowe, Conrad Anker, and filmmaker David Bridges were reconnoitering the massive south face of the mountain, which they eventually hoped to ski down. Suddenly, a huge cornice on the summit ridge thousands of feet above the men broke loose and hurtled toward them. Anker ran one way, Lowe and Bridges another. Anker survived with lacerations and broken bones, but his two teammates were entombed in ice. The bodies of Lowe and Bridges were never found, just as the bodies of Anatoli Boukreev and Dimitri Sobelev have never emerged from the snows of Annapurna's southwest face.

Incredibly, Simone's long fall brought him to rest exactly at the site of the team's Camp I. (No doubt the spacious shelf had served as a catchment basin for the avalanche.) Simone realized his good fortune when he spotted a red tent only footsteps away. The zipper door was frozen shut, but he got it open by stabbing the tent with a crampon point and pulling the zipper with his teeth. Inside the tent, he found spare gloves and a down jacket. As he later wrote, "I put [the jacket] on and in agonising pain pulled the mittens over my bleeding hands. That was a fantastic way to stop the bleeding. They stuck to the deep cuts and staunched the flow of blood."

Then he had to make a cruel choice. He might spend hours trying to find his friends, probing in the avalanche debris, hoping against hope that one or both of them had survived and could be dug out. But that effort would probably cost him his own life. Moreover, as he put it, "The avalanche front was so wide that any attempt at searching for them would be sheer folly."

Instead, he knew that he had to begin his descent immediately. "Go!" he hectored himself repeatedly.

Below Camp I, fixed ropes still hung in place, but Simone's hands were so damaged that he could not hold on with them. Instead, "I devised a way of twisting the rope two or three times round my arm and lowering myself using friction. It worked, clumsily, but it worked."

On the descent, Simone threw caution to the wind. He jumped crevasses and several times leapt off seracs that he estimated to be as high as 15 meters, his landings cushioned by the deep powder of the recent snowfall. Ten hours had passed since the three men started their climb that morning. Simone had had nothing to eat or drink, and now he felt weary with the loss of blood.

At last he reached the Korean Base Camp site. But 3,000 vertical feet of terrain still yawned between him and base camp, at 13,000 feet. Even worse, there was no beaten track to follow below the Korean site. He would have to plow his way through the deep drifts every step of the way. As he later recalled that gutsy effort,

> I carried on down anyway, even though by now it was only thirty or forty steps at a time. Then I would collapse into the snow and stay there for at least a minute and a half. I no longer remember how or when, but I reached the foot of the face, managing to find a way to put almost

> 1,500 meters behind me by sheer desperation and inventive climbing techniques.

Throughout his descent, Simone talked out loud to himself, ordering himself to keep moving. The "third man" phenomenon is a kind of hallucination that many explorers have experienced in survival situations: a pair of climbers or trekkers will become convinced that a third person accompanies them, usually just out of sight behind one's shoulder. The third man is typically a benevolent being, urging the stranded refugees toward safety. Now Simone began to hear his own voice as a second climber exhorting him not to quit. In *Cometa* he vividly captures the dialogue between these two alter egos:

> The thought that kept going round in my mind more and more obsessively was that there would be nobody there at base camp, so I might as well give up anyway and await my end.
>
> "Coward, get up! I said GET UP! Now's the time to show me if you've got any guts! Count up to ten and then get up and get going, hear me?"
>
> 1-2-3-4 . . . 10 and my legs straightened up. I took ten steps and then collapsed.
>
> "Great, great! I knew you could do it. You can make it, you can. Now count to ten again and then up."
>
> 1-2-3-4 . . . 10 and ten more steps and then down again.
>
> "That's the way. Like that."

I've never experienced the third-man phenomenon myself. But such extraordinary climbers as Reinhold Messner report its happening to them time and again on 8,000-meter peaks. I can well believe that, rather than serving as a delusional distraction, the extra voice can spur men and women in extremis to last-ditch efforts they might otherwise not be capable of.

After hours of stumbling and resting and driving himself onward, Simone caught sight of the tourist lodge that had served as the team's base camp. The sun had set, but a bright moon lit up the landscape. Although he was sure no one was there, he called out, "Phurbaaa!" several times. No one answered. Simone counted steps and trudged on. Then, amazingly, he heard a call in response: "Simoneee!"

> I looked up and saw Phurba waving his arms merrily on the brow of the moraine a few paces from base camp and about half a kilometer from me.
>
> "I've made it! Perhaps it's not all up with me after all."
>
> I immediately felt a surge of new strength and morale and answered Phurba with, "*Come here! Please come here!*"

But then Phurba disappeared behind a hillock of snow, and Simone's cries went unanswered. He had just begun to think that the Sherpa was a hallucination when, some ten minutes later, Phurba popped into sight again. And he was not alone: another person walked beside him.

> The two of them came quickly towards me, Phurba carrying a thermos of hot tea. Totally unaware of what had happened, he had made tea before coming to meet me. As normally happened at base camp, he had decided to welcome our return to camp with a hot drink.
>
> As they drew nearer to me I could see they were looking behind me, obviously trying to see where Anatoli and Dima [Dimitri] were.
>
> A few minutes later Phurba stood before me and I can

> still remember his horrified stare. Without waiting for him to speak I told him: "Phurba, there's been a terrible accident. Anatoli and Dimitri are dead."
>
> He asked no questions and gave me his shoulder to lean on as I walked. It was then I saw who the other person was.
>
> It was Cecilia, the girl we had met and got to know at Hot Spring. She did not say a word and her face clouded over with sadness. Taking the thermos out of Phurba's hands, she immediately gave me the hot tea. I drank several cupfuls and only then did Cecilia break the silence by saying, "Be brave, Simone, you're safe and now we can help you."

The only reason base camp was not deserted was that Cecilia had taken Anatoli up on his invitation to visit the team's headquarters, and had recruited Phurba to guide her there. Inside the hut, Simone collapsed on a bed, while Phurba started cooking. Then,

> Cecilia sat down beside me, helped me take off my crampons and boots and get into the sleeping bag and then she began calmly getting me to talk and making me feel safe. Every now and again she asked how I felt and where it hurt. She also caressed my face and with that I fell instantly asleep.

Simone's ordeal was not over. Besides the palms of his hands being cut open to the bone, he had suffered a pair of deep burns from calf to inner thigh where the rope that had gotten tangled around his leg had sawed grooves. He was certain that he could not manage the long hike down to the native villages. He needed to be rescued by helicopter, and there was no time to waste. Intensifying Simone's urgency was the dreaded obligation of telephoning Linda Wylie to tell her that Anatoli was dead.

Exhorted by Simone, Phurba took a scrap of paper with the phone number on it of the team's logistical contact, a Sherpa named Nima Nuru, and set out that evening to hike to Gandrung. Cecilia stayed in the lodge, nursing Simone and brewing up hot drinks. In a heroic effort, the cook whom the whole team had so maligned during the early days of the expedition hiked fifteen hours straight through the night to reach Gandrung, but the telephone there was still out of order.

The only fallback was the office of the Annapurna Conservation Park ranger, which made radio contact with Pokhara for a brief interlude every morning. The exhausted Phurba carried his scrap of paper onward to that office. A warden radioed Pokhara, and after a while, Nima Nuru was on the other end of the transmission. Shocked by the news of the disaster, Nima managed at once to hire a private helicopter. By midday, remarkably enough, the chopper approached the lodge that had served as the expedition base camp. As Simone later wrote, "I got out of the sleeping bag half-dressed and, without putting on my boots, ran out of my refuge just like an American soldier in Vietnam. The pilot had already opened the door of the helicopter and I just threw myself in on my stomach."

There was no room in the chopper for Cecilia. In the end, the gutsy Argentine "tourist" hiked out to the lowlands on her own. She and Phurba had performed the heroic deeds that ensured the survival of Simone Moro.

The chopper took Simone to Kathmandu, where Nima drove him to a French clinic. A shocked woman doctor cleared away the makeshift bandages Cecilia had applied and cut off tags of ruined skin. The next day, Nima took his friend to a hospital where, under local anesthetic, Simone had the torn tendons in his fingers repaired. Even in shock, he demanded of the physician, "Will I still be able to climb again?"

Now Simone had to face the ordeal of calling Linda Wylie and telling her that Anatoli was dead. As soon as she came on the line, she sensed that something was wrong. But when Simone blurted out the news, she started crying, wailing over and over, "No! It can't be."

At this juncture, Simone made a strange about-face. It may be that guilt over having abandoned his partners without probing for their bodies was his motivation. Standing amid the debris of the avalanche on December 25, he had been certain that his friends were dead, but now he had second thoughts. As he recalled in *Cometa*,

> It was then I felt I ought to give her one last ray of hope in order to help her accept what had happened and give her time to take in the full meaning of the tragedy.
>
> "Linda! I said I hadn't seen them since, but I can't be absolutely certain they're dead or that there's nothing more to be done for them. I'm telling you this because the point where the avalanche stopped is just a few meters from our last tent. After the accident I couldn't see properly and I only looked for Anatoli and Dimitri for a few minutes. In the tent there are provisions and gas for a week. If they got out of the avalanche after I'd gone and managed to reach the tent, even if they were injured they could survive for several days. I don't want to raise false hopes, I'm just saying this is a possibility. That's why I'm promising you I'm going to get a helicopter today and go back up to the avalanche."

At once, Wylie endorsed the plan, offering to pay for the helicopter search, and she made plans to come to Kathmandu herself.

Despite his exhaustion and his injuries, Simone not only hired a helicopter but insisted on riding in the passenger seat to guide the pilot back to the scene of the accident. It was still only December 28, a mere three days after the cornice had collapsed. But now the weather had closed in. Despite a number of attempts to fly through the clouds, the helicopter was unable to get anywhere near the team's Camp I at 18,000 feet, where the avalanche debris had come to a halt.

Meanwhile, a team of Kazakh climbers prepared to come to Nepal, intending to search for their compatriots on the ground. Dimitri Sobelev, of course, was a Kazakh, and by 1997 Anatoli had lived in Kazakhstan for the past sixteen years.

On December 30, Simone flew home to Italy. He had only begun to process his grief. On Annapurna he had lost what he would call "my best friend and the companion of my Himalayan climbs." But it was not the mountain that was to blame. In a retrospective comment in *Cometa,* Simone offers a manifesto about risk in mountaineering with which I heartily agree:

> I could not hate the mountain and I do not feel that way even today. A killer mountain exists only in the stupid vocabulary of journalism. A mountain does not kill, does not take anyone, you can't conquer it or challenge it. It remains unmoved in the face of both man and time.

A little more than a week later, the Kazakh team, overcoming daunting obstacles and bitter cold, reached the scene of the accident. They found the red tent still pitched in place, but no sign of Anatoli or Dimitri. Upon their return, the Kazakhs contacted Simone. "They told me," he reported, "how difficult and dangerous it had been to get up there and that around the tent there were great splotches of blood—mine. Even though I had given up all hope, the news came like a knife-thrust to my heart; it finally registered with me that I was the only survivor."

The route on Annapurna that Anatoli, Simone, and Dimitri attempted in December 1997 remains unclimbed today—in either winter, spring, or fall.

Simone not only recovered from his injuries, but he returned to Himalayan mountaineering, where he pulled off a string of landmark ascents. In 2002 he won the David A. Sowles Memorial Award from the American Alpine Club after he gave up his own attempt on Lhotse to rescue an English climber who would otherwise have died. Simone's crowning achievement may have come in February 2009, when he and Denis Urubko made the first winter ascent of Makalu, the world's fifth highest peak. This much-sought-after goal had taken the life of my great friend J.-C. Lafaille, when he vanished above his high camp on an extremely bold solo attempt in January 2006.

The publication of *Above the Clouds* in 2001 served in part to rescue from oblivion the writing and climbing philosophy of Anatoli Boukreev, who had the misfortune to become, thanks to the Everest disaster of 1996, one of the twentieth century's most misunderstood alpinists. Although Anatoli's body has never been found, he is honored with a memorial plaque to climbers who have lost their lives on Annapurna that stands in the Sanctuary below the south face. There, someone has engraved one of Anatoli's pithiest sayings. It serves, I believe, as the perfect epitaph to his dazzling career: "Mountains," Anatoli once wrote, "are not stadiums where I satisfy my ambition to achieve. They are the cathedrals where I practice my religion."

EIGHT

MY ANNAPURNA

After I climbed Broad Peak in July 2003, I had thirteen of the fourteen 8,000ers under my belt—all except Annapurna. I realized that for a third time, I would have to face the mountain that scared me more than any other, or quit the whole game. At times I actually considered ending my Endeavor 8000 with only thirteen of the highest peaks on my ledger, if Annapurna remained beyond the boundaries of my scale of acceptable risk. After all, I'd tried the mountain twice, and both times I'd backed off because I'd decided there was no way to avoid the extreme objective dangers that Annapurna posed. Why should I hope that things might change in my favor this time around?

In the end, though, my stubbornness won out. I felt that I had to give Annapurna a third try, confronting the mountain face-to-face before making my final decision. By 2004, I'd spent seventeen straight years campaigning among the 8,000ers. In a real sense, it had become my life's work. Temperamentally, I can't stand not finishing a project I've worked so hard on—in a metaphor I often use, I need to hammer the last nail into the deck. So I applied for an Annapurna permit for the spring of 2004.

Then I got an interesting offer. David Breashears invited me back to Everest, on an expedition during which he would shoot footage for an ambitious movie planned by the acclaimed British director Stephen Daldry, who, despite having no climbing experience, had become fascinated with the 1996 tragedy on the mountain. As in 1996 on our IMAX expedition, in 2004 my role on the team would be climbing leader in charge of logistics. Veikka Gustafsson would also be part of the crew. He and I thought we could get a jump on Annapurna by first acclimatizing on Everest. If the timing worked out, we'd fly back to Kathmandu after the filmmaking trip, then head a few days later in to Annapurna. The permit on which I'd secured places for Veikka and myself was held by a husband-and-wife team, the strong climbers Ralf Dujmovits and Gerlinde Kaltenbrunner.

Acclimatizing on another peak and then climbing Annapurna quickly had been a scheme I'd contemplated for some time. This seemed the perfect program. I promised David Breashears, however, that Veikka and I would stay on Everest until we were completely done with our work. We wouldn't leave early just to get to Annapurna at the right moment.

Stephen Daldry's intention was to make not a documentary but rather a semi-fictionalized version of the complicated events of that tragic spring, reducing the plot to a drama revolving around Rob Hall, Scott Fischer, and Beck Weathers. But he wanted the real mountain on film, and he also wanted to get an authentic feel for life on Everest, so he came to base camp with us and spent five weeks there. One day I roped Daldry up and got him through the lower part of the Khumbu Icefall, where he reached 19,000 feet—a pretty good effort for an out-of-shape chain-smoker.

The pay was good, the filming was fascinating, and Everest seemed almost tame compared to Annapurna. Along with getting the footage Daldry needed, several of us, including David, Veikka, and me, reached the summit without the slightest mishap. It was the sixth time I had stood on top of the highest mountain in the world.

Seven years later, however, Daldry's film remains on the back burner. Most of us suspect that it will never get made, but we still hope that the footage we shot might be resurrected in some other film about Everest 1996. For Daldry, the primary stumbling block seems to be finding a screenplay that tells his story in a concise and comprehensible manner, while still doing justice to what really happened on the mountain.

As it turned out, we stayed on Everest until well into May. By the time we got back to Kathmandu, Veikka and I realized that we didn't have time to go after Annapurna before the summer monsoon hit. In Kathmandu, we learned that four mountaineers, including not only Dujmovits and Kaltenbrunner but also my Kazakh friend Denis Urubko, had successfully climbed Annapurna by the original French route. It must have been, I guessed, a season with relatively safe conditions on the north side of the mountain. Had I somehow missed the perfect season? I was tempted to kick myself for having passed up that golden opportunity, but I consoled myself with another of my favorite mantras: *You can always go back. The mountain will always be there.*

I didn't want to try Annapurna in the autumn season, so I bided my time and got another permit for the spring of 2005. Veikka would be my partner for the thirteenth time on an 8,000er. We originally planned a simple two-man attempt, but when a couple of my sponsors gently suggested that it would be good to come back from Annapurna with first-rate photos, I decided to invite a third climber. I'd never before had a professional photographer along on one of my expeditions just for the sake of taking pictures, nor had I ever felt any pressure to do so, but I immediately thought of Jimmy Chin. Jimmy was not only a top-notch shooter, but also a very accomplished mountaineer and rock climber. If anything, I felt, he would add strength to our team. He'd been with us on Everest in 2004, reaching the summit with David, Veikka, and me, and we'd all gotten along handsomely.

The plan I concocted for Annapurna in 2005 should, I thought, reduce the hazards to an absolute minimum. The three of us would go first to Cho Oyu. I'd climbed that mountain in 1996, but neither Veikka nor Jimmy had. We'd use an ascent of Cho Oyu as our acclimatization training run. Then we'd fly out to Kathmandu for a brief respite, helicopter in to Annapurna, and go up the French route as fast as we could. I'd worked this scenario on a number of previous "twofers," starting in 1994, when I'd climbed Lhotse just a week after climbing Everest. Then, in 1999, I'd gotten up Manaslu and Dhaulagiri back-to-back, and Nanga Parbat and Broad Peak in 2003. (In 1995 I'd pulled off my only "threefer," climbing Makalu, Gasherbrum I, and Gasherbrum II in quick succession. It was almost a "fourfer," but we'd had to turn around just 300 feet shy of Everest's summit only ten days before we reached the top of Makalu.)

Meanwhile, however, my home life was growing ever more busy and involving. On October 25, 2004, Paula gave birth to our third child, a beautiful girl whom we named Anabel. I had seen over the years how the strain on Paula of my going off to the Himalaya year after year was taking its emotional toll. When I set out on an expedition, she would be home managing the kids and our house. The daily business tasks that I usually took care of, such as returning messages and booking speaking events, now became her responsibility. On the road, I tried to help out by satellite phone, but there was only so much I could do. Paula had always been completely supportive of my Endeavor 8000. Knowing how getting out in the mountains energized me, she'd never have dreamed of asking me to quit climbing. But she also knew just how dangerous Annapurna was. By the spring of 2005, moreover, I was forty-five years old. I felt in as good shape as I'd ever been, but there was no avoiding the fact that the simple gung-ho resolve to get up 8,000ers that I had in my late twenties had evolved into a more complex and ambivalent passion. In the early years, when I was living by myself, it was easy to leave Seattle and head off to the Karakoram or the Himalaya.

Now each departure for an expedition meant a wrenching separation from Paula and the kids.

Until it was set in stone that we were really going back to Annapurna in 2005, the magnitude of that decision didn't really hit me. When the expedition was still five months off, or four, it seemed like a distant cloud on the horizon. But then it became two months before we started, then one. I started having sleepless nights. In the wee hours my thoughts grew dark: *Oh, shit! I've gotta go do this.* Yes, I'd publicly announced I was going back to Annapurna, but at the core of my resolve was a commitment to myself.

I didn't want Paula, or anyone else, to see my anxiety, so I tried to keep it hidden. But at night, even on the mountain, you're always more fearful—that's when the deepest, darkest thoughts flood through your head. The next morning, under a sunny sky, the doubts and fears tend to evaporate. In a similar way, the buildup to an expedition can seem more stressful than the expedition itself. As I tossed in bed, I'd sometimes tell myself, *Ed, just go to Annapurna. You'll feel much better when you're standing at the base of the mountain.* Yet the strain through those winter months was cruel. I'd never felt that kind of foreboding before.

In April we finally flew to Kathmandu. After rounding up gear and food, we drove in trucks from the Nepalese capital across the border into Tibet, until we reached the end of the road at a village called Tingri. From there, we made our way on foot, with yaks carrying our loads, to the Cho Oyu base camp. The climb up the mountain's flanks went smoothly. We were there early in the spring season, so we had the mountain virtually to ourselves. By April 20, Veikka, Jimmy, and I were established in our high camp at 23,300 feet. We would set out for the summit at two o'clock in the morning.

A storm delayed us for a day, but we got ready to go in the wee hours of April 22. Only fifteen minutes out of camp, however, Jimmy collapsed in the snow. As Veikka and I hovered around him,

I was alarmed to hear Jimmy slurring his speech, and he admitted that he couldn't catch his breath. To me, the symptoms were all too suggestive of the onset of cerebral edema. Jimmy insisted that if he just took a short rest, he'd be ready to go again. He really wanted to make the summit.

Against our better judgment, Veikka and I waited while Jimmy rested, then we set out together once more. Almost at once, Jimmy collapsed again. That was it, as far as I was concerned. I wasn't going to take any further chances.

On previous expeditions, when I was serving as a guide, I'd sometimes ordered clients who were moving too slowly or starting to show signs of altitude sickness to turn around. It's hard to dictate to someone who's dreamed about and saved his dollars for years in the hope of getting to the summit of a big mountain that he has to give up his goal and go down. But not heeding those warning signs is asking for trouble. My job as a guide was to make those tough calls, and I never had any qualms about laying down the law with clients.

Yet this was different. Jimmy wasn't a client; he was an equal member of our expedition. The only thing he lacked was age and experience. Cho Oyu was my twenty-ninth attempt on an 8,000-meter peak. I'd never before ordered a partner on a Himalayan climb to do anything, but now I was as firm with Jimmy as I would have been with a client. "I'm afraid that's it, Jimmy," I said. "You can't go any higher. And we have to get you down as fast as possible."

Once he accepted my edict, Jimmy was great about it. Not wanting to sabotage Veikka's and my chances for the summit, he offered to stay in high camp while we pushed for the top. But that's asking for it, too, if you've got cerebral edema. The only sure cure is to get to a lower altitude as fast as possible. (Back in the States, a doctor to whom Jimmy described his symptoms concluded that he was most likely suffering from pulmonary, not cerebral, edema. The lack of oxygen due to his condition afflicted his brain with hypoxia, which caused his slurred speech and uncoordinated movements.)

The upshot was that I went down with Jimmy, while Veikka pushed on solo to the top. The climb meant much more to him than to me, since I'd climbed Cho Oyu before. It was his ninth 8,000er. Only four years later, he would become the seventeenth mountaineer to climb all fourteen, only the ninth to do so without supplemental oxygen.

I really didn't mind giving up the summit of Cho Oyu. Getting Jimmy down safely was paramount. And I was greatly relieved when, back at base camp, he recovered dramatically. Soon he was almost his normal self again.

By April 25 we were back in Kathmandu. In only a few days, we would helicopter in to the north side of Annapurna. Now we had a discussion that was every bit as painful as my overruling Jimmy's wishes at high camp on Cho Oyu. Jimmy wanted to give Annapurna his best shot. He was feeling fine again, and with his youthful drive, he was raring to go.

Once more, I had to veto his hopes. It wasn't simply a question of whether taking care of Jimmy might undercut my single-minded determination to push up the French route on Annapurna. It was Jimmy's welfare that clinched my veto. It would simply be too risky for him to go as high as 23,000 feet (not to mention all the way to the 26,545-foot summit) so soon after his collapse on Cho Oyu. Edema doesn't always recur the next time a climber who's been flattened by it goes high, but the chances of its striking again only two or three weeks later are hugely magnified.

I'll confess that a slightly selfish agenda also contributed to my edict. This would be Veikka's and my third attempt on Annapurna and, regardless of the outcome, almost certainly our last. I did not want to compromise our chances in any way, and the possibility that Jimmy could get sick again as we made our rapid ascent seemed too great a risk.

So I had to tell Jimmy the terms on which Veikka and I would consent to his coming with us on Annapurna. It was a tough call for me, since disappointing my friends is not one of my strong suits. It actually took me a few days to work up the courage to tell Jimmy my decision. As long as he was well, he could hang around base camp, shooting pictures to his heart's delight. He could even go with us to the next camp, at the start of the north face. But he was not going to join us on the climb itself.

It was a bitter pill for Jimmy to swallow, but he did so with grace and magnanimity. In the end, he climbed with us to Camp II, at 19,000 feet. He shot lots of great photos of Veikka and me at base camp and just above. And he was a fine companion whose support throughout the expedition meant a lot to Veikka and me. Would that more ambitious high-altitude mountaineers were capable of the kinds of self-sacrifice and loyalty Jimmy displayed that May!

Veikka and I had decided that on our third attempt on Annapurna we'd give the 1950 French route a shot. It seemed the fastest and most direct line to the top, and now, well acclimatized from Cho Oyu, we hoped to race up it in as few as three days. This despite the fact that in 2000, as we sat at base camp and watched avalanches pour down the huge concave bowl across which the French route makes a beeline upward and left, that part of the face had seemed ridiculously dangerous. Yet, year after year, climbers managed to repeat the French route without catastrophes. Veikka and I had concluded that conditions in 2000 had been about as bad as they ever get. Besides, we knew by now that there really was no safe route on Annapurna. The French line was, so to speak, the least of all evils.

We'd learned in Kathmandu that two other expeditions were already on the mountain on the north side. One was an Italian team led by Silvio Mondinelli. I recognized his name but didn't know much about him. I'd soon learn that Silvio was going for his twelfth 8,000er on Annapurna. The other team was also Italian, co-led by Christian Kuntner, who, like Reinhold Messner, was a German-speaking climber from the Italian Tyrol. Christian, like me, had all the thirteen other 8,000ers under his belt; this would be his fourth attempt on Annapurna.

We flew in on April 30, leaving Kathmandu in the midst of a lightning storm, but landing on a shelf below the north face in clear weather. We had scarcely gotten our tents pitched at our grassy base camp when Silvio's team paid a visit. "V[ery] v[ery] nice guys," I wrote in my diary. We learned that they'd already been on the mountain for forty-one long days. They'd fixed ropes all the way up to 23,000 feet and were ready to go for the summit, but they'd been waiting for more than a week for the weather to be right. I was impressed by their caution and patience. During the next couple of days, we visited each other's camps. The Italians couldn't have been more hospitable. In their dining tent, they treated us to good cheeses and prosciutto and coffee and chocolate, and often we would walk back to our camp with our arms full of Italian goodies. All we had to offer in return was Pringles and beer!

Then Silvio said, "Come with us!" It turns out they knew all about Veikka's and my two previous attempts on Annapurna. They were offering to let us join forces with them and use our ascenders on the fixed ropes they'd already placed, which would save us an immense amount of time and effort. It would mean that we could climb alpine style, having to traverse that dangerous face only once on the ascent. Yet, inwardly, I hesitated, since I had played no part in fixing those ropes myself. Still, it would have been absurd, not to mention cluttering up the mountain, for us to lay a whole parallel string of fixed ropes right next to theirs just to demonstrate our independence. Veikka and I gratefully accepted Silvio's offer.

We spent a day packing heavy loads up to a secure site at 15,000 feet that we turned into a gear depot. The weather was holding fine. Champing at the bit, the Italians planned to climb on May 3 to Camp II, spend the night, then push on to a camp just above the notorious Sickle, the ice cliff that brows the whole face. They had pinpointed May 5 as their summit date. If all went well, we might be right behind them. Our acclimatizing on Cho Oyu was paying its dividends now. Veikka and I were in top shape. I wrote in my diary, "Everything 'feels' right. We'll soon know. . . . Relax now & get head space." Could climbing Annapurna really be this easy, after all the anguish I'd expended over the prospect?

But then the weather changed: fog swallowed base camp, thick clouds rolled over the mountain, and a light snow fell. Each afternoon we packed up, ready to go; each evening, we made the decision to wait another day.

Four days came and went with no progress. Veikka and I studied the face, expecting to see the gigantic avalanches that had so frightened us in 2000. But something seemed different this spring. The mountain looked far more stable and quiescent. We allowed our hopes to soar, even while the bad weather kept us confined at base camp.

During this lull, I called Paula on our sat phone. Missing her and the kids was as excruciating as ever, but by now I was really focused on the challenge at hand. Before the trip, she'd had a sense of anxiety almost as deep as mine. In hopes of easing both our minds, I'd decided to carry the sat phone all the way up the mountain to keep her updated on our progress. Normally, Paula didn't want me to call her from a summit, knowing that was too soon to claim success. But this time we agreed that a call from the top of Annapurna would be a good thing.

On May 7 we got a favorable weather report from Michael Fagen, a precision meteorologist back in Seattle whom I'd hired to monitor conditions half a globe away. (This has become a standard tactic on Himalayan climbs. Those geniuses sitting behind their computers studying satellite imagery can give a far more accurate forecast for a single mountain such as Annapurna than anything we'd get over the radio from Kathmandu.) We planned to head up on May 8. I wrote in my diary, "It's now or never. Feels as good as it's going to. Will get more of a feel as we move tomorrow."

On the eighth, it took us ten hours to climb from base camp to Camp II, where we found three of the Italians installed. The crux of the expedition, I thought, would come on the next day, when we had to dash up and across what I called the Gauntlet, that frightfully exposed face down which in 2000 we'd seen the avalanches pour. I knew we'd want to make that vulnerable climb as quickly as possible.

The next morning, Silvio and a fifth Italian arrived at Camp II very early, planning to join us on the push to Camp III. Since they'd already stocked their highest camp, the Italians had to carry almost nothing in their packs, while Veikka and I lugged forty-five pounds each. But that meant that the Italians could break trail for us up the Gauntlet. We were off at 4:30 in the morning. Everything went as smoothly as we could have hoped, and we arrived at Camp III, at 22,300 feet, after eight hours of nonstop climbing—nonstop be cause there was only a single place en route where we thought it was safe to pause and rest. That evening I wrote in my diary, "Glad to finally get the tent up, etc. Ugh! Hope to not have to do that again." By "that," I meant the crossing of the Gauntlet, during which my heart had been in my throat the whole time.

I was pretty wired—the culmination of an eighteen-year quest might come the next day. We still had 4,000 feet to climb to reach the summit, but from what I knew from other expedition reports, that endless snow slope above Camp III was relatively safe, with only a few mildly technical passages. At that altitude, it would be a long haul, but I'd made comparable pushes in the past to the tops of other 8,000ers. Early that evening, however, the wind picked up and clouds moved in again. We went to sleep still hopeful—or rather, tried to go to sleep. I didn't get a wink all night. No matter how many times I'd been stuck in a tent in similar circumstances, that night of May 9–10 was psychologically grueling.

All through the dark hours, our tent flapped violently in the wind. The sound alone kept us awake, but on top of it, ice particles that condensed on the roof from our breathing kept falling in our faces. If you covered your face with your sleeping bag (Veikka and I shared a single bag, draped over us like a down comforter), you couldn't breathe. By 4:00 A.M. with the wind as strong as ever, I knew we would have to be resigned to a day of waiting. But all through May 10 the wind never relented. At some point I wrote in my diary, "Sucks! . . . No way to move today. Wind all day—hard to rest!!"

Our tent was pitched only 75 feet below the Italian tents, but in the wind, it would take an inordinate effort to get dressed and clump up to their campsite—across several small hidden crevasses that, though probably harmless, were enough to give us pause. Instead, we shouted over the gale. "There's no way!" I called out. "Too windy! We'll talk to you again in twenty-four hours." The Italians shouted back their agreement.

We spent the day nibbling on banana chips, cashews, dried pineapple, and salami. We stayed hydrated with soup and tea. Several times each we suited up simply to get out of the claustrophobic confines of the tent and shovel the windblown snow off it. Peeing into a bottle inside the tent was no big deal, but the process of taking a crap outside on a steep slope with snow blowing into your pants was an ordeal. No matter which way you faced, the wind would shift direction at the critical moment and you'd be doused with stinging snow. Fortunately, our small intake of food meant a small output of waste, minimizing the number of forays we had to make out into the cold to take care of business.

Veikka and I got up at midnight on May 11, hoping for a break in the weather, but the wind and whiteout were as bad as ever. We crawled back under our sleeping bag, despondent at the thought of another day of inaction. In the Himalaya, there's nothing more mentally arduous than waiting out a storm at a high camp. It's hard to get warm. We didn't have a book to read, and as for conversation, Veikka and I had already told each other everything that was in our minds. In addition, the very act of talking seemed to waste precious energy, so we kept our conversations short. We just lay there counting the minutes like convicts in a prison cell. Beneath it all, we heard a constant undertone of gloom—the prospect of defeat. My diary records the torment: "Wind all night again. No sleep. No way to move so will stay another day. We really *don't* want to go down & have to come back up. That would suck!!"

The sleeplessness debilitates you. On top of that, Veikka and I were running short of food and gas canisters for the stove. Sometime on the eleventh, Silvio called out, "Do you guys need anything?" I shouted back, telling him about our dwindling supplies. He called out, "We have plenty!" Once again, the hospitality of the Italians was reassuring, and we were deeply grateful for their presence.

A couple of the Italians were smokers. It's funny, but as hard as it was to hear each other yelling over the wind, with our camps 75 feet apart, we could sometimes smell the smoke from their cigarettes. We took that as a sign that all was well with them. But that day, one of the Italians bailed. "I just can't handle the waiting anymore," he said. We were sorry to see him go down.

During our enforced idleness at Camp III, I kept Paula updated via the sat phone. Every time I reached her, though, she assumed we were on the verge of leaving for the summit or were already on our way. Learning that we were still delayed, she felt a small thud of disappointment. But she rallied her spirits and boosted mine with unfailing optimism.

Shortly after noon on May 11 the wind died at last. We planned to get up at 1:30 A.M., check out the conditions, and, if they were tolerable, give it a go. We thought we could be out of the tent and headed up by 3:00 A.M. We figured that the final 4,000-foot climb could take eight hours or more. My last diary entry on May 11 was like a plea to the mountain gods: "Finally?? We hope tomorrow is the day. Otherwise we have to go down. Don't want *that.* Pleezze give us a chance."

We stuck to our schedule, getting up at 1:30. One of the last things I did as we got ready to go was to call Paula and tell her of our departure. But no matter how hard I tried, I could not get a signal from the sat phone. Of all the times for the device *not* to work, this was the worst. In my frustration I threw the phone into the corner of the tent, knowing it would be a lump of useless weight in my pack. I was able to radio down to Jimmy Chin at base camp and ask him to call Paula, to tell her we'd launched our summit bid. We would carry the radio to the summit instead of the phone.

We didn't even take the time to brew up a hot drink. Breakfast consisted of a granola bar apiece. I carried a single liter bottle of water, which I knew in the bitter cold would turn to icy slush, and several tubes of energy gel, which is one of the easiest things to eat when you're on the go at high altitude. That's not much food and liquid to sustain a 4,000-foot climb, but I'd learned over the years that I barely ate much of anything on a summit day anyway, so it seemed pointless to carry additional weight. It may be hard to understand how climbers can push through as many as eighteen hours of hard labor during a round-trip summit day with almost nothing to eat or drink. The fact is that it's often too cold to stop, you're simply too focused on the task at hand, and the extreme altitude messes with your appetite to the point where you have little or no desire to eat.

I carried with me a small camera, some willow wands to mark the route, a light 25-meter rope, and a single snow picket to anchor that rope. Normally I carry even less, but on this crucial ascent, which might be my last on an 8,000er, I didn't want to regret having left behind some piece of gear I might need.

Weeks before, the Italians had fixed a rope above Camp III to secure our passage through a small ice cliff. Above that, in the early hours, we fixed a couple more ropes; they would serve not only to make descent easier, but also to help us find the way to the top of the ice cliff if we got down in whiteout or after dark. The slope was quite steep right out of camp, and after two days of inaction, the effort took our breath away. But then we climbed into a wide, open snow basin. The Italians had left camp first, but Veikka soon overtook them and went into the lead. In all our climbing together, I'd never seen Veikka stronger. I could keep up with him, but I never closed the gap between us.

It was fiendishly cold that morning, in part because we were in perpetual shadow, as the sun, hidden behind the slope above us, never hit the face. I had on everything I could to stay warm—fleece jacket under my down suit, face mask and neck protector, goggles and mittens—and still it was all I could do to ward off the polar chill. Despite my double boots (plastic outer, foam-lined inner) encased in insulated overboots, my toes kept threatening to go numb, so as I climbed I wiggled them constantly to keep the circulation flowing. In and of itself, that simple act takes concentration and energy. My thoughts flew back fifty-five years to Herzog and Lachenal on this same slope, as they felt their toes go numb. Lachenal had stopped twice to take off his inadequate leather boots and rub his toes, but Herzog had charged on, all but oblivious to the numbness in his feet, already rapt in his mystical trance.

Everybody was having his own private battle with the cold. After three or four hours, I looked down and saw only three climbers below me, not four. When one of the Italians briefly caught up with me, I asked, "Where's Silvio?" "His feet too cold," the man answered. "He turn around." *Poor Silvio,* I thought. This close to seizing his twelfth 8,000er, after nearly two months of struggle on Annapurna, he had had to throw in the towel. Yet at the same time I admired his good judgment. No mountain is worth losing your toes for. As it turned out, Silvio would return to Annapurna two years later, climb it successfully, and close the loop on his own fifteen-year campaign to reach the top of all fourteen 8,000ers.

I'd started placing the willow wands above the last fixed ropes, but we had so few that I had to string them out at great distances from one another. Still, they could prove invaluable on the descent if the weather turned bad.

The monotony of the vast summit slope was cruel in its own right. As I later wrote in my diary, "Continuous grade—relentless. No place to stop/sit, only squat." I'd planned to shoot photos on the way up, but now it seemed too cold and too much work to stop, take off my mittens, and risk frostbite for the sake of a picture. For the same reason, I didn't bother to take off my pack to get out my water bottle or the tubes of energy gel.

Another factor that made the climb arduous was that we couldn't see the summit pyramid—it was hidden behind the top of the seemingly infinite slope up which we trudged. It was hard even to judge our progress, as we "ran laps" on our treadmill of featureless snow. "Dig deep & focus on rhythm & pace," I later described the discipline I had to muster on May 12.

The wind had sprung up, making the day even colder. Veikka and I hardly exchanged a word—shouting over the wind, like getting out my camera, just seemed too much work, and besides, during our climbs together we were used to long stretches of silence. Each of us moved upward in his own private capsule of cold.

At last I saw the final rock band. I thought it was only half an hour above us, but it actually took us two more hours to reach it. The scale of this upper north face was truly monstrous. Finally we got to the band. The gully that split the cliffs was easy to find, and we discovered an old fixed rope snaking through it. We knew better than to trust that weathered cord by pulling on it, but we used it to guide our way up the narrow couloir.

Above the rock, instead of the summit we so dearly longed to see, a series of snow bumps, each slightly higher than the previous one, stretched into the distance. It was past noon, but the cold and wind were relentless. We kept moving. Then, still in the lead, Veikka yelled out the first words I had heard him utter in hours: "That's it!" It looked like just another snow bump, but as we wearily closed the gap and clambered atop its crest, we could see that there was no higher ground anywhere around us. We were on the summit of Annapurna. Since leaving camp that morning, it had taken us eleven long, cold hours to get there.

It was 2:00 P.M. Veikka and I hugged each other as tightly as we could, feeling clumsy with cold. My mind was racing: *Oh, my God! It's not just my fourteenth, it's Annapurna. That in itself is an amazing achievement. And I've finally pulled it off.*

For weeks, I had imagined that if I got to the top of the mountain, I wouldn't be able to hold back the flood of emotion and tears. Somehow, though, I didn't start crying now. I teared up a little, but the full release of my feelings would have to wait till I got back to base camp. On top of Annapurna, Louis Lachenal and Jerzy Kukuczka had felt only a numbed nothingness. That wasn't what hit me now. My whole body seemed to vibrate with joy and a sense of fulfillment, but it was checked by a certain rational alertness. Maurice Herzog's mystical rapture was very far from my own mental state on the summit.

That rational calm was the safeguard I'd carried with me on all thirty of my Himalayan expeditions. The climb wasn't over. As I had always told myself, *The summit is only the halfway point.* We had climbed Annapurna, but we still had to get down safely. And as it would turn out, on no other mountain that I'd ever climbed—

except perhaps K2 in 1992—would the challenge of the descent exact all the skill and endurance I possessed.

On the summit, I finally got out my camera and took a few pictures. I shot some snaps of Veikka, then handed him the camera so he could take portraits of me. I turned on our two-way radio to tell Jimmy Chin at base camp about our triumph. "This is one of the happiest days of my life," I said, "and one of the hardest." In the background, I could hear other climbers at base camp cheering our success. I asked Jimmy to call Paula on the sat phone we kept at base, so that she'd know we'd made it. Since my own sat phone had stopped working that morning, relaying the news through Jimmy was the next best thing to calling her myself.

We spent almost an hour on top. I wanted to savor every sweet moment of this profound turning point in my life. After a little while, Veikka and I peered down the massive south face, which pitched dramatically away from just below our feet. Out of that gulf, Don Whillans and Dougal Haston had emerged in 1970, forging the first ascent of the face, and somewhere down there J.-C. Lafaille had managed his desperate retreat in 1992, after Pierre Béghin fell to his death, taking all the duo's hardware with him.

Finally we started down. We met the three Italians just as they reached the summit ridge. Shaking their hands, we wished them good luck. All three went on to top out on the true summit shortly after 3:00 P.M.

My first premonition that the descent was going to be problematic came as the usual afternoon clouds rolled in. Before long it was snowing lightly, and the mist thickened until we were in genuine whiteout. Now, I knew, the willow wands would be critical to our finding our way. In some places the new snow was knee deep. At this point, Daniele, the strongest of the Italians, caught up to us. Instead of climbing down single file, the three of us spread out parallel, increasing our chances of intercepting each of the widely spaced wands.

All this took an inordinate amount of time. Sometimes we had to sit down and patiently wait for a gap in the mist to get a glimpse of the next willow wand. It grew later and later, but one by one, we found each of the markers. I could see, however, that new snow was starting to pile up. I started to fear that the upper anchors of the fixed ropes, below the last wand, would get drifted over.

On the way up, just above the topmost ice screw anchor, I'd placed a pair of wands as a landmark for where the fixed ropes began. At last we found those wands, but now it was 6:00 P.M. and starting to get dark. Still, I thought, it should be a piece of cake from here back to the camp. Once we were on the fixed ropes, we would have a continuous handline stretching all the way to our tents.

The upper anchor ought to be just below us, around a tiny corner, screwed into a wall of ice a few feet off the ground. But as I turned that corner, I saw nothing there. "What the hell?" I muttered.

A sense of dread crept over me. This was how things could turn serious, I knew. Daniele insisted, "I know the way. Follow me." We climbed farther down, but nothing felt right to me. Nor did it to Veikka. We had our headlamps on, but they illuminated only a cone of ground ahead of our feet. After we'd flailed around in the snow for a while, finding no sign of the fixed ropes, Veikka said, "I don't remember climbing this. We need to go back up and traverse a bit to the right." I trusted his judgment, which had always been uncanny when it came to route-finding. Had we kept descending in line with Daniele's hunch, it was entirely possible we would have missed Camp III altogether and found ourselves stranded in the dark on unknown terrain on the huge north face.

It grew later and later, and we got more and more tired. Around

9:00 P.M., the weather started to improve. The stars came out and the wind died. The possibility of spending the night out occurred to me. At an altitude of around 23,000 feet, I figured we could survive, but a bivouac in the open wasn't a prospect I looked forward to. We were pretty sure we were close to the place where the fixed ropes led down over the ice cliff, so I started to drag my boots through the snow, hoping my crampons might snag the rope lying buried in the slope.

Then, suddenly, I felt my crampons scrape and stick on something. I pulled that something loose, and joyously recognized it as fixed rope. But it wasn't the uppermost rope. Whatever happened to make the upper ice screw anchor disappear puzzles me to this day.

We didn't get back to our tents until 10:00 P.M. Except for our rest on the summit, we'd been going for nineteen hours straight, with very little to eat or drink. Seldom on any of my Himalayan expeditions had I felt so exhausted. But that night, I still had the strength to write in my diary, "TODAY WE DID IT! UN-BE-LIEVE-ABLE! DREAM COME TRUE!"

The other two Italians didn't make it back to camp that night, but Daniele told us not to worry about them. As it turned out, the men accidentally broke through a small crevasse somewhere on the summit slope and decided to take refuge inside it. After a grim bivouac, they pushed down in the morning. At Camp III, Veikka and I finally slept for the first time in days, and slept more deeply than we had in weeks. In the morning, when we smelled cigarette smoke wafting on the breeze, we realized the whole team was safe.

That day, May 13, we resolved to push all the way to base camp. Veikka and I dashed down the Gauntlet for the last time. No debris, thank God, came hurtling through that basin while we were there. At Camp II, Charley Mace, my partner from K2 in 1992, who was on Annapurna with another small team, had kindly stashed a pair of water bottles for us. We swigged them down almost in a single gulp. Up at Camp III, Veikka and I had left behind our small tent, stove, and sleeping bags for Charley to use on his attempt several days later.

Now, at Camp II, we were able to strip off our down suits for the first time in days. We were shocked to see how loosely the clothing under the suits hung from our emaciated bodies. We retrieved the rest of our gear and started down. We were very tired, but we weren't going to stop short of base camp.

Then, just as it had the day before, clouds moved in and we found ourselves in whiteout again. We were off the north face proper, but we still had to wend a circuitous path through a small icefall and over domes of rock and snow. The wands with which I had marked the route had melted out, fallen flat, and were now buried under new snow. We were so close, but once again we started wandering like zombies. Many times we had to sit and wait for a clearing to get our bearings once again. I cursed the mountain to myself, *Come on! Give us a break!* As I later wrote in my diary, "Annapurna would not let us go!"

We got on the radio with Jimmy, who tried to guide us to camp by describing landmarks. He was like an air traffic controller talking a plane he couldn't see into a smooth landing. As we descended the final stretch of ice, Jimmy, Silvio, and several others hiked up to greet us at the toe of the glacier. There was a momentary break in the whiteout, and we saw them below us, cheering and waving.

When we met, Silvio gave me a tremendous bear hug, lifting me off the ground. Six years later that hug is indelibly etched in my memory of the expedition. It came from a warm and generous man whom I had only recently met and who, in ways too numerous to count, had helped Veikka and me climb Annapurna. Silvio epitomized what we call "the brotherhood of the rope," the code by which climbers selflessly go to the aid of their teammates, or even of other climbers not on their team.

The guys had brought our trekking shoes, into which we

changed for the last easy hike to base camp. And they'd brought us beer and juice, which we guzzled like men who had reached an oasis after crawling across a desert. They'd also brought Pringles, the first food that we'd had the luxury of eating in more than twenty-four hours.

Finally my emotions broke. I've almost never cried on a mountain, but there, below the north face of Annapurna, I let it go. Not full-on sobbing, but tears, hidden by my sunglasses. Choked up, unable to speak, I felt vaguely embarrassed, but too full of relief to care. Veikka and I hugged each other without a word.

Forty-five minutes later we reached base camp. As I wrote in my diary that night, "Great to be on solid, flat earth with grass!" At last I had put the specter that had haunted my sleepless nights all winter to rest. I had climbed Annapurna. It was still hard to grasp, but in the coming weeks and months, my sense of fulfillment would bloom and flourish like some wild exotic plant. It had taken eighteen years for me to complete my quest. The future, it seemed, held nothing but gratification and joy.

EPILOGUE

GODDESS OF THE HARVESTS

At first, however, my sense of fulfillment had to be put on hold. On May 11, 8,000 miles away from Annapurna, a different drama from my push to the summit was playing itself out. At our home in Bainbridge Island, west of Seattle, Paula had picked up the phone at 3:00 P.M. It was Jimmy Chin, telling her that Veikka and I had just set out for the top, at 3:00 A.M. on the twelfth, Nepalese time. During earlier conversations, I'd told Paula that I thought it ought to take us eight hours or so to go from Camp III to the summit.

All the rest of that afternoon and evening, Paula waited in silence. By 10:00 P.M. she was almost holding her breath. Eleven P.M. came and went, then midnight. Paula's mood steadily darkened.

At that time, Veikka and I were still two hours from the summit, pushing up the interminable slope below the final rock band. Part of my mind was acutely aware that eight hours had passed since we had set out. Step after arduous step, as I realized that our progress was slower than I'd anticipated, I knew that I ought to signal Veikka to halt, dig the two-way radio out of his pack, and call Jimmy with an update. But aside from the cold and the unrelenting steepness of the terrain, the sheer effort it took to keep moving seemed to rule out stops of any kind, even to take a swig from my water bottle. Veikka and I needed all the concentration we could muster to have a chance of getting to the top. Aware that Paula must be growing anxious, I tried to send her a kind of telepathic message: *Be flexible, babe. You know that eight hours is only a guess.*

At base camp, Jimmy himself had started to worry. Loyal to the end, he felt that he had to give Paula some kind of bulletin, so he called her again. "They left at three A.M.," Jimmy said, "but we haven't heard from them since." Jimmy probably felt that a no-news-is-good-news message was better than silence. But his call only ratcheted up Paula's anxiety. She went to bed, but she couldn't sleep. She hadn't said a word about what was happening on Annapurna to Gil or Ella—there was no point inflicting her own fears on our kids. (Anabel, at seven months, was too young to understand.)

In the months before the expedition, my own darkest moments had come in the middle of the night, when I couldn't sleep. It's not surprising that the same sort of angst now assaulted Paula. She curled up in a fetal ball as one scenario after another ran unchecked through her head. We could have been caught in an avalanche. One or both of us might have taken a fatal fall. The cold and wind could have forced us to seek shelter under a serac, where we might be slowly freezing to death.

As the minutes ticked by in our dark bedroom on Bainbridge Island, Paula gradually became convinced that one of those scenarios must have come true. *Something's gone wrong,* she said to herself. *Eddie's not coming home.*

In retrospect, it's easy to dismiss that kind of gloomy conviction as a fantasy borne of fear and love. But it's so utterly real when it washes over you. Just eight months after I got back from Annapurna, Katia Lafaille endured a comparable night of terror and despair. Attempting his incredibly bold solo ascent of Makalu in winter, J.-C. called Katia, at home in southern France, on his sat phone to tell her he was setting out for the summit. He promised to call her again in just a few hours, when he had reached the base of the final couloir leading to the top. The hours came and went. Katia grew frantic. Unable to bear the tension by herself, she e-mailed me. I tried to calm her down, e-mailing back, "There is always hope. Please give him time to come down."

But this time Katia's worst fears were realized. J.-C. never made that call. And though Katia eventually flew to Nepal, helicoptered to the Makalu base camp, and then flew around the mountain, she never gained the slightest inkling as to what had happened to J.-C. He had simply vanished somewhere high on the mountain.

Now, in the night of May 11–12, as Paula lay curled up in our bed, her anxiety suddenly morphed into anger. She had always supported me in my quest to climb the 8,000ers, suppressing her fears because she knew how much those great mountains meant to me. All at once, an underlying fury rose to the surface. *Screw you!* she cursed me silently. *How am I going to tell the kids?* Now she rehearsed over and over again the manner in which she would break the terrible truth to Gil, Ella, and Anabel.

Then the phone call came from Jimmy announcing the triumphant news that Veikka and I had reached the summit. Paula's darkest thoughts dissipated, as she imagined the gratification that my finally getting up Annapurna must have brought me. Yet I'd always told her how important it was to keep one's guard up on the descent. *Getting down is mandatory.*

At 6:00 A.M. on the twelfth, Paula got out of bed and tried to start what she pretended was a normal day. But once more the hours marched by, and there was no new call from Jimmy. During those hours, Veikka and I were floundering around in the dark, trying to find the fixed ropes that would guide us back to Camp III. Once more, we were overdue.

At last, of course, Paula learned through Jimmy that we were safe in camp. And a day later I was able to phone her from base camp. And only five days after that I was back home. Yet Paula could not so easily let go of the anger that had assailed her in the middle of what she felt was the worst night of her life. So at first she couldn't fully share my joy. During my first days home, I felt that I was walking on eggshells. Rationally, Paula knew that I had not been able to afford the luxury of keeping her, through Jimmy, abreast of every stage of our progress above Camp III. But the feelings stirred up so intensely during that agonizing night were not so easy to dissolve.

Then, out of the blue, came another shock from Annapurna. As I was enjoying my first full day home, the second Italian team, co-led by Christian Kuntner, had started up the French route. Just above Camp II they'd started to traverse left across a steep gully. It was a natural funnel for debris coming down from above, so you wanted to get across that gully as fast as possible. But Christian paused there for just a few seconds, as he shot some footage with his video camera.

Everyone on the mountain heard the sharp crack. An avalanche had broken loose from above. Christian never had a chance. Big blocks of ice struck him, tore him loose from his holds, and carried him several hundred feet down the face. He was still conscious when his teammates got to him, and was even able to start down on his own two feet, with others helping him. But only minutes later, he started spitting blood: internal injuries had taken a grim toll. The rescuers got Christian back to Camp II, but he died less than three hours after the accident.

In Bainbridge Island, when I got the news, I was deeply unsettled. Was the route I'd climbed on Annapurna a game of Russian roulette after all? I'd crossed the same gully on the way up and on the way down. Was it just luck that the avalanche hadn't struck when I was there?

Given Paula's lingering vexation upon my return from Nepal, I was afraid at first to tell her the awful news about Christian. But when I did, she responded with equanimity. "Christian was just in the wrong place at the wrong time," she said. "And maybe the conditions were different when you crossed the gully."

Still, I remained shaken—and all the more grateful that I was done with Endeavor 8000. That spring, there had been three of us on Annapurna who had climbed eleven or more 8,000ers. Silvio Mondinelli, Christian Kuntner, and I were equally strong and talented mountaineers. But Silvio had had to turn back, and now Christian had lost his life. Only I had reached the summit and gotten back safely. I felt not the slightest urge to congratulate myself for succeeding while the other two had not. On Annapurna, no matter how much you try to control the risks, to a certain extent you're always rolling the dice.

It was very fitting that Veikka Gustafsson was my partner on my last 8,000er. We'd first climbed together on Makalu in 1995, and on Annapurna in 2005 we paired up for our thirteenth expedition. That's far more trips to the Himalaya and Karakoram than I've shared with anyone else.

There was a slight language barrier between us at the beginning, but year after year, Veikka's English got better. (Needless to say, I never attempted to master Finnish!) The reason I kept going back time and again with Veikka was that both temperamentally and in terms of climbing skills, we meshed almost perfectly.

The only year during that decade that we didn't climb together was 2003. That summer, I got up Nanga Parbat and Broad Peak with J.-C. Lafaille, while Veikka was turned back in the spring on Kangchenjunga by bad weather and snow conditions. I think we both felt a bit out of sorts in 2003, as we missed the comfort and routine of the partnership that we had crafted during the previous eight years. With J.-C., I had begun to feel a comparable comfort and routine, but it takes time to form the kind of bond that Veikka and I had.

One of the things I liked about Veikka was that he was very easygoing. Nothing seemed to fluster him. He wasn't picky when it came to mediocre food or crappy housing conditions in the third world. He was always patient, never in a rush to finish a trip and get home. He could be serious when the occasion called for it, but he had a great sense of humor as well. I don't think I ever saw him lose his cool. We could be together for hours without speaking, without even feeling the need to speak.

Yet, at the same time, Veikka was a thoroughly gregarious guy. On the 8,000ers, he usually took the lead in terms of introducing himself and me to other teams on the mountain. And he had a genuine curiosity about natives and their cultures. In treating our Pakistani or Nepalese Sherpa camp staff, Veikka was extremely fair, and he never condescended to them, as so many earlier Western expeditions had, with their neocolonial "sahib-coolie" attitudes.

It seems a little strange to me, given the depth of our friendship, that I haven't seen Veikka since we parted ways in Kathmandu after Annapurna 2005. We've stayed in regular touch ever since, phoning and e-mailing each other frequently. I still consider Veikka one of my absolute best friends. And I was his most enthusiastic cheerleader as he pursued his own goal of climbing the fourteen 8,000ers. After Annapurna, he had four to go: Kangchenjunga, Gasherbrum I, Gasherbrum II, and Broad Peak. He got up Kangch in 2006. In 2008 he came up with an audacious plan to knock off the remaining three in a single expedition, since they're relatively close together. If you're going to travel that deep into the Karakoram, why not try to climb all three back-to-back?

Veikka succeeded on Gasherbrum II but had to turn back just 300 feet short of the summit of Gasherbrum I, as he climbed alone toward the top in worsening weather. On his way out from the Gasherbrums, he easily climbed Broad Peak, finishing the ascent we had just missed together in 1997.

In the summer of 2009, Veikka went back to Pakistan to go

after Gasherbrum I. I didn't envy him that long, hot, dusty walk up the Baltoro, which I'd made so many times myself. Just back from my own seventh ascent of Everest, I followed Veikka's expedition day by day on the Internet. When I read that he'd topped out on July 26, I had tears in my eyes. As I mention in the previous chapter, Veikka became the seventeenth climber to close the loop on the 8,000ers, and only the ninth to do so without bottled oxygen.

I called to congratulate Veikka as soon as he was reachable by telephone. He was extremely happy, but he was also certain that his 8,000-meter career was over and done with. Knowing full well how dangerous the big mountains are, he had no desire to tempt fate again. Having closed that chapter of his life, he was ready to move on to other pursuits.

In the spring of 2010, Veikka married his girlfriend, Henna Meriläinen (Miss Finland of 1994). That summer they had a baby girl, whom they named Selma. And in the summer of 2011, Paula, our kids, and I traveled to Finland to spend two weeks with Veikka and his family. We had a great time reliving past exploits and plotting new ones. I still believe that the two of us will join forces once again to perpetrate some grand adventure—just not another climb of an 8,000er!

No mountain has ever haunted me the way Annapurna did. Before I finally got to the summit, I started thinking of the peak as my personal nemesis. (I even titled a chapter in *No Shortcuts to the Top* "Nemesis: Annapurna.") The mountain occupied my waking thoughts (and more than a few of my nightmares) for many days over five years, but it never became a true obsession, as it had for my friend J.-C. Lafaille. When J.-C. got to the top in 2002, he unabashedly called his triumph "revenge" on the peak that had killed his mentor, Pierre Béghin. I never lost a partner on Annapurna or any other mountain, but even if I had, I wouldn't have referred to my success in 2005 as revenge.

It's tempting to make a black-and-white distinction between obsession and commitment, to regard commitment as a good, even necessary, condition for attacking a difficult objective, while seeing obsession as leading to unjustifiable risk and sometimes disaster. But that's not the claim I wish to make. It may be that commitment and obsession are simply different points on a continuum. Yes, J.-C. was obsessed with Annapurna, but I never climbed with a partner who had a cannier judgment of risk than he did, and he was absolutely the last of my teammates I ever expected to die in the mountains. J.-C. was simply willing to shave the margin between safety and danger a lot thinner than I was.

And he went at the highest mountains in the boldest of styles. He was proof of Messner's dictum that to become one of the world's truly great mountaineers, you have to focus on steep, very difficult, previously unclimbed lines. There were some who regarded J.-C.'s plan to climb Makalu solo in the heart of winter as verging on the suicidal, but not me. I actually thought he might pull it off—he was so talented, so smart, and so good at getting out of trouble.

J.-C. had set his sights on closing the loop on the fourteen 8,000ers himself. He had planned to save Everest for last. And he told me in confidence that he was going to attempt the world's highest mountain in truly spectacular fashion. Exactly what he was scheming up for Everest, however, he never told me—nor, I would guess, anyone else, not even Katia. We're left to wonder what that crowning deed might have been.

By now, I've been on eleven expeditions to Everest, and reached the summit seven times. But there's no way I'd try Annapurna again. It's just too frightening and too dangerous. Someday, however, I'd love to go back to base camp on the north side and just hang out at our grassy base camp, where I spent so many stressful days before our climb. Over the years, that spot had become a significant place for me, but in 2005, I was so focused on the upcoming ascent that I couldn't really relax there and luxuriate in its beauty.

The case can be made that Annapurna is the deadliest mountain in the world. Accurate statistics are hard to come by, but a Spanish mountain chronicler named Rodrigo Granzotto Peron calculates that as of August 2010, 183 climbers had reached the top of Annapurna, while 61 had died attempting the mountain. It's become a standard gauge of danger on the highest peaks to calculate the ratio of fatalities to summiteers. Thus the Annapurna ratio is exactly 33 percent. Everest, by contrast, has a ratio of "only" 9 percent. K2 comes close to Annapurna, with a balance hovering around 25 percent. No other mountain in the world is in this ballpark.

The subtitle of my K2 book was *Life and Death on the World's Most Dangerous Mountain.* A few sharp-eyed critics argued that I should have saved that epithet for Annapurna, based on the stats I've just cited. But there are many ways of measuring "most dangerous." When I claimed that K2 was the most dangerous, I had in mind not only the technical difficulty of the mountain but the extremes to which climbers were willing to push themselves to grasp at success there. In this sense, "dangerous" is a subjective criterion. "Deadliest" is a term that can be calculated, as in the ratio of ascents to fatalities.

K2, in other words, is a harder mountain to climb by the easiest route, the Abruzzi Spur. But the French route on Annapurna, while technically not extreme, is scary as hell. Reinhold Messner puts it succinctly: "Annapurna has the most dangerous standard route of all 8,000ers." And the great Swiss speed climber Ueli Steck chimes in, "Annapurna isn't the toughest summit, but there is always danger when someone climbs the mountain." The distinction between "dangerous" and "deadly" may seem like mere sophistry, but it makes intuitive sense to me.

The differences between K2 and Annapurna are further illustrated by the events of the last three years. In 2008 on K2, eleven climbers died in a single thirty-six-hour period, in one of the worst catastrophes in Himalayan history. Then, in 2009 and 2010, although many good climbers were on the mountain, not a single person reached the summit. On Annapurna in the spring of 2010, in an unprecedented season, no fewer than twenty-six climbers got to the top of Annapurna, seventeen on a single day, April 27. Evidently the normally treacherous snow and ice conditions on the north face relented, allowing whole waves of mountaineers to charge up the route. There was a single fatality, attributed not to avalanche or serac but to acute mountain sickness.

Aesthetically, Annapurna is not the most beautiful of the 8,000ers. It lacks the sheer, sweeping, pyramidal grace of K2, which I consider the most stunning of the fourteen highest peaks. Annapurna's south face, to be sure, is one of the most striking and formidable precipices in the world. But in general the mountain is defined by its jumbled complexity. It boasts some of the longest high ridges in the Himalaya, in particular the east ridge by which we attacked the mountain in 2002 and the southwest ridge that Simone Moro and Anatoli Boukreev were heading for in 1997. Annapurna's faces are festooned with hanging glaciers, chaoses of seracs and crevasse fields, and ill-defined rock-and-snow ribs, most of which culminate not in the summit but on crests along the various ridges. Yet that very complexity is what makes the mountain difficult and dangerous. There are no broad, smooth basins leading to high plateaus, as there are on other 8,000ers. Almost everywhere you climb on Annapurna, you tend to keep looking up, wondering what kinds of debris might come crashing toward you at any minute.

The origin of Annapurna's name belies the danger of the mountain. It is a Sanskrit cognomen, usually translated as "Goddess of the Harvests," but more literally and more prosaically as "Full of Food." Evidently the name derives from the streams and rivers that flow down to the lowlands from its glaciers, making the growing of crops possible. The natives who live in the mountain's shadow seem never to have approached its base. When the French tried to solve the labyrinthine approach to the north face in 1950, they could find no villagers anywhere who had the slightest idea how to get to that side of the mountain.

"Goddess of the Harvests" makes an unromantic label for such a great peak, at least compared to the Tibetan name for Everest, Chomolungma ("Goddess Mother of the World"), or Kangchenjunga, Nepali for "The Five Treasures of the Snows." Yet thanks to the remarkable exploits recounted in this book, and to the mountain's irrevocable status as the first of all the 8,000ers to be climbed, the name Annapurna reverberates with its own romantic power in the world of adventure.

Six years after I finally got to the summit of Annapurna, that achievement—and the whole campaign of Endeavor 8000, which Annapurna capped—still infuses me with a profound sense of fulfillment. When I give talks and slide shows about my climbs in the Karakoram and the Himalaya, I always try to share with the audience my belief that what you learn on a mountain can translate into overcoming challenges in other walks of life.

Thus I will always be puzzled by the great mountaineers—among them, Louis Lachenal and Jerzy Kukuczka—who felt not fulfillment on achieving the goal of a lifetime, but emptiness, numbness, no emotion at all. For a few climbers who got to the top of Annapurna (I think of Don Whillans and Dougal Haston in 1970), a certain numbness made tactical sense, for they had to turn around almost at once and keep their act together to get back to their highest camp in a gathering storm. Lachenal's numbness on the summit was directly linked to his awareness that his feet were frozen, that he was probably going to lose his toes, and possibly his life. But Kukuczka's emptiness on reaching the top of his fourteenth 8,000er was existential. It was as if he had suddenly come face-to-face with the dilemma "Now what will I do with the rest of my life?" Kukuczka's frame of mind conjures up the legend of

Alexander the Great, having won his greatest battle, weeping because he had no more worlds to conquer.

My chronicle about K2 was full of controversies, betrayals among members of a single team, and ill-advised decisions that led to fatal outcomes. The most heroic chapters in the mountain's history, such as the 1938 and 1953 American expeditions, played out as failures in the strict sense that the teams failed to get to the summit. In my mind, however, those two expeditions will always resonate as successes because of how the teammates came together in the face of extreme hardship and tragedy.

The history of Annapurna is utterly different. It is spangled not so much with follies and fiascos as with daring ambition and brilliant triumphs. The French first ascent against all odds; the courageous British siege of the south face, the hardest climb performed to that date in the Himalaya; Loretan and Joos's truly gutsy ascent of the east ridge and descent by the north face; Kukuczka and Hajzer's first winter ascent; Lafaille and Iñurrategi's journey into another world on the east ridge; Messner and Kammerlander's determined push in violent winds up the northwest face and ridge—all these exploits rank among the finest deeds performed in the Himalaya. Even the disaster that struck Moro and Boukreev on the southwest face came as the tragic denouement of a visionary campaign.

We can be sure that some of the world's best climbers will continue to tackle Annapurna. The very fact that it's regarded as the deadliest mountain in the world will be a motivating factor for some of those aspirants. And for anyone trying to climb the fourteen 8,000ers, Annapurna is necessarily on the tick list. Without that incentive, some mountaineers might regard the mountain as too risky to justify the attempt.

What's more, there are still significant "firsts" to be achieved on Annapurna. By now at least nine different routes have been put up on the massive south face, but there remain untouched ribs and gullies that promise new lines. The route that Simone and Anatoli were attempting on the southwest face, then over the Fang and along the southwest ridge to the summit, stands as a challenge for the boldest mountaineers of the next generation. Eventually, perhaps, climbers will accomplish a complete traverse of the mountain, up the southwest ridge, over the top, and down the east ridge—or vice versa.

As early as 1979 a Frenchman, Yves Morin, attempted a ski descent of Annapurna. He made it 4,000 feet down to a steep ice section at 22,300 feet. There, still on skis, he attached his ascender to a fixed rope, but got it jammed. In trying to extricate himself, he died of exhaustion. The full first ski descent (by the French route) came in 1995, by a pair of daring Slovene brothers, Davo and Andrej Karnicar. By the time they reached the base of the wall, however, Andrej had suffered bad frostbite of his toes; he had to be evacuated by helicopter.

Two climbers have come very close to pulling off the first solo ascent of Annapurna. In 1991 another daring Slovene, Slavko Svetičič, attempted a new route on the west face. He got to 25,900 feet—only around 600 feet below the summit—before he had to bivouac in hurricane winds. Traversing below the summit, Svetičič managed to descend the French route. This astounding feat went all but unnoticed in the Western climbing world. Four years later, Svetičič faced an even more daunting challenge: a solo climb of the west face of Gasherbrum IV, arguably the most difficult mountain in the Karakoram. High on the route, he was stalled by bad, loose rock and a heavy snowstorm. After waiting a whole day in a bivouac, he started down. Some Koreans at the base of the peak thought they saw the man descending, but then clouds swallowed the mountain. Svetičič was never seen again.

In 2007 yet another Slovene, Tomaž Humar, completed a dazzling new route on the south face alpine style and solo, although he went only to the east summit, not to the true apex of Annapurna. Two years before that climb, on Nanga Parbat, Humar generated wild acclaim in his home country but international criticism from other climbers after he was plucked from a possibly foolhardy bivouac in a perilous helicopter rescue. Then, in 2009, on another bold solo attempt, on a peak called Langtang Lirung in northern Nepal, Humar died after he broke his leg in a long fall, succumbing to his injuries and hypothermia before anyone could mount a rescue on the remote mountain.

The remarkable deeds performed by the likes of the Karnicar brothers, Svetičič, and Humar only go to show just how dangerous a mountain Annapurna is, and will continue to be. This makes us ponder all over again what may be the greatest deed in Annapurna's history: its first ascent. No matter how many times I've thought about that climb, pulled off in a mad dash during the last two weeks of May, with the flimsy gear of 1950 and a complete ignorance beforehand of the mountain's topography, I come away from the French achievement in a state of stupefied awe.

In the long run, perhaps the greatest blessing of mountaineering is the fellowship it bestows. For me on Annapurna, my friendship with Neal Beidleman and Michael Kennedy, partners on our aborted 2000 attempt, was sealed in a bond that lasts to this day. In 2002, I began a partnership with J.-C. Lafaille, whom I consider the best climber I ever roped up with. His disappearance on Makalu in 2006 is a loss that still grieves me deeply. Finally, going to Annapurna with Veikka Gustafsson three times, and standing on the summit with him in 2005, solidified the finest partnership I ever found in the mountains.

I suppose that guys can forge such friendships playing in a softball league or hanging out in a favorite pub, but it's hard to believe that those linkages have the lasting intensity of a good partnership in the mountains. By his own testimony, Simone Moro found in Anatoli Boukreev the best friendship of his life, and I know that Simone still grieves for Anatoli as I do for J.-C. On Annapurna, Reinhold Messner cemented his bond with the best partner of his own climbing life, Hans Kammerlander. Despite their differences in temperament, Don Whillans and Dougal Haston developed on the south face in 1970 a teamwork unequaled in British mountaineering, ended only by Haston's untimely death in 1977. And one of the most legendary brotherhoods of the rope ever devised, that between Louis Lachenal and Lionel Terray, reached its apotheosis as they saved each other's lives on the epic descent from Annapurna in 1950.

That kind of fellowship in mountaineering can even transcend generational gulfs. On November 9, 1996, I was a guest of honor at a black-tie dinner for the Himalayan Foundation in San Francisco. Six months earlier, I'd reached the summit of Everest as part of David Breashears's IMAX expedition, after we'd helped get some of the climbers injured in the debacle of May 10–11 down the mountain. By then I'd climbed eight 8,000ers, but I wouldn't say I was a famous mountaineer. That evening, to my shock, I found myself seated at a table between Sir Edmund Hillary and Maurice Herzog. I remember thinking, *I'm not worthy of this. What am I doing sitting next to these guys?*

Herzog was impeccably dressed, as I'd heard that he always was when making public appearances. I watched out of the corner of my eye as he hoisted his wineglass between his palms, since all ten of his fingers had been amputated at the first joints in 1950. I couldn't stop thinking, *This is the man!*

It was Herzog's *Annapurna,* after all, that had first made me want to become a mountaineer. I'd bought a copy in a used bookstore in my hometown of Rockford, Illinois, in 1976, when I was sixteen. Since then I'd read the book countless times.

Knowing Herzog was going to be at the dinner, but hardly imagining that I'd get to sit next to him, I'd brought along my copy. Now I got up the nerve to turn to him and ask, "Could I please have you sign my book?" He nodded and smiled. Opening the book to the title page, he grasped a pen between his palms and wrote a short inscription. Later I read it. Herzog had written:

For Ed Viesturs,
My compagnon of Himalayas,
My very best regards.

Herzog's signature was a flamboyant scrawl.

In May 2005, when I got back from Annapurna, I took down my copy of *Annapurna* and opened it to the title page. The dinner in San Francisco came thronging back, along with my thrill upon first reading the inscription. Fifty-five years before I'd stood on top of Annapurna, Maurice Herzog had been the first human ever to reach that apex in the sky. Now we were linked in a kinship of shared adventure that transcended the fact that we'd never before met—a kinship the likes of which few human pursuits can engender.

I put the book back on the shelf. It's hard to feel much better than I did then.

ACKNOWLEDGMENTS

Of all the mountains in my life, Annapurna was the most pivotal. The classic account of the first ascent, *Annapurna,* which I eagerly read as a kid, was the spark that ignited my climbing ambition. Some thirty years later, as I stood on Annapurna's summit on the afternoon of May 12, 2005, I reviewed the personal journey that the book had launched for me as a teenager. My first debt, then, is to Maurice Herzog for writing *Annapurna*. I know by now that scores of young men and women have been as inspired by Herzog's tale as I was to enter the mountaineering arena.

I also want to thank Paula, my loving and supportive wife of fifteen years. As I worked my way through one expedition after another, it was she who allowed me to spread my wings above the clouds. She understood the commitment and recognized the risks but nonetheless believed in me every step of the way. Her emotional and psychological support gave me strength and lightened my load.

Thanks also to Veikka Gustafsson, my climbing partner of ten years—the easygoing, rarely flustered, always positive ropemate. Each year as we came down from a Himalayan climb, Veikka's first question to me was, "What shall we climb next year?" He understood that the journey itself was more important than a successful ascent, and that with patience, the time would come when we'd be allowed to reach the next summit.

As Veikka and I traveled toward Annapurna in the spring of 2005, we could not fathom what course our future might take. After two previous failed attempts on the mountain, we could scarcely imagine how fortunate we would be with the outcome of that season. The mountain itself seemed completely different from previous years—colder, better solidified, relatively quiet—almost inviting. One of the cornerstones of our successful ascent was the friendship and the partnership we received from the five-man Italian team led by Silvio Mondinelli. The groundwork the Italians laid in establishing fixed ropes on key sections of the route, and their invitation to us to join forces on our final push to the summit, were crucial to our success. The monstrous hug that Silvio gave me as Veikka and I stepped off the mountain upon our return from the summit was a moment worth a thousand words.

Jimmy Chin, expert mountaineer and superb photographer, gave me vital support from the lower camps on Annapurna in 2005. And I'm grateful to Jimmy for supplying the stunning photo that graces our dust jacket cover. Caroline Hirsch spent months arduously researching historical photos for this book. Anne-Laure Treny provided excellent help in translating the pithy and complex prose of Erhard Loretan in his remarkable memoir, *Les 8000 Rugissants*.

Last but not least, I want to thank my coauthor, David Roberts, for helping to craft our third and (we hope) not last book together. Thanks also to our tireless literary agent Stuart Krichevsky and to his diligent colleagues Shana Cohen and Jennifer Puglisi. At Crown, we were handsomely served by the shrewd eye of our editor, Charles Conrad, and by the many details skillfully handled by his assistants, Hallie Falquet and Jenna Ciongoli.

Just as this book was going to press, I learned about the death of Erhard Loretan on the Grünhorn in the Swiss Alps, as he and the client he was guiding took a long fall from the summit ridge. It seems unthinkable that a man who had achieved some of the boldest ascents in Himalayan history should have died on a relatively easy peak in his alpine backyard. I met Loretan only once, in a brief encounter in a restaurant in Kathmandu, but there was no mountaineer in the world whom I more admired. His death shocked and saddened me almost as if I had lost a personal friend and partner. May the account in this book of Loretan's astounding traverse of Annapurna with Norbert Joos in 1984 serve as a testament, however inadequate, to one of the visionary geniuses of mountaineering.

BIBLIOGRAPHY

Blum, Arlene. *Annapurna: A Woman's Place*. San Francisco: Sierra Club Books, 1980.

Bonington, Chris. *Annapurna South Face*. New York: McGraw-Hill Book Company, 1971.

Boukreev, Anatoli. *Above the Clouds*. New York: St. Martin's Press, 2001.

Boukreev, Anatoli, with G. Weston DeWalt. *The Climb*. New York: St. Martin's Press, 1998.

Frost, Tom. "Annapurna South Face," *The American Alpine Journal* vol. 17, no. 2 (1971).

Hawley, Elizabeth. "Kangchenjunga, Ascents and Tragedy." *The American Alpine Journal* vol. 38 (1996).

Herzog, Maurice. *Annapurna*. New York: E. P. Dutton & Co., 1952.

———. *Renaître* (Rebirth). Paris: Editions Jacob-Duvernet, 2007.

Houston, Charles, and Robert H. Bates. *K2: The Savage Mountain*. Guilford, Conn.: Lyons Press, 2000.

Hunt, John. *The Ascent of Everest*. Seattle: The Mountaineers Books, 1993.

Krakauer, Jon. *Into Thin Air*. New York: Villard Books, 1997.

Kukuczka, Jerzy. *My Vertical World: Climbing the 8,000-metre Peaks*. London: Hodder & Stoughton, 1992.

Lachenal, Louis. *Carnets du Vertige* (Vertigo notebooks). Chamonix, France: Editions Guérin, 1996.

Lafaille, Jean-Christophe, with Benoît Heimermann. *Prisonnier de l'Annapurna* (Prisoner of Annapurna). Chamonix, France: Editions Guérin, 2003.

Lafaille, Katia. *Sans Lui* (Without him). Paris: Bernard Grasset, 2007.

Loretan, Erhard. "Annapurna, First Ascent of East Ridge and Traverse." *The American Alpine Journal* vol. 27 (1985).

Loretan, Erhard, with Jean Ammann. *Les 8000 Rugissants* (The roaring 8,000ers). Fribourg, Switzerland: Editions La Sarine, 1996.

Messner, Reinhold. *All 14 Eight-Thousanders.* Seattle: Cloudcap, 1988.

———. *Annapurna: 50 Years of Expeditions in the Death Zone.* Seattle: The Mountaineers Books, 2000.

Moro, Simone. *Cometa sull'Annapurna* (Comet on Annapurna). Milan: Corbaccio, 2003.

Perrin, Jim. *The Villain: The Life of Don Whillans.* London: Hutchinson, 2005.

Rébuffat, Gaston. *Starlight and Storm.* New York: E. P. Dutton & Co., 1957.

Roberts, David. "Driven to the Edge." *National Geographic Adventure* (May 2006).

———. "The Prisoner of Annapurna." *National Geographic Adventure* (February 2003).

———. *True Summit: What Really Happened on the Legendary Ascent of Annapurna.* New York: Simon & Schuster, 2000.

Terray, Lionel. *Conquistadors of the Useless.* London: Victor Gollancz Ltd., 1961.

Viesturs, Ed, with David Roberts. *K2: Life and Death on the World's Most Dangerous Mountain.* New York: Broadway Books, 2009.

———. *No Shortcuts to the Top: Climbing the World's 14 Highest Peaks*. New York: Broadway Books, 2006.

Wielicki, Krzysztof. *Crown of Himalaya: 14 x 8000*. Kraków, Poland: Wydawnictwo, 1997.

Willis, Clint. *The Boys of Everest: Chris Bonington and the Tragedy of Climbing's Greatest Generation*. Cambridge, Mass.: Da Capo Press, 2006.